Foreign Aid and Journalism in the Global South

Foreign Aid and Journalism in the Global South

A Mouthpiece for Truth

Jairo Lugo-Ocando

LEXINGTON BOOKS
Lanham • Boulder • New York • London

Published by Lexington Books
An imprint of The Rowman & Littlefield Publishing Group, Inc.
4501 Forbes Boulevard, Suite 200, Lanham, Maryland 20706
www.rowman.com

6 Tinworth Street, London SE11 5AL, United Kingdom

Copyright © 2020 The Rowman & Littlefield Publishing Group, Inc.

All rights reserved. No part of this book may be reproduced in any form or by any electronic or mechanical means, including information storage and retrieval systems, without written permission from the publisher, except by a reviewer who may quote passages in a review.

British Library Cataloguing in Publication Information Available

Library of Congress Cataloging-in-Publication Data Available

ISBN 978-1-4985-8335-0 (cloth)
ISBN 978-1-4985-8337-4 (pbk)
ISBN 978-1-4985-8336-7 (electronic)

Dedication

To Everette E. Dennis, whose professional and academic life has been, and continues to be, exemplary and whose contributions to our field are larger than life. In a short time, while working together, I got to appreciate his commitment to journalism education.

Contents

1	Introduction	1
2	The Imposition of Common Sense	29
3	How Journalism Came to Be in the South	53
4	Journalism and Postcolonial Aid	93
5	Spreading the Ideology of Objectivity	107
6	Educating and Training Journalists in the South	119
7	Foreign Aid for Media Development in the Digital Age	137
8	Shaping Values and Practices	157
References		169
Index		201
About the Author		205

Chapter 1

Introduction

In order to understand the historical role of foreign aid in shaping journalism as a political institution in the Global South, one only needs to see the remarkable convergence of values and aesthetics in news reporting across the globe. Indeed, one of the most interesting findings of the Worlds of Journalism Study (WJS) research project is the overall convergence of normative claims and deontological aspirations among journalists from all over the world with regard to news values and journalistic ethics (Hanitzsch, 2016; Mellado & Van Dalen, 2017). If well, the WJS project also highlights that there are important caveats within these normative professional aspirations, cultures, and practices, the survey nevertheless conclusively suggests important overlaps regarding ethical aspirations and stances among news reporters across the globe.

Consequently, it is crucial also to study the historical process of cultural convergence that set about today's professional ideology. One that is characterized by the overlapping normative aspirations toward the ideal of professional autonomy; one that claims universality with regard to journalists' deontological approaches and practices (Deuze, 2005; Hanitzsch et al., 2010; Singer, 2007) and that centers upon the ability of news reporters to be independent from government and corporate pressures in the pursue of factual-based truth. It is a mind-set that is closely interconnected to the notion of objectivity, which despite criticism, continues to be paramount in the conceptualization of journalism as a professional and independent field (Maras, 2013; McNair, 2000; Ward, 2015).

Moreover, as some of the findings of the WJS project underlines, the idea of "professional autonomy" is strongly associated with detachment and non-involvement, both of which are considered essential journalistic functions by those interviewed across the globe. The journalists surveyed in this project equally value notions such as impartiality, reliability, and factualness of information, as well as adherence to universal ethical principles such as accuracy (Hanitzsch et al., 2011), despite important cross-national and cross-cultural differences.

The prevalent interpretation, so far, as to how these values became so widely shared and spread around the world is that the current news cultures and practices that have characterized professional mainstream journalism somehow emerged "naturally" from the process of industrialization and commercialization of the US press and that it then became adopted as a universal notion by other societies from around the globe. As Michael Schudson suggested some years ago,

> Journalism is not something that floated platonically above the world and that each country copied down, shaping it to its own national grammar. It is something that—as we know it today—Americans had a major hand in inventing. (Schudson, 2008, p. 188)

This proposed interpretation of how journalistic values "from the West" became the ethical threshold for the rest of the globe derives from the assumption that the notions of journalism and democracy are not only historically intertwined in both the public imagination and professional practice, but also by the belief—still held today—that they were "naturally" underpinned, albeit more subtlety, by the emergence of the Market Society in the West as a historical development. For some, this accounts for a great deal of the formation of journalism as a political institution and its associated practices and professional ideologies. It is an explanation that suggests that the process of commercialization and consolidation of market economy was the key driver for the emergence of this particular model of the press and its consolidation as the archetypical type of news provision (Conboy, 2004, 2006; Mott, 1941).

It is perhaps important, at this point, to clarify what I mean by "West" when using the concept in this book. I am very aware of the problematic nature of the term and how unprecise it is in terms of geography—as it also incorporates countries such as Australia and Japan. Hence, the use of the term here is not so much to denote a geopolitical configuration but instead a sociopolitical construction that incorporates liberal democracies that operate within a context of free market and that often aligned themselves within particular international and multilateral collaborative arrangements, such as NATO, the United Nation's system, Organisation for Economic Co-operation and Development (OECD).

These countries are able to exercise international power by means of resources and military intervention and share a past that is intertwined with the colonial and neocolonial enterprises that dominated the late 19th century all the way to the 1990s. Although they are not homogenous in terms of interests and foreign policy, one can say that there are far more overlaps than divergences in that respect. In relation to the journalism models being exported by these countries by means of foreign aid, there are certainly key differences between the US, European efforts, and, let us say, Japan. However, they converge overall in the fundamental support for models that underpin democracy and free market economy. Few of these efforts and resources go to government-own media and in most cases, if not almost all, Western aid has historically underpinned private media (including commercial and nonprofit).

These accounts also tend to present this process as occurring in quasi-political neutral terms (Anderson, 2018; Schudson & Tifft, 2005). In this context, one of the key notions in journalism norms, that of journalistic objectivity, has been interpreted to be a by-product of commercialization, political changes, and technological advances that emerged in the Anglo-Saxon world as a guiding principle between the 1890s and 1930s and which was closely associated with the rise of the mass audiences for newspapers (Muhlmann, 2008, p. 2). In this sense, prevalent historical versions argue that the ideal of a positivist definition of "objectivity" became a dominant discourse among journalists since the appearance of modern newspapers in the Jacksonian Era of the 1830s in the backdrop of the democratization of politics, the expansion of a market economy, and the growing authority of an entrepreneurial, urban middle class (Banning, 1998; Schudson, 1976).

It was the end point of the consolidation of the Enlightenment as a political project (Lugo-Ocando, 2008; Nerone, 2013; Schiller, 1981), which translated into a prevalent positivist deontology for news reporting. Accordingly, the notion of journalistic objectivity is seen by many historians and experts as a universal and core professional value in the mainstream newsrooms that "occurred" or "happened" as a phenomenon, "naturally" deriving from particular events and circumstances that lead to a press far less committed to advocacy and political mobilization and instead increasingly concerned with expanding its commercial audiences and remit. This view has been adopted as the most important explanatory theoretical framework within debates around professionalization and freedom of expression (Ryan, 2001; Steel, 2013; Ward, 2015) as to why it became the dominant form of journalism around the world.

According to this view, one of the reasons as to why there seems to be such a remarkable convergence of values and professional aspirations across so many practitioners operating in different societies—who nevertheless display such distinctive backgrounds—is because these were values developed as historical formation, which were underpinned by the seemingly universal development of the political economy of the press (Banning, 1998; Conboy,

2004; Muhlmann, 2008; Schudson, 1976). Accordingly, it is one explanation that—by assuming the universality of the principles set in the West—has narrated a history of journalism in which the current dominating values spread from the center to the periphery (Golding, 1977; Hampton, 2010; Schudson & Tifft, 2005).

A COUNTERVIEW

These historical accounts are mostly right in the interpretation of how values and normative aspiration got disseminated across the globe. They are also sound when providing an explanatory theoretical framework for the overlaps observed across the globe. However, these explanations fall short when examining the roots of the formation of these values and do not seem to sufficiently recognize the degree of diversity in the conceptualization of both journalism practice on the ground and journalism as a political institution in each constituency in the Global South. Moreover, these accounts persist in interpreting the emergence of "professional journalism" solely as a natural derivation of the marketization of the press.

These historical interpretations are often offered without properly exploring possible agency and interventions in the formation of journalism both as a professional practice and as a political institution in the Global South. Hence, assessing the thesis that rather than a "natural occurrence" in which the South just copied the grammar of the North, standards, practices, and professional ideologies were also a product of a "contested orchestration" that involved both the imposition from the top against counter-flows and resistance from the bottom by means of native models and expressions of news gathering and dissemination that were already there.

To be sure, my thesis is that the process of "modernizing" journalism practices—as we know them today in the South and, the shaping of journalism as a political institution in the mirror image of its Western counterparts—was carried out by establishing an umbilical cord to the ideologies underpinning liberal democracy and the market economy. This link took the form of a deliberate effort to expand cultural hegemony in the face of the challenges posed by the rise of the mass society and (revolutionary) forces that threaten the economic and political order at that time. Firstly, within the United States and Europe and later on across the globe.

In so doing, I contend the prevalent suggestion that the spreading of the normative values that today characterize professional journalism practice in the Global South, or at least in a great part of it happened "naturally" and "only" as a collateral effect of the expansion of media markets. Instead, I argue that we should also think of journalism in the Global South as a colonial and postcolonial enterprise that aimed at a form of nation-building exercise, which, in turn, responded to the type of "collective imaginary" proposed by Benedict Anderson (2006 [1983]).[1] One that was, at the same time, a cultural tool designed to open new capitalist markets for the new centers of power and forms of hegemony being set in the United States.

Following this line of inquiry, I suggest that mainstream professional journalism in the South should not be conceived only as a historical and natural "occurrence" that happened in one place and that then was copied in others but one that rather developed simultaneously and in parallel in many places as part of a larger process to construct nationhood, which nevertheless faced opposition and resistance from the ground. Consequently, mainstream commercial journalism in the Global South was an exercise of nation building in the same terms suggested by Professor Barbie Zelizer (2017) when referring to the United States: one which started with the colonial and neocolonial enterprises between the late 19th century and first half of the 20th century and that morphed later into more sophisticated forms of cultural hegemony across the Global South. One that over the years was resisted, contested, and embraced at the same time.

In saying this, I am not disagreeing with the prevalent interpretation, which has argued that journalism was exported to the Global South as a projection of geopolitical power through cultural hegemony (Golding, 1977; Schudson, 2008). On the contrary, my own argument is based partially in this assumption. However, I am suggesting that this process of dissemination encounter already-existing models of ethics and practices in a set of diverse forms of journalism in these very places. In fact, contrary to colonial narratives that claim how empires "build civilization" and institutions—often portrayed in the metaphor that it has turned "empty deserts" into cities and brought progress by means of technology and science to remote corners of the uncivilized world (Fitzgerald, 2007; Pappe, 2007; Tharoor, 2018)— in reality, communication forms that can be considered journalism already existed in the many places in the Global South (regardless of some Western scholars and practitioners wanting to acknowledge that or not).

There is an enduring myth that we also see permeating into many histories of journalism recycled in a diversity of forms for which the North "invented" journalism. Instead, as I will argue here, the North just tried to impose particular professional standards that reflected its own ideology of truth. Moreover, as I will also argue, the dissemination of journalism norms and values was part of bringing about modernity upon existing forms of communicating news in the South and channeling them into particular mainstream models that could help underpin overall hegemonic power. These attempts to impose modernity by means of a particular form of journalism were met, however, with resistance and contestation in many places. Indeed, research in this field shows that journalists in the Global South conceptualize universal professional values and the possible impact of a universal ethics code in a variety of manners and are suspicious of a Western-imposed set of values or a code (Rao & Lee, 2005). Indeed, this process of imposition was met with resistance and subject to counter-flows while facing competition from other powers such as the then emerging Soviet Union, which also tried to build its own ideological empire with its own promises of modernity.

What I mean in this book by "imposition" is not a situation in which people in the Global South where forcibly and by means of violence made to adopt a particular model of journalism (although that is part of the story too, particularly in colonial and Cold War settings such as Kenya and Chile). On the contrary, many newsrooms were all too eager and rapid to adopt standards and practices from the West as they saw it as a role model to fallow. Instead, the notion of imposition that I use here is one of ideological significance, which denounces the imperialist project that excludes, subordinates, and erases local cultures and subaltern voices by creating a system where particular knowledge is considered legitimate and others are not (Freire, 2018 [1968]; Spivak, 2010 [1988]).

I argue here that it was these tensions between imposition, contestation, and political competition that influenced mostly the native forms of journalism and the development of their own grammars across the globe in what they are today, particular and specific to each constituency. In some cases, this grammar was more similar to what the North tried to impose and in other more autonomous, hence showing the power and limits of disruption of foreign aid. Consequently, in certain places, the local grammar took a form of its own in ways that reflected more the traditions that already existed in those societies, while in other, it simply emulated a carbon copy of the North.

In reflecting on these points, my invitation is to explore in more detail continuities and disruptions in the formation of journalism across the globe, and perhaps more importantly, to challenge common assumptions that have left aside "agency" and "nation building" in the overall historical interpretation of the development of journalism as a professional body in our side of the world. In opening these questions, I am inviting the reader to understand news values such as objectivity, balance, and fairness within broader national and international efforts seeking hegemonic status or resistance in an increasingly globalized world. A world that fundamentally changed in the 20th century with the rise of the United States as a superpower and the Great Transformation that led the world to the Market Society Karl Polanyi (2001 [1944]) refers to and the overall confrontation to the Soviet Union during that century.

In this book, I am concentrating on how Foreign Aid for Media Development, one of the multiple elements in this process, has historically help to foster and shape particular models of professional practice and normative aspiration in news reporting, which develop distinctively over time in different parts of the world. In so doing, this book explores the agency of Foreign Aid in underpinning a particular model of news gathering and dissemination as part of a larger exercise to project hegemony in order to replicate a cultural and political paradigm of society across the Global South and expand markets. It is my argument that this exercise was met with resistance and the final outcomes were reshaped by a diversity of forces leading to a nuance in the way journalism is practiced around the world. This was an outcome that was not necessarily expected by many of the original donors and that continues to defy our understanding of what journalism is and its role in society.

So, let us start by acknowledging that at the center of these efforts of hegemonic projection of power and postcolonial attempts of nation building, there was an orchestrated effort by the West to achieve geopolitical and ideological influence, particularly after the Soviet Revolution of 1917 (Kenez, 1981; Knock, 1992). These efforts extended all over the cultural realm and included literature, arts in general and journalism in particular (Lemberg, 2019; Parker, 2016; Saunders, 2000) and had a central role in defining the shape of political institutions in liberal democracies during the 20th century. Which is why it is profoundly baffling that the most important political event of the 20th century—one which split the world into two halves and that was an underlining cause of World War II, going on to dominate culture and society all way through the 21st century—is so absent in the historical accounts of the formation of professional journalism in the West. This, despite the fact that from the start, journalism in modern times is defined in contraposition to the Soviet "propaganda" model (Lippmann, 2010 [1920]; Siebert & Schramm, 1956), where journalism undertook its own shapes and forms (Hopkins, 1965; Resis, 1977).

The aims by which the model of journalism practiced in the United States was exported to the Global South could nowadays be characterized as part of the broader efforts of "public diplomacy"; an effort that was designed to win the hearts and minds of those in that part of the world. These aims encompassed from the beginning a series of actions and approaches in order to influence public opinion and counter the threat of communism abroad. Over the years, this meant allocating resources and efforts in order to influence the future shape of media systems in the Global South so as to make them a mirror image of the dominant powers of the time. This part of what capitalism in general was doing with all areas of the economy by exporting cultural models that reproduced consumer ideology while expanding markets. However, there was a significant difference; by expanding news markets the centers of power were also co-opting the agenda of newly independent states and projecting hegemony over former colonies (Mujica, 2006 [1982]; Schramm & Atwood, 1981).

This is the way we can argue that media development during the Cold War was mostly about winning hearts and minds of the masses in the Third

World and it was intrinsically linked to exposure to modern commercial mass media (Chakravartty, 2009). In the case of those allocating resources from the West the idea was to replicate a model of media operations and journalistic practice that saw itself anchored in liberal democracy and operating under private ownership. One that could only be independent and free, it was assumed, if it faced market competition and embraced scientific objectivity in its nature (Lippmann, 2010 [1920]). Other efforts, during the Cold War, would instead try to replicate the media model of the Soviet Union in places such as Angola, China, Cuba, and Vietnam (Peycam, 2012; Santamaria, 2018). The normative assumption of truth was also central in the professional ideology of socialism's reporters, but it was one that saw structural issues and class struggle as the ultimate truth and that rejected illusions of "freedom of expression" as bourgeoisie decoy by those who own the media and the rest of the means of production (Brovkin, 1998; Hopkins, 1965; Kenez, 1981).

All and all, these efforts to promote media systems and journalistic practices in the Global South sought to embrace modernity. Therefore, the 20th century saw an influx of Foreign Aid destined to achieve these goals by supporting media "modernization"—a term that was broadly interpreted by both sides in the Cold War—and that led not only to support the development and creation of media outlets and media infrastructure (Schramm, 1964, 1971) but also, and somehow more importantly, to foster particular news values and journalistic approaches that emulated those in the United States and the USSR. In this sense, "modernity" broadly came into journalism as aesthetical ideological formats that determined ethics and standards. This increasingly came to be emphasized after the end of World War II, when Foreign Aid for Media Development took the form of investment in media industries, the training of journalists, communication educational programs, and widespread subsidies to create or sustain particular news media outlets.

Having said this, the examination of the relationship between foreign aid and media development should not be limited to looking at what happened during the Cold War period as it not only preceded this conflict but also continued to play an important role in shaping journalistic cultures in the Global South long after the fall of the Berlin Wall. Indeed, in the past twenty years alone, just the expenditure in media development assistance by Western agencies has skyrocketed to way over US$ 600 million (Brownlee, 2017, p. 2278). Moreover, far from being "dead"—as Dambisa Moyo (2009) would want us to believe—foreign aid remains an influential and effective force in shaping organizations and public institutions around the globe (Bräutigam & Knack, 2004; Jenkins, 2001).

Over the years, foreign aid has been corporatized and securitized, this by not only making it part of the security and defense prerogatives but also turning it into a profitable business for many private corporations. Consequently, it has now, nevertheless, larger tentacles and is far more influential than it ever was. Today, government expenditure on foreign aid has surpassed initiatives such as the Marshall Plan after World War II (Lomøy, 2011) although where and how it is allocated is not as transparent or visible as it was in the past as it is now being mostly outsourced to Third Sector organizations, which do not have the same level of accountability. By being privatized and then channeled through a complex web that avoids the type of check and balances that it had in the past, taxpayers in the North continue to pay for media development but in some cases in less accountable ways.

While Senator Frank Church (1924–1984) was able to determine the responsibilities of those involved in overthrow of Salvador Allende in Chile by tracing the origins and destinations of the covert and overt aid provided by the US government (Barnes, 1981; Bernstein, 1977), today's network of Foreign Aid for Media Development presents a far greater challenge for general governance of aid, transparency, and accountability. Not only because it is channeled with far more opacity, as it is increasingly allocated through outsourcing to third parties but also because intentions and outputs are far less clear and more complex. In today's world, we find journalistic enterprises carrying out investigative reporting that have exposed the interests and wrongdoings of precisely those who have funded, directly or indirectly, these same news enterprises, as was the case of many of the independent journalistic organizations that, as part of an international consortium of journalists, exposed the Panama Papers (Hudson, 2017; Obermayer & Obermaier, 2017).

Over the years, foreign aid directed toward media development has become more complex, particularly around its nature, objectives, and final outcomes. Nevertheless, those allocating this aid have also shown a remarkable ability to disseminate values and normative aspirations across the globe. So, my inquiry is: How were these key ideas, values, practices, and notions around an ideal of journalism professionalization disseminated across the globe, and what allowed Western values—particularly those forged in the United States and Great Britain—to become such a standardized and almost axiomatic set of principles among journalists in the Global South?

In answering these questions, I am not seeking to invalidate current historical accounts around historical "occurrence" in the North—which might still be valid there—but rather open up the debate for complementary and alternative interpretations of journalism histories in the Global South, where existing theoretical explanatory frameworks seem inadequate, given the fact that the rich histories of journalism in the southern part of the globe have yet to be incorporated more thoroughly and comprehensively into the wider narratives about how journalism became to be what it is today. I believe that this exercise could also help us advance a better understanding of how journalism became a source for power struggles rather than a true force for social accountability and justice, both in the center and the periphery, of world geopolitics.

The thesis of this book is that far from being a "historical occurrence," notions such as objectivity, fairness, and balance—now central to our understanding of professional journalism in the Global South—were fostered, at least partially, through orchestrated efforts disguised as—what we call today—foreign aid for "media development."[2] In so doing, international donor nations—and later own private ones—had the intention of promoting particular models of journalism that reflected the type of liberal values set in their own societies. This was part of a set of ideological, geopolitical, and strategic efforts to replicate similar models of liberal democracy around the world while, in the specific case of the United States and Western Europe, helping to contain the spread of communism.

Indeed, some of the most important efforts to replicate liberal democratic institutions and the market economy—that is, exporting the US model or the cultural "Americanization" of world society (Appy, 2000; Mattelart, 2002)— can be traced to Woodrow Wilson's quest for a new international world order (Ambrosius, 2002; Knock, 1992) and his struggle to confront the nascent Soviet Union. However, anti-communism in the United States was not, as many assume, a monolithic enterprise. In fact, it seemed more a kaleidoscope of different interests that was only able to come together at particular times of history, thanks to the galvanizing effects of major events such as the Soviet Revolution, Great Wars and then, afterward by the building of the Berlin, the Korean War, Cuban crisis, the Vietnam war, and other similar events (Powers, 1998).

For journalistic practices being forged during the First and Second Red Scare, this meant the use of the norm of objectivity as a way of presenting a response to communism, which had become an ideological alternative to many workers' movements from around the world. This became even more so some years later, during the McCarthyism era, when journalistic objectivity became de facto a virulent anti-communist exercise in defense of freedom (Maras, 2013, p. 130). Therefore, these periods set the tone for how world politics was reported in the Great Press in the North as well as in many newsrooms in developing countries that aimed at emulating them (Alvear & Lugo-Ocando, 2016; Diaz-Rangel, 1976; Mujica, 1982).

I suggest, consequently, that international aid efforts to foster media development are key in explaining the spread of particular models of journalism education and practice in many of our countries. Moreover, they are crucial in understanding how these models became hegemonic as part of the increasing expansion and globalization of Western media systems throughout the 20th century. By exporting their models while excluding local and native practices, they enabled the Western news media to play broadly the same role at an international level as it already played in the past at a national one. Furthermore, as some authors have suggested, the international media systems became one of the key mechanisms by which developing countries were brought within the common cultural hegemony of Western capitalism (Elliott & Golding, 1974, p. 229) even if at times this was challenged by the then Soviet Union's own cultural and ideological expansion (Stevenson, 1988; Thussu, 2006).

In her work, Diana Lemberg has documented thoroughly how the US government and news organizations deployed systematic efforts to shaped media systems and journalistic practices around the world after 1945 under the banner of the "free flow" of information, showing how the push for global media access acted as a vehicle to project US power. She has examined how information diplomacy and development aid coming from Washington were intrinsically linked to wider efforts of propaganda during the Cold War, while highlighted the nature of US efforts to circumvent foreign regulatory systems in the quest to expand markets and bring their ideas to new publics decades following World War II. All this is a part of wider efforts to win the hearts and minds of people in the Global South (Lemberg, 2019).

In more recent times, replicating these models in the Global South was underpinned by aid programs that shaped curriculums in journalism schools, funded exchanges of leading scholars, allowed journalists and editors in the Global South to study abroad, helped set training programs, and even supported particular journalistic projects with resources for infrastructure and financial operations. These efforts also included supporting journalism practice itself in the wider context of foreign intervention and public diplomacy. These ranged from the money that the Central Intelligence Agency channeled toward El Mercurio newspaper to help overthrow Salvador Allende in Chile back in the 1970s (Alvear & Lugo-Ocando, 2016; Corvalán, 2003) to the more recent support of the Konrad Adenauer Foundation and the Open Society of George Soros to foster independent journalism NGOs in the Global South (Cook, 2016; Requejo-Alemán & Lugo-Ocando, 2014), including the programs to train broadcast journalists in Africa, Latin America, and Asia by leading European broadcasters such as Radio Netherlands and Deutsche Welle. I suggest that all these aid efforts need to be contextualized within the larger framework of "public diplomacy" (Cull, 2008; Nye Jr, 2008) rather than just see them as media development initiatives.

In fact, in order to understand how convergent news values and normative claims became endowed into journalism around the world, we need to examine more carefully and critically the relationship between foreign aid and media development. However, I must warn the reader that I am not attempting to present a comprehensive history of Foreign Aid for Media Development, although historical accounts are central to the analysis. My intention is instead to use history in my own effort to understand the current state of Foreign Aid for Media Development in ways that are more critical and meaningful for us in the Global South. This is an exercise that has certainly been initiated already by several scholars (Abbott, 2016; Park & Curran, 2000; Paterson, Gadzekpo, & Wasserman, 2018; Wasserman, 2017). This analysis, however, cannot only be performed in terms of the North-South relationship nor be narrowed to the US efforts and programs toward particular regions, but needs to be also widely open to include historical and present efforts as well as other geopolitical initiatives that have not been traditionally accounted for.

This is because in the same way US and Western European foreign aid has had an effect upon shaping journalism cultures and organizational practices in certain countries, other streams of foreign aid were also instrumental in modeling journalistic practices in places such as Cuba and Eastern Europe under the Soviet influence. This in addition to other examples from donor countries such as China and Japan, all of which have also tried to advance their own public diplomatic efforts in places such as Africa and Asia. By making this multidimensional analysis, one can also ask why certain aid efforts were more effective than others in the Global South even before the fall of the Berlin Wall and, why the Western set of values and aspirational journalistic deontology became so prevalent despite important competing alternatives in each period of time.

Let us be clear, the allocation of foreign government resources toward media in the Global South is not a new phenomenon (Bushnell, 1950). On the contrary—and to cite an example—we can find that the Spanish empire promoted and funded a great number of publicly managed and privately owned pro-colony newspapers in Latin America as early as the 17th century (Earle, 1997). These international aid efforts were followed years later by the new Black Republic of Haiti, which supplied Simón Bolívar in 1815 with a print and resources to establish in Venezuela a pro-independence and pro-abolitionist newspaper (Blackburn, 2006; Fischer, 2013) and subsequent financial and logistical support from Great Britain to also foster new media outlets in that country. In fact, as is widely documented, the geopolitical struggles of the old European empires were key in the development of the international media systems and particularly in relation to news agencies (Boyd-Barrett, 1980; Boyd-Barrett & Rantanen, 1998; Frère, 2015; Paterson & Sreberny, 2004) as it continues to be exposed today as in the case of the recent diplomatic standoff between Saudi Arabia and Qatar in relation to Al-Jazeera (Aldroubi, 2017). In this sense, Marie-Soleil Frère (2012, 2015) has convincingly argued that the interventions of the great European powers of the time shaped the media systems in their then African colonies, which explains partially the distinctiveness of the Francophone and Anglophone media systems of today in that part of the world.

Important ideological paradigms coming from the North have also been crucial in determining the organization and nature of a series of media systems around the planet. To give an example, the notion of "free flow of information," which provided an international justificatory framework for "journalistic objectivity" and that was used in the backdrop of the McBride Report (2003 [1980]) to counter international demand for a new information order and greater state involvement, has been central in defining resources and policies around supporting the development of media systems in the Global South. To be sure, the debates around the New World Information and Communication Order (NWICO) were in fact ideological struggles that tried to challenge, in the shadow of the Cold War, the dominating status of Western media representations and journalistic cultures (Lemberg, 2019; Lugo-Ocando & Nguyen, 2017; Mujica, 2006 [1982]; Sparks, 2007). Therefore, it is important to remind ourselves that the whole system of beliefs in the South behind normative professional aspirations, such as journalistic objectivity and other news values, have been—historically speaking—part of or by-product of broader geopolitical and ideological struggles.

KEY CONCEPTS

In order to discuss these issues, I use two very problematic categories that are far from universal or axiomatic in reference to the way they have become historically conceptualized and defined. In this sense, both are ideological notions that conform to specific historical and societal contexts and as such can only be examined within these same particular frameworks. Take the case of the concept of "foreign aid" and what it means in those terms. Often associated with foreign government interventions, it is, however sometimes, neither "foreign" nor can strictly be considered "aid." Neither can we say that nowadays it is solely official or allocated only by governments, as a great chunk of the resources deployed comes from the private sector or directly from the public (as in the case of donations, crowdfunding or money transfers/consignment).

Foreign aid has been often defined as a voluntary transfer of public resources, from a government to another independent government, to an NGO, Third Sector institution or even individual (Lancaster, 2008, p. 11). The ethics of foreign aid normatively claim that it aims to transfer resources (skills, know-how, capital, goods, or services) from a country or international organization for the benefit of the recipient country or its population. However, because aid can be economic, military, or emergency humanitarian (following natural disasters), it implicitly has a series of problematic issues as it enables "intervention" (Baldwin, 1969; Lugo-Ocando & Nguyen, 2017).

The other concept is that of "media development," which is as problematic as the above notion of foreign aid. Overall, media development refers to a separate albeit overlapping set of processes and initiatives, which development agencies, government, and international nongovernmental organizations (NGOs) try to engage with to strengthen the media sector in a particular country in the Global South; particularly in supporting "press freedom" (Vokes, 2017). Regularly linked to modernity and progress, development policy and efforts that try to foster media systems in the Global South have received important criticism from many scholars and practitioners. For Jesus Martin Barbero, for example, media development was, and continues to be, a key concept for those planners wanting to "bring modernity" to places such as Latin America. As he pointed out,

> Without it, planners would have been unable to break, for example, cultural links between, let us say, indigenous people and the land. It was thanks to the creation of a media landscape that mirrored that in the West that planners were able to introduce new cultures and re-shape worldviews, which made possible the acceptance of property rights over the land, the water and the air thanks, all this while introducing techno-deterministic notions in those societies. (Barbero, 2010)

Other scholars concur, as they see also a link between the use of foreign media to foster modernity as part of a wider effort to introduce notions of private property and land ownership that went against societal practice that are rooted in pre-Columbine cultures that survive even today, this despite of some criticism that Foreign Aid does not enough to promote private property rights, which—according to many in that field—are necessary for economic development (Leeson, 2008; Merrill, 2006; Saurin, 1996).

For all intents and purposes, Foreign Aid for Media Development became over the years an influential factor in disseminating news values and normative aspirations. Resources were transferred within the increasing expansion of Western media systems, which enabled the news media outlets in the Global South to play broadly the same role as they already played, at a national one, in the developed countries.

As some authors have suggested, the international media systems are one mechanism by which developing countries were brought within the common cultural hegemony of Western capitalism (Elliott & Golding, 1974, p. 229). At the center of this expansion and also underpinning the emerging discourse regime of "common sense" was "modernization," which was a political strategy that would be used as the justification to advance liberal democracy and the free market in the Third World. At the time of the Cold War, it was believed that US assistance would enable the transition of "traditional" societies into modernity, undertaking approaches that steer toward liberal, democratic, and capitalist directions (Latham, 1998, 2000),

> The problem, however, was that the United States did not possess a monopoly on transformative power. As Rostow and other strategists argued, one of the fundamental dangers in the world was the possibility that, in conjunction with trade, aid, and guerrilla warfare, the Soviets would succeed in projecting an image of Communism as the most efficient method for modernizing the underdeveloped regions and as a system closing rapidly on the sluggish American frontrunner.... Modernization, therefore, became a battle of image and identity as much as it was one of program and policy. (Latham, 2000, pp. 86–87)

The other aspect to take into consideration is that media development has manifested itself in multiple forms in the Global South.

Nevertheless, I focus here on one type of Foreign Aid for Media Development that is allocated to promote a particular type of journalism model. The reason for this focus is that media development in the context of journalism and liberal democracy has had the effect—intentionally or not—of consolidating the notion of common sense in the public debate and in so doing, it has brought about a paradigm that still defines the way citizens see the world around them. In this sense, foreign aid directed toward media development has aimed at changing the terms of reference for political debate in many places in the Global South. Most of these efforts have been directed at fostering media systems that replicate those of the donors while promoting values related to liberal democracy and the market economy (LaMay, 2009; Requejo-Alemán & Lugo-Ocando, 2014).

One fundamental aspect of Western aid is that it tries to place emphasis on securing media independence and professional autonomy for journalists (Myers, 2014; Uche, 1991). Therefore, many of the projects around this particular trend of aid are directed toward projects that are directed to advancing the agenda of a "free press" and particularly, nowadays, in promoting "diversity." However, by subordinating aid to projects that fall within these aims, they take a particular form, which ends up subscribing to ideologies. As I will discuss in a future chapter, we can see that in the majority of the cases that relate to these aid projects, particularly from Western donors, we find a focus on replicating the models of journalism that serve both liberal democracy and the market economy under the notions of free flow of information and objective news reporting.

Thanks to this, all ideologies have been rendered invisible in the newsroom while "market economy," the true and only ideology explicitly articulated, is presented as factual analysis and considered "natural" as an explanatory framework (Harkins & Lugo-Ocando, 2017; Harvey, 2007). In relation to specific newsbeat such as poverty, to put one example, this has led to a predominantly individualistic account of poverty and social exclusion that is constructed through the voices of elite sources and that reflects market ideology while claiming objectivity and factual analysis (Harkins & Lugo-Ocando, 2019; Lugo-Ocando, 2014).

Within this discussion, I have also included terms such as "media assistance" in the discussion. Media assistance emerged as a significant aspect of development work in the 1980s and the 1990s, particularly following the end of the Cold War and the dissolution of the former Soviet Union. It evolved from relatively modest programs with minor donations of equipment and training tours for journalists to long-term, multifaceted projects with multi-million dollar budgets (Price, 2002). Media assistance refers to resources and support provided to existing media outlets in order to improve their ability to contribute with the consolidation of liberal democracy. It is distinctive from, although closely related to, media development in that the latter deals with the broader set of policies and actions that are directed toward creating capabilities on the ground regardless of the political function of the media. Media assistance focuses on the resources provided to specific media outlets while media development includes a wider set of aspects including improving media access and literacy among the public.

Other categories that I will be using in this book are those that refer to the Global South and the Global North. I am very aware of the flawed baggage that these two notions carry with them and how problematic they are in the light of history and current society. I am also well aware of how these categories are used to generalize and paintbrush, with a single stroke, what are by any means very distinctive realities or essentialize a variety of countries in one single region (Lugo-Ocando, 2008). Nevertheless, a category such as Global South is a useful term that evokes a particular place and history, one that reflects society and institutions (Braveboy-Wagner, 2009). I have used these categories more as a metaphor of power and wealth rather than in relation to geography.

REVISING ASSUMPTIONS

Some scholars have already explained the formation of journalistic practices in the Global South from a hegemonic perspective (Golding, 1977; Mujica, 1982; Smith, 1980), particularly in relation to how these practices were "transferred" within the colonial and postcolonial settings. Other authors concur with this by extending the argument into the transferring of these practices and news cultures as part of wider hegemonic exercises during the Cold War (Papoutsaki, 2007; Parameswaran, 1997). This analysis continues by all means to be adequate as an explanatory framework, mostly because it suggests (although does not mention) a multiplicity of elements that have enabled the prevalence of particular journalism paradigms. No less, for example, the role of international news agencies and international broadcasters in setting the standards for the rest of the news actors at both a national and a supranational level (Boyd-Barrett, 1980; Boyd-Barrett & Rantanen, 1998; Paterson, 2005, 2011).

However, where there is a gap within our understanding is in the analysis and explanations around particular factors, such as foreign aid, which I argue here have contributed to establishing and supporting particular models of journalism. One of the key arguments of this book is in fact that, given these colonial and postcolonial settings, we should not treat the process that led to the prevalence of the Western paradigm of journalism only as a "historical occurrence" derived only from changes in the political economy of the media but rather recognize the presence of agency. I argue that there was in fact "standardization by imposition and contestation." That is, a process in which the values and practices associated to the news media in the centers of power were transferred to subordinated actors (colonial or market-dependent societies) in the South by creating professional aspirational thresholds, which enable for particular values to be adopted as part of a prevalent status within most journalists' worldviews.

This process of "professionalizing" social practices such as that of producing and disseminating news then helped replicate and reproduce practices and normative cultures under particular aesthetical forms in the newsroom around the world even in cultures and places where they remain contested. This is because the quest for "truth" in news reporting became, over the past two centuries, a matter defined exclusively by the Western ideal of rational enlightenment and liberal values (Martinisi & Lugo-Ocando, 2015, p. 440). This created a setting with normative goalposts, which acted as a Weberian ideal type for those who wanted to become news reporters. This suggests that the standardization of global culture in actual started during the Enlightenment thanks partially to the political power that was underpinned by the accumulation of capital from the transatlantic slave trade (Bailey, 1990) and by technology, that is, the role that the printed press had in political mobilization (Eisenstein, 1980, p. 148). It is a process that can be better explained in relation to Benedict Anderson's (2006 [1983]) notion of an imagined community, something that suggests that the media can foster a common culture and therefore a common sense of shared national identity and belonging (Parker, 2016, p. 14). However, and in all fairness, the standardization of global culture is not new. From ancient times, Phoenicians, Greeks, Romans and, more recently, the British Empire achieved a degree of cultural hegemonic imposition within their respective empires by fostering a general perception of shared culture that included syncretic forms of religion, political institutions, language, and other forms of collective expression (Hall & Rose, 2006).

At all times, empires have partially exercise cultural hegemony from the center by allocating power and legitimacy to communities of communicators who are locally trusted as legitimate sources of news and knowledge. For example, in their seminal analysis of the pre-columbine American society, Beltrán, Herrera, Pinto, and Torrico (2008, p. 180) highlighted how Mesoamerican civilizations created spaces to exchange information and news in their cities and how they had individuals who mediated this information. In the case of the Andean civilizations, this was the "Taki," who had a way of signing the events that had occurred so people in the cities and towns knew what was happening. It is important to underline that the "Taki" had to offer a "historical" and "very accurate" account of the events. The person who was commissioned by the town—not the authorities but the people themselves—had to offer accounts of events, people, and places was known as "takikamayok," which meant something like "registrar" or "person who remembers." In addition, the person's narrations had to be accessible given the format of a song and at the same time register details and facts of the events being narrated (Millones, 2007; Varón Gabai, 1990).

The difference between those forms of reporting in the ancient world and that of modern journalism that acts as an "interpretative community" (Zelizer, 1993, 2009) is both the industrial-shape aesthetics in the forms of news dissemination (which for a period left little room for other forms of presentation) and that today's news accounts center around the consumption of news as determined by the Market Society's logics. By this I mean that today's professional and mainstream journalism exercise is in fact not that different in its core function as a social practice from those in previous periods in humankind; that is, that all societies have exchanged information among the members, which in nature could be defined as truthful and accurate accounts of what happens or what we call today news. However, in today's modern world, the way this message is produced and disseminated presents a different aesthetics; one that is shaped by ideology, which over the years has become hegemonic and dominant. This ideology is summed up in the notion of market-driven economy characterized by privately owned property and means of production—and, by the construct that we have come to call liberal democracy.

The dissemination of news in modern times requires the same amount of "trust" that the Taki demanded in the pre-Columbus era in Peru. However, today's trust seems to depend to the objective nature of what is being reported and this is understood as providing the information without a political bias. Indeed, contrary to the advocacy pamphlets among workers' organizations in the 19th-century England, in the modern ideological setting of the market society, news has been deprived from its explicit political and ideological stance and subordinated instead to a "neutral" practice that reports the world with no emotions and no opinions but only the "facts."

This is what we find today at the forefront of these notions of standardizing the pursuit of "quality" and "ethics" by means of journalistic objectivity, which has been a fundamental tool for the articulation of a particular worldview where ideologies around social progress are rolled back in favor of a particular type of factual analysis (Lugo-Ocando, 2014, p. 174). Indeed, the concept of journalistic objectivity is employed by the modern newsroom as a way of detaching news coverage from engaging with wider structural social and economic issues. Western news coverage often stopped from referring to structural issues—such as inequality in relation to class struggle—as this was an approach that was considered to be "too ideological" in most newsrooms and gave instead an overview based on the overt facts (hence, only referring to poverty in a manifest manner).

Thanks to these practices, many explicit references to ideologies in the mainstream newsrooms in the Global South have been rendered invisible while "market economy," the true and only ideology explicitly articulated, is presented as factual analysis (Lugo-Ocando & Nguyen, 2017; Steel, 2013). In relation to specific news beats, such as poverty, by way of example, this has led to a predominantly individualistic account of poverty and social exclusion that is constructed through the voices of elite sources and that nevertheless reflect market ideology while claiming objectivity and factual analysis (Harkins & Lugo-Ocando, 2019; Lugo-Ocando, 2014). The mainstream news media in that part of the world, as I will discuss later on in the book, has adopted—although with degrees of contestations—the aesthetical framework into its own professional ethics and news cultures of producing and disseminating news.

In this book, I argue that throughout journalism's modern history in the Global South, there were overt and covert efforts to "standardize" it as a US-Western corporate practice (as opposed to a less homogenous social practice; i.e., citizen journalism), which was launched and supported from the center so as to underpin the expansion of liberal democracy and market-driven economy as an ideology. These efforts were particularly emphasized after the Soviet Revolution and the end of World War I. They included the creation of journalism schools and training facilities for reporters, the setting, dissemination, and adoption of a manual of styles—some years later—the expansion of the Associated Press (AP) as a news provider that also set values and standards and, the more general use of Foreign Aid for Media Development as a tool to implement these efforts (González & Torres, 2011; Horne, 2017; Silberstein-Loeb, 2014). This is why we need to understand these efforts, at least with regard to North-South relations, in the larger context of public diplomacy, geopolitics, and ideological struggles; in other words, as a set of efforts to project soft power. That is the ability to affect others to obtain the outcomes one wants through attraction rather than coercion or payment. In this sense,

> Public diplomacy has a long history as a means of promoting a country's soft power and was essential in winning the cold war. The current struggle against transnational terrorism is a struggle to win hearts and minds, and the current overreliance on hard power alone is not the path to success. Public diplomacy is an important tool in the arsenal of smart power, but smart public diplomacy requires an understanding of the roles of credibility, self-criticism, and civil society in generating soft power. (Nye Jr, 2008, p. 94)

The push for the creation of a particular type civil society in nations of the South was always seen as an attempt to reinforce market economy (Ehrenberg, 2017; Rueschemeyer, Stephens, & Stephens, 1992); this is because it meant expanding the so-called middle class and private ownership in general so as to secure hegemonic power. I say a particular type of civil society because Latin America had one, as Carlos A. Forment (2013) has well documented in relation to the period of 1760–1900. So, the type pushed in the postwar period tended to be consumer-oriented and politically aligned with the institutions of the bourgeoisie political system.

Therefore, far from just an "associational" view of the common, we need to place these efforts to "modernize" civil society that took place in the Cold War in terms of Gramscian logics; that is, by seeing the capitalist state as being made up of two overlapping spheres, a "political society," which rules through force, and a "civil society," which rules through consent. It is in pursuit of this consent that efforts at "modernizing" journalism took place in the Global South. Indeed, Foreign Aid for Media Development was at the center of these efforts to shape civil society in those countries; this by spreading values of Western journalism that subsequently helped to underpin the notion of "common sense" in the public imagination as a core value to make sense of the world while constructing social reality around the wider paradigm of the "Market Society" (Polanyi, 2001 [1944]).

MEDIA DEVELOPMENT

The efforts toward media development in the context of journalism and democracy has had the effect—intentionally or not—of consolidating the notion of common sense in the public debate, and, in so doing, it has brought about a paradigm that still defines the way citizens see the world around them. This is one of the most enduring influences of the "modernization" of journalism; one that has helped to establish the language of "common sense" as the hallmark for political discussion in the public sphere and that nowadays assists in the advancing of right-wing agendas (Lugo-Ocando, 2018; Pickering, 2001; Rosenfeld, 2011).

Journalism, as a political institution, has played a key role in setting the parameters for political debate among citizens in a way in which the public examination of society by individuals is considered only legitimate when it is driven by "factual" examination rather than by opinion or ideological analysis. For journalists of the past two centuries, this last issue has translated into the motto "comment is free, but facts are sacred" enunciated by one of the most emblematic editors of *The Guardian* newspaper, CP Scott (1846–1932). However, for journalists in the Global South, this has meant, in addition, emulating the Western model of journalism practice by focusing on the "facts" provided by institutional authorities—which are referred as "expert sources"—as legitimate sources of information, even when these authorities were not legitimate in places where there was no democracy at all or transparent institutions of governance (Alvear & Lugo-Ocando, 2016; Olukotun, 2004).

Accordingly, this "common sense" simplifies political debate to intuitive narratives that allows for superficial explanations of society's wrongdoings while displacing the blame for them to "the other," while "individualizing" the issues and de-structuralizing the analysis (Harkins & Lugo-Ocando, 2016a). By being absorbed and then becoming embedded in the organizational cultures of the newsrooms and professional networks, journalists working in the mainstream news media enable and reinforce such types of discursive regimes. They have done this by normatively claiming to adopt "journalistic objectivity" as a core normative value that assumes that one needs to be "scientific and rational" in order to achieve truth. In so doing, journalism has become a hegemonic institution in modern society, which has helped set and protect the parameters of political engagement by linking them to the values of the Enlightenment as a political project while underpinning over time the discourses of power of the ruling elites (Harkins & Lugo-Ocando, 2016b, 2017).

This had the effect of creating a particular culture within journalism, one that aspired to be scientific in the ideal set by positivism. However, in trying to emulate the scientific community, journalists also tend to confront the key problems of the scientific community, which tends to stick to existing worldviews—or paradigms as Kuhn (2012 [1962]) called them. Instead of constant innovation, scientists tend to discard anomalies and new discoveries until the existing paradigm is too flawed to remain as an explanatory framework in the face of scientific evidence. The problem for journalists is exactly the same but aggravated by the fact that their "paradigms" in the political and social world not only tend to last longer and be far more resistant to change, as they are deeply ideologically rooted and bound to political and corporate interests (or as Marx would suggest, the dominant ideas of the time, which are the ideas of the ruling class, tend to prevail and rule).

Far from being critical of the discourses of power, journalists tend to embrace them and adopt them in their own interpretation of the world (Harkins & Lugo-Ocando, 2016b, 2017). In the face of new evidence, even when it contests existing worldviews, journalists might interpret it differently to other particular members of their professional community. In other words, although journalists may want to see themselves as a "scientific community"—as Lippmann (2010 [1920]) once suggested—they fail to appreciate that their pursuit of truth is a very different one than that of natural scientists as rather than being scientifically centered, their quest for truth is profoundly ideologically defined and bounded to their own worldviews.

Nevertheless, over the past 100 years, this appearance of being scientific and seemingly constructing their narratives upon objective "facts" has allowed mainstream journalism as a political institution—at least in the United States and the United Kingdom—to push other forms of journalistic practices to the margins while presenting "structural analysis" as being too "ideological," "emotional," or "irrational" to be taken seriously and therefore restricting it to the margins of the public debate.[3] To be sure, as this particular way of practicing journalism consolidated over the years as a universal model and became accepted as legitimate, other forms of journalism practices around news production and dissemination became increasingly marginalized from the mainstream debates as they were considered propaganda and opinion (González & Torres, 2011; Janowitz, 1975; Schudson, 2001). Therefore, reducing these other formats and practices of communicating news to non-scientific expressions, which was something that would be synthesized in the notion of Four Models of the Press (Hampton, 2010; Siebert & Schramm, 1956).

Because of this, notions such as "journalistic objectivity" became historically intertwined in the public imagination—and among journalistic values—with freedom and democracy, while "structural analysis" and "dialectical materialism" became associated with propaganda, ideology, totalitarianism, and oppression. In this sense, it is claimed that journalism can only operate fully as a watchdog in a system that gives these professionals the freedom to present the "facts" beyond and in spite of any ideological consideration (Gauthier, 1993; McNair, 2000; Mindich, 2000). The argument has been, for many years, that journalism needed to be objective and this can only happen, arguably, in the context of a system in which individuals can make rational and free political choices (McNair, 2000; Overholser & Jamieson, 2005). Consequently, one of the unresolved dilemmas during the Cold War was how to promote journalism in places that lacked democracy or if these practices under repressive regimes, supported by the West, could be considered journalism at all (the Soviets as we will see later in this book had their own dilemmas). This dilemma was particularly exacerbated during the Eisenhower administration (1953–1961) as it started to sponsor a series of military coups, that is, ordering troops to Lebanon to thwart an uprising by Muslim rebels that supposedly had communist involvement. The Eisenhower Doctrine, as it became to be known, stated that it was best to have a pro-Western dictatorship than pro-Soviet democracy. It led to interventions and military support to despots in Guatemala, Iran, and many other parts of the Third World, although it did not deter Fidel Castro from coming into power in Cuba through guerrilla warfare (Statler & Johns, 2006; Takeyh, 2000).

It is important to say, however, that there was not necessarily linearity in the adoption of these journalistic values, nor did they go uncontested across the Global South. On the contrary, there was a distinctive gap between initial intentions and final outputs of these types of interventions.

The idea that American (US) journalism just hovered from the top and spread into the Global South societies its values can be easily challenged on the ground and certainly that is one of the core tasks of researchers in the pursue of De-Westernizing media studies as the superb effort deployed by Michael Bromley and Vera Slavtcheva-Petkova (2019) in their work on global journalism has shown. Moreover, as many of these aid efforts toward "media development," which initially colluded with dictatorships and authoritarian regimes in order to protect strategic interests in subservient markets and colonies, such as the newspapers set in India and African nations during the colonial time, went later to help instead to unleash the same forces that they were aiming to subdue (Chatterjee, 1993; Parameswaran, 1997). Similarly, many of the attempts that were originally set up as hegemonic projects ended up becoming spaces for contestation in which journalism was only partially co-opted in relation to its ability to challenge discourses of power in those societies.

If well Foreign Aid for Media Development has played a pivotal role in shaping journalism in the Global South, it has done so by undertaking different approaches and means. In a variety of cases, the end result was very different from what was originally anticipated by the donors. There are countless cases in which the same resources that were allocated to establish a particular type of hegemony ended up becoming the trigger to unleash the forces to contest the established power. As we will explore in this book, these apparent contradictions between what foreign aid initially aimed at and its final output is something that can help explain also—at least partially—the discrepancies, challenges, and re-interpretations of the dominant journalism aspirational paradigm found by the WJS and others across the South

(Mellado, Moreira, Lagos, & Hernández, 2012; Skjerdal, 2012) in relation to divergent normative aspirations across the globe.

Far from a cause-effect view that assumes straightforward relations of dominance and dependence, I suggest that the relationship between foreign aid and media development efforts and policies in the Global South is a phenomenon that continues to be much more complicated and dynamic than the traditional critical analysis has led us initially to believe. Rather than being just an effort to develop a sort of "Maquilas of Power" (Lugo-Ocando, 2008, p. 1) to reproduce hegemonic institutions in the South, Foreign Aid for Media Development has also provided a series of unintentional outputs that have shaped journalism as a social practice in ways that were initially not intended, therefore becoming manifestations of subversion and contestation. This is something that calls for a research agenda that is urgently necessary in times in which journalism is re-inventing itself (Anderson, Downie, & Schudson, 2016; Peters & Broersma, 2013).

UNDERSTANDING MEDIA DEVELOPMENT

Another important aspect that we will study in this book is the aid structures through which media development programs have been put in place in the Global South. They follow, as we will see in this book, complex mechanisms, which vary according to each specific case and the nature of both the donor and the political goals of the different parts. As one officer from a related NGO pointed out,

> The flow of funds often comes from donors (rich governments, private corporations or individuals). It then reaches agencies (multilateral institutions), and it is at this point funnelled to the recipient country through the implementers (NGOs, local partners, etc.). Support for independent media is one of the main fields for many Western donors, which tend to operate through either very transparent or obscure funding schemes.[4]

Because of this, it is very difficult in some cases to track specific projects and establish clearly the origin of certain funding streams. In those cases, media development projects are particularly difficult to map, as they are scattered across different sectors and funding instruments. It is rather emblematic that media aid programs, which are aimed at enhancing freedom of expression and transparency, are at times so obscure and secretive (Brownlee, 2017, p. 2281).

One of the most important aims of this book is precisely to highlight these contradictions and what they mean for today's re-invention of journalism—not only in the Global South but also in the North—where professional news reporting is being challenged by the demise of the traditional political economy of the news media, the rise of everyday new technological challenges and the de-politicization, fragmentation, and transformation of the news audiences. It is time, as I will argue throughout the book, to accept that any rethinking of professional journalism, at least in the Global South, needs to start by challenging its colonial and postcolonial settings that shaped its past and that continue to define its present. This last point, not only by leaving behind traditional dichotomies that may no longer be valid in some cases—such as the state versus the private in the models of public service broadcasting (Fuenzalida, 2000; Lugo-Ocando, Caizalez, & Lohmeier, 2010)—but also by accepting that the convergence of values and practices was not simply a random occurrence. Only then, as I intend to discuss here, the Global South will be better placed to rethink journalism in a way that responds better to the needs and aspirations of those living on the periphery of wealth and power. This is not a marginal enterprise destined to create a footnote in the new history of journalism in the 21st century but instead my effort is directed to help us rethink journalism through a particular perspective, one that happens to be that of the majority of those living on this planet.

The book is divided in chapters, starting with the introduction, which explains the objective and aims of the book as I have done so far in this chapter. The second chapter then goes to argue how the news media in the West came to embrace the language of common sense as a defining discursive regime of the news. It then discusses how this discursive language sets the parameters for news reporting that became the basis for normative aspiration and professional standards. This section goes on to explain how the language of common sense was firstly imposed in countries such as the United States and the United Kingdom and then follows that spread across the Global South.

The third chapter continues with the discussion about normative aspirations and standards that were imposed in the Global South as a broader historical process of projection of power and extension of the markets. The section discusses in depth the role of class struggles during the 20th century in shaping a particular way of doing journalism and mainstream news media. This is followed by a fourth chapter that discusses foreign aid and media development in the context of colonial and postcolonial settings. Chapter five focuses on disseminating the notion of factual news and particularly in relation to the notion of objectivity. The chapter argues that this type of approach to reporting is effectively an ideology that has been presented as a natural norm, that is to say that it has been assumed as universal and natural to news reporting. It is a norm that has its own geopolitics and that has played a crucial role in underpinning international policies relating to both media development and media assistance.

In chapter six, I discuss how educating and training journalists in the South has played such a central role in allowing not only the adoption of normative aspirations and professional standards but also how it was crucial in the adoption and reproduction of the models of news gathering and production. In so doing, the chapter assesses issues, overlaps, and discontinuities in the way foreign aid has funded journalism education across the globe. The seventh chapter examines Foreign Aid for Media Development in the digital age and tries to map what takes place on the ground. This is done by assessing what particular donors do on the ground and the specificities of each program. It looks at various examples across the Global South and uses them to illustrate current trends and approaches in the field. The chapter goes on to look at how aid is being channel to underpin and support the type of investigative reporting that is no longer performed by traditional mainstream media, also referred to as legacy media.

Finally, chapter eight provides a critical summary of the main conclusion that one can derive from this discussion. It explores how aid has helped shape values and practices of journalism in the Global South. It argues that this is perhaps the most important contribution toward the formation of journalism as a profession and as a political institution. It also discusses key philosophical aspects and argues the importance of contestation and resistance to the imposition of modernity in the formation of journalism in the South.

ACKNOWLEDGEMENTS

This book grew from initial discussions during a series of meetings and events funded by the Arts and Humanities Research Council in the United Kingdom, which awarded my colleague Chris Paterson and I a grant (AH/P00606X/1) to set a network around these topics. Thanks to these resources, we were able to organize a series of three symposiums, one in Leeds in the United Kingdom, a second one in Cartagena de Indias, Colombia, and a third one in Accra, Ghana, between 2017 and 2018. These meetings were part of the research network, which allowed scholars from Africa and Latin America to examine the global power relations and geopolitics of foreign aid that since the end of World War II has been substantially directed toward disseminating a specific model of journalism practice and education aligned with the interests of donor nations. The symposiums explored how the imposition of particular models of journalism practice have been central to the "modernization" efforts in the Global South and need to be conceptualized within the broader international development paradigm. This network looked at journalism practice, journalism education, and critical journalism studies in the context of the impact that foreign aid and assistance has had in these regions and how this has affected the ability of these developing regions to foster a critical and independent media sector.

This research network produced several publications, including two special issues of two separate journals, most of which have been used to substantiate some of the discussions in this book. However, it was perhaps the ability to network and discuss with scholars working in this field that perhaps proved more valuable to me. I never imagined that this topic, which at the time we considered a niche, would attract such a variety of talented and acute scholars and high-quality works. It was in interaction with them and particularly with my colleagues in the network project that I came to elaborate upon the key ideas I have discussed here. Hence, I would want to thank firstly my dear friend and former colleague at the University of Leeds Chris Paterson in the United Kingdom. His support, ideas, and intellectual exchanges provided the grounds for this book. I would also want to thank professors Cosette Castro at the Catholic University of Brasilia (UCB) in Brazil, Audrey Gadzekpo at the University of Ghana, Maria Soledad Segura at the Universidad Nacional de Córdoba in Argentina, and Herman Wasserman at the University of Cape Town in South Africa, who became fellow travelers and close friends in this intellectual journey.

The book as well as the research project was widely inspired by Professor Barbie Zelizer's ideas about the formation of journalism in the United States as a nation-building exercise, which she presented succinctly to us at the University of Leeds back in 2017. In numerous occasions, before and after that we met at the fringes of conferences and events and talk about the implications of such a perspective not only for the United States but also to the rest of the world. So, to her, I express also my gratitude for such important discussions.

Some key parts of the book were also made possible by other sources of funding. This included the Theodore C. Sorensen Fellowship from the John F. Kennedy Library and a Research Grants for Scholarship from the Truman Presidential Library & Museum. I am deeply grateful to the staff of these two libraries, who helped and assisted me in this project by allowing to explore a series of documents that were essential to understand the history and context of foreign aid. In this sense, I would also want to thank the staff from AP archives in New York and the Dwight D. Eisenhower Presidential Library & Museum in Abilene, Kansas, who were all immensely helpful and supportive.

In the journey to develop this book, I also had the pleasure to exchange ideas and receive feedback from practitioners and researchers in the field in a diversity of locations and places from around the world. They are a small but very active group of individuals, practitioners, and academics, who are producing ground-breaking research in this area. There are: Susan Abbott, Mel Bunce, Nicholas Benequista, Winston Mano, Toussaint Nothias, Martin

Scott, and Kate Wright. To them, my gratitude for their friendship and feedback over the years. From a very small place of discussion about these and other related topics, we have gone to a proper platform of debate.

I would specially want to thank Professor Martin Conboy, with whom I debated for long hours about these topics in our own trenches at the University of Sheffield in the United Kingdom. Under a heavy artillery of arguments and counterarguments, the discussions were pivotal in exploring these ideas. His work makes him undoubtedly one of the pre-eminent journalism historians but his great knowledge and wittiness also make him a formidable intellectual adversary and friend. Equally, my gratitude goes to Professor Silvio Waisbord for his comments and feedback. No doubt that Silvio, who himself is one of the most solid voices in our field, has been a champion when promoting the scholar work of Latin America and the Global South in general; a true bridge that connects knowledge across the globe. Both of them made this work much better than the original draft was. However, and goes almost without saying although it is an important clarification, I am still sole responsible for flaws and shortcomings in this monograph.

Finally, to Maria Alejandra D'Lacoste, my wife, who has joined me in this adventure that we chose to call life and whose newlywed patience made this book possible.

NOTES

1. According to this last concept, a nation is a socially constructed community, imagined by the people who perceive themselves as part of that group (B. Anderson, 2006 [1983], pp. 6–7). For him, the media also creates imagined communities, through usually targeting a mass audience or generalizing and addressing citizens as the public, while also creating imagined communities through the use of images to which the people can relate to.

2. I should point out that media development is not often used in academia. Many academics prefer to refer instead to media for development or media for social change. However, given the distinctive meaning in the context of this piece, I have decided to use it, although I am well aware of the problematic dimension that is brought into discussion by incorporating such a label.

3. Let us not forget that these debates around scientific/rational approaches against irrational/ideological did not only happen in the West. In the Soviet Union, for example, they were also at the center of discussions (Ings, 2017; Pollock, 2006).

4. Interview with NGO official on February 5, 2020. Identity withheld at the request of the interviewee.

Chapter 2

The Imposition of Common Sense

Very often, mainstream journalism is credited for having played a key role in setting the parameters for modern political public debate in ways in which the wider examination of society by individuals is considered only legitimate when it is de-emotionalized and driven by "factual" analysis rather than by opinion or ideological structural deconstruction (Glück, 2016; Koch, 1990). This function of the press was developed in a time in which the progressive opening to the masses of the bourgeois public sphere was also occurring. One that was aided, at least partially, by the rise, not only of the mass media—including newspapers, theatres, museums, and so on (Habermas & Habermas, 1991, p. 43)—but also by increasing literacy rates since the 19th century and the growing unionization of workers and politicization of society in more general terms.

However, in parallel to this opening, there was at the same time an important restriction to other important public spaces. One that had started in the 16th century, consolidated in the 17th century, and that by the 18th century was an established norm. Land closure of what was, until then, "common land" and, the privatization and appropriation of common property by individuals in places such as England and North America, meant not only limiting access to means of production and subsistence for many but also pushed the displacement of large segments of the population into the new urban dwellings that gave birth to the public sphere as we know it today (Blomley, 2007; White, 1969).

In Europe as well as in its colonial overseas sphere, the process of state formation and property formation went hand in hand. The formation of centralized bureaucracies and armies was deeply linked to land being commodified as part of the incipient expansion of the markets (Greer, 2018, p. 355). Property appropriation—which included turning humans into slaves—was not only central to this but also in supporting the industrial revolution as a whole; establishing both, the ownership of the mills and of the black slaves from Africa that generated the capital to fuel that revolution (Eltis & Engerman, 2000; Inikori, 1989). In this sense, the historical and ideological foundations of modern journalism reflected the opening of the public sphere in the terms set by liberal democracy and also by the need to guarantee property rights set by the early capitalist trends mentioned earlier. Since the dominant ideas of the time are those of the class that owns the means of production (Claeys, 2018), one could argue that liberalism, which provided the ideological basis for modern journalism, reflected, according to Lenin (1919), both the political institutions set by the ruling class and the need to preserve the structure of private property.

Although this analysis might seem nowadays démodé, one element still stands out, that journalism as a commercial and mainstream enterprise has an ethical and professional commitment to preserve private property. This is not only because it is still the basis of the political economy that sustains it but also because private ownership of the media has historically defined and secured, in the collective eyes of many, its own independence, freedom and professional autonomy. This is the case at all the levels of the media; local, national, and global. Marxists are right when they point out that the media sphere is a bourgeoisie sphere even if this also provides access to other voices and at times and enables scrutiny of corporations and elites. Beyond the complexities relating to who participates in the debates and how much is exclusive of a particular class, the fact remains that most journalists in the West by definition will only conceive a viable free press if this is under private hands and detached from the state (Knight, 1982), with perhaps the exception of the public service broadcasters tradition in Europe. Yes, there is the question of the very European notion of public service broadcasters, but these are media outlets that reflect rather the aspiration of impartiality and balance than of press freedom. All in all, there is the historically strong belief that the media had to be in private hands as a way of securing independence from the state, something that has only become more prevalent over the years.

Modern journalism was born and bred within this scope and as part of a liberal project that had this as part of its scaffoldings. As such it has had to deal with the tensions between normative claims of free speech to all and its underlining protection of private property, which unequivocally underpins the power of the ruling class. It has been able to manage these tensions and even reconcile both elements by increasingly adopting the language of "common sense." This allowed journalism as a collective professional body—with the exception of the radical expressions that were soon overrun by the market—to claim being a defender of freedom, a watchdog against the powerful and the unified voice of "the people" (or the "public" as it was later assumed).

News became a commodity, that was industrialized on a mass scale and that catered for all publics (and classes) in a way that was allegedly neither ideological nor politically biased.

Consequently, thanks to this reconciliation, this form of "industrialized" news media, capable of mass production and mass dissemination of news, was central to the construction of an ideal of nation in multicultural places such as the United States. However, it was one which was also strongly anchored upon the identity of "property owner" later evolving so as to be anchored, particularly after World War II, upon the notion of "consumer." As such, the news media became a glue of the social fabric and a core identifier of what it meant to be "American" (Lugo-Ocando, 2008; Wood, 1991) in the case of the United States. This was the exact construct that became the model that would be later exported throughout the Global South with the help of foreign aid.

INITIAL PARAMETERS

Given this background, it is crucial to understand the history as to how the philosophical foundations of Western modern journalism—or what has been called the "philosophy of truth" (Hearns-Branaman, 2016)—derived in today's prevalent form of news reporting. In this sense, one can argue that the modern parameters for public debate have been ultimately defined in the past 130 years by media interventions.[1] These interventions consisted mainly—at least until almost the end of the 20th century—of a process dominated by the mass production and dissemination of news in a way that replicated the rest of what the Industrial Revolution did for other areas of the economy. It reflected what José Ortega y Gasset called the "Rebellion of the Masses" (1993 [1929]) or the arrival of the mass-industrialized society into the public sphere. One that occurred in certain particular terms set by the legacy of the Enlightenment and bourgeois' rationale (Adorno & Horkheimer, 1997 [1944]) but that also galvanized the rise of a working class that demanded more rights and further access to power.

Even before the Russian Revolution in 1917, elites had already put their ear to the ground in relation to the role of the news media in political agitation among the working class. By the middle of the 19th century and all the way to the beginning of the 20th century, many authors had expressed profound concerns about the rise of the "masses" (Le Bon, 2010 [1897]; Ortega, 1993 [1929]; Tarde, 2010 [1895]). Their work synthesized the elites' misgivings and misapprehensions in relation to the effects that rapid urbanization—in the backdrop of the Industrial Revolution—was having upon politics, particularly regarding how the new urban masses were rapidly becoming a threat to the status quo. Their writings reflected some of the worst elite's fears of that time: that these masses would take over power by a world revolution. These fears, one must add, were not completely unfounded concerns as several revolutions and uprisings had characterized this period, which saw the working class at the center of political struggles (Rapport, 2009; Read, 2008).

One of the pivotal fears centered around the role of the media, particularly radical newspapers, in stirring the masses and contributing to political uprisings (De Balzac, 2009 [1843]; Eley, 2002; J. D. Popkin, 1990). It is possible to see these fears toward the masses as an example of moral panic; one that was not completely unfounded as the press had had indeed a central role in agitating workers in many parts of the world (Curran & Seaton, 2009; J. D. Popkin, 1990). Even many newspaper owners, who by then had become part of the new industrial setting (Brendon, 1983; Seldes, 1938), started to express their own reservations against that part of the press that remained vociferous, committed, and militant in the workers' struggles. There were important precedents for these concerns as historians have widely documented the way authorities in the United Kingdom, to give an example, imposed the first newspaper tax way back in 1712; one that was intended to place limits on newspapers' readership and curb radicalism (Curran, 1978; J. A. Smith, 1990). Similar concerns were also raised in the United States by editors and newspaper proprietors who themselves had initially supported radicalism in the past only later to go on and call for limits to the populist and "pro-negro" press (Hogan, 1984; Horne, 2017b). In the United States, curbing the radical press was strongly associated with reactionary responses to anti-slavery struggles, the populist-alliance between poor whites and blacks, and the emergence of workers' unions (González & Torres, 2011). In fact, one could argue that since the 18th century, there were orchestrated efforts to limit public access to the press, a product of the fear of its ability to mobilize the public.

It was in the context of these growing fears when the Russian Revolution of 1917 happened, which came as a shock to the US and European elites as it summed up all of their fears. Here we were, in the face of potentially the most threatening menace of the worldwide workers' revolution. One that proposed a completely different world order and that challenged, not only the property of the means of production, but also that threatened to disrupt the world markets and status quo given the initial support from the masses. The birth of the Soviet Union was, in the elites' eyes, the "cataclysmic event" they feared and one that was even more than the World War that was still going on; several authors have suggested, for example, that once of the reasons for German rendition was partly due to the internal upheavals in the face of workers' strikes and actions (Hagedorn, 2007; Read, 2008).

It was in this context that news organization consolidated their willingness to turn "news" into a mass-consumed product that was then able to attract audiences' attention in such a scale that could convert these same audiences into a commodity for products, services, and power. This rise of the mass media also operated on ideological and cultural levels as it provided the societal platform for the mass consumption of ideas. Despite the fact that newspapers had existed long before the press developed as a mass medium or had the ability to attract a mass readership (Conboy, 2004; Gorman & McLean, 2003; Winston, 2002) it was only in the industrial period that they gained such massive inroads into the public mind (Pettegree, 2014). This helped to crystalize the ability of the news media, collectively, in fostering power to sell and mobilize masses in the United States and Europe. It was this ability to create hegemonic mechanisms in the hands of the bourgeoisie that many, years later, would want to be replicated in other parts of the world, first with the pro-colonial newspapers in the late 19th century and later with foreign aid efforts after World War II and during the Cold War. For example, as some authors have suggested, the use of the media in underpinning Giuseppe Garibaldi as a political leader and hero were pivotal in his efforts to unify Italy as a nation (Riall, 2007).

Subsequently, any historical account of how this model of journalism was exported to the Global South has to start by acknowledging that newspapers in the United States—as with other key political institutions in that country—were set in terms of envisaging both as a nation-building exercise and keeping in mind "property" as the cornerstone for liberty (Epstein, 2003; Siegan, 2018), particularly in relation to the independence of the individual in the newly formed nation from the state (which they saw as the King). In this sense, the ideas of the English philosopher and physician, John Locke (1632–1704), regarding property were intrinsically embedded into how the rights around freedom of expression were later conceptualized. Regarded as one of the most influential thinkers of the Enlightenment, he is often considered as the "Father of Liberalism" (Dunn, 1982; Tully, 1982). Locke was an empiricist who followed the tradition of Sir Francis Bacon (1561–1626), whose work greatly affected the development of epistemology and political philosophy.

In his Second Treatise of Government, Locke (2016 [1690]) presented his theory of property rights, which was mostly rooted in laws of nature. In it, he had identified the right of individuals to exercise control over the land and other material resources. In fact, he argued that ownership of private property is a natural right of every individual and that this right pre-existed government. For him, it was as inalienable as the rights of life, liberty, and the pursuit of happiness and therefore it must be protected in the same way we should protect other inalienable rights. However, Locke's treatment of the issue of private property did not fall within the canons with which we use to conceptualize today property rights and therefore his theory remains highly controversial among scholars and is often used to justify everything from laissez-faire to the welfare state and to full-blown socialism.

What is important, however, was how over history many have linked the Founding Fathers to the US interpretations of freedom made by Locke and how this, in turn, was linked to the notion of property with individual freedom as this would become central to the development of US political institutions by being included in the Declaration of Independence (Handlin & Handlin, 1989; Manion, 1949). Locke's work would go on to help shape many of the institutions of the new world (Brewer & Staves, 2014; Ward, 2010) and by extension after the 1940s to return to Europe to reshape theirs. It is there where we can find the reason as to why centuries after, politicians and government officials would start using the term "Un-American" to refer to activities that went against not only the United States but also against the free market and private property (Davis, 1971; Nielsen, 2001). This would be a strand of thought deeply enshrined into journalism, as many such as Walter Lippmann argued that "private property was the original source of freedom and that it was still is its main ballpark."

Journalism as a US political institution became part of that same "liberal" superstructure that defined the US and post–World War II modern political institutions. One that inherited from the Enlightenment its quest for scientific truth based on reason and knowledge. Nevertheless, it is one institution that would be equally indebted to the build-up to the Industrial Revolution and in particular to the growing philosophical defense of private property as a way of protecting individual rights against the monarchs (the state). Therefore, the type of journalism that grew on US soil tried, from the start, to bring about reason and deduction into the public debate within the same types of parameters that the Enlightenment put into play for the natural sciences but with the caveat that it placed equal importance on the defense of the "private" and particularly of private property as an enabler of individual freedom. This mainly, reflected in a landscape of local and national newspapers that operated under private citizens and in contraposition to the state (Atton & Hamilton, 2008).

From this, it is possible to argue that the discursive setting that defines today the discussions within the news media space, those that are being exported to the Global South as a model to follow as we speak, is a direct result not only of journalism's aspirations to be scientific but also of the overall consolidation of the "private" domain into public life (Fitzgerald, 2007). This is why, even today, after the emergence of public service broadcasters in Europe and foundation-sponsored digital-native journalistic initiatives, it is difficult to think of a "free" press other than that which is privately owned and commercially viable. Furthermore, this defense of "private property" has been historically underpinned by Malthusianism as an explanatory framework.

This is because in addition to the widely publicized warning against unlimited growth of the population versus scarce resources-referred to as the geometric of population growth against the arithmetic of available resources-, Thomas Robert Malthus was also able to advance the even more perverse argument that in order to administrate efficiently these resources the elites had to secure property rights of the land and other resources (Harkins & Lugo-Ocando, 2016b; Ross, 1998).

Therefore, journalism not only subscribed to the Enlightenment as a political project but also embraced broadly the bourgeois' rationale on private property and market. Victor Pickard (2015) has identified this as the "discursive capture," arguing that attempts to reform the US paradigm of journalism and news media—referring to the Hutchins Commission in the 1940s and the Waldman Report of 2011—have been constrained by the fact that conceptualizations around the role of the press in that country are implicitly defined by pro-market and property rights ideologies.

REASONS AND NEWS REPORTING

Journalists claim to adhere to aspirational values of scientific objectivity as a way of achieving "reason" while assuming that private property and market is the way if maintaining the necessary independence from any state imposition and underpin professional autonomy. The logic behind this is that in order to achieve its goal of political independence and to perform reason one needs the media not to be in the hands of the state and instead be privately owned and subject to the free market of ideas (Hearns-Branaman, 2016; Steel, 2013). This became the framework upon which the sense of professional autonomy in journalism would be built over the past two centuries, one that gives reporters the ability to claim legitimate authority over truth and achieve public trust to the accounts of the human world that they report.

This unwritten social contract that awards public trust to journalists and a privileged position in society, in exchange for performing the role of watchdog to power, makes journalists a sort of a professional community that can exercise authorial control over the news. Their central claim for this is to be able to produce scientifically objective and impartial understanding of human affairs (Anderson, 2018; Zelizer, 1993) and therefore provide "reason" to governments and people. Moreover, their normative aspiration is that somehow their craft is supporting the common good because of its own ability to deliver a truthful account of the things they report upon (Carlson, 2017, p. 35). In other words, journalism as a profession is able to claim authorial domain over truth upon its own ability to emulate a particular type of rationality, that of the Enlightenment, in the way that it presents the news stories as scientific. By this, it is meant, not subject to partisan opinions but grounded in reason but a type of reasoning that is only independent because it is not subject to the state thanks to the fact that it is exercised by means of the privately owned media.

This last idea translates in the fact that mainstream Western modern journalism can also be viewed as a positivist enterprise in that it claims authorial control over truth on the basis that the information that it disseminates is derived from sensory experience (calling it factual), which, in turn, is interpreted through reason and logic. One of the reasons why Western mainstream journalism, as a collective community, undertook such as angle was its quest for scientific validation. To be fair, it was not only journalism that fallowed this path as positivist thinking gave birth to most of the branches of modern social science today (Bryant, 1985; Burtt, 2014; Stengers, 2000). Hence, these "positivist foundations" are not a footnote in the history of news reporting but a fundamental aspect that helps explains its nature, professional cultures, and current deontology. The grammar of Western journalism is certainly one defined by positivism, which is crucial in understanding its stance toward objectivity and truth (Durham, 1998; McNair, 2006; Wien, 2005).

As a strand of Western philosophy, positivism confines itself to the data of experience, excluding its way a priori or metaphysical speculations. Positivism argues that all knowledge regarding matters of fact is based on the "positive" data of experience and that beyond the realm of fact is that of pure logic and pure mathematics. This explains why the Western paradigm of journalism has been so keen in linking itself with the use of data, something that dates back decades but that more recently has been undertaken in a much bigger fashion (Anderson, 2018; Borges-Rey, 2016; Martisini and Lugo-Ocando, 2020). Indeed, a key element of the paradigm of journalism that was exported to the Global South is its closeness with an ideal of truth shaped by data, particularly in relation to mathematical data as a way of underpinning truth in their news narratives (Lugo-Ocando & Faria Brandão, 2016; Martinisi & Lugo-Ocando, 2015).

Journalism, which now sees itself as a discipline of knowledge, with its own epistemology, has embraced positivism in the same way that sociology did in the past, which came to be associated with the very idea of a social science and the quest to be scientific (Bryant, 1985, p. 1). Not surprisingly, and given the initial association between journalism and sociology in the United States, the journalistic mainstream community embraced similar approaches toward truth. Journalism, that imperfect "vessel of truth" as Michel Schudson once describe it (2009, p. 108), saw "facts" as truth and tended to assess them in a positivist fashion.

Consequently, the professionalization of journalism aspired to follow the pathway of disciplines such as sociology, anthropology, and modern economics, that also sought to interpret the world in a "scientific" manner (Muñoz-Torres, 2012; Wien, 2005). However, it additionally developed a collective rational that was empiricist in such a way that it related more to the type of positivism predicated by Auguste Comte (1798–1857) than to the natural sciences. Moreover, in doing so, it assumed a long-standing, love-hate, relationship with sociology, which followed a similar pathway toward datafication (Anderson, 2018). Hence, journalism was and continues to be, particularly today with the rise of approaches such as Data Journalism, a social practice that sees itself as an objective effort that is empirically driven and that aspires for factual truth that is mostly positive-based (or as Comte would call it, mathematical).

Journalism as a professional body was in its way able to argue for "objectivity" and "impartiality" as core normative values, something that assumes that the social world can be analyzed throughout the same type of "scientific rationality" as that of the natural world. This argument depends, of course, on the ability of those who analyze it "to have the independence to apply the necessary reason." However, and this is a key point of the argument, contrary to natural science it derived "truth" not from experimentation—led to test assumptions—but by appealing to people's popular common sense, hence taking for granted the assumptions themselves as truth.[2] This assumption derived from the notion that there were certain "truths" that we intrinsically held and that reflected universal and axiomatical moral understandings of the world.

Journalist came to embrace the 'common sense' language as a way of reiterating also their commitment towards the 'common good'. In other words, making news accounts as appealing, accessible, and overall as reasonable as possible in order to connect with the general public by claiming that they represented the voice of the people in their objectives and language. Reporters from the start embraced the idea that not only their stories need to reflect the "facts"—and by these they meant what everyone knew—but that also -and at the same time- that they had a role as storytellers (Bird & Dardenne, 2009; Roeh, 1989) who could connect with people's '"common sense"' by making sure that their language, narratives, and discourses reflected the common ideas of the times, which were considered to be the truth (speaking the "evident" truth).

This approach had also an economic reason; the industrialization of journalism meant the expansion of its markets—which now included vast segments of the population—that needed to be reached by a standardized form of news that could be exchanged as any other commodity (Jackson, 2009; McManus, 1992). What was seen as a source of information and entertainment for a small elite went on to occupy important public spaces in society and be more inclusive while becoming a full large-scale corporate enterprise (Black, 2001; Conboy, 2004). Indeed, running in parallel—and closely intertwined—with positivism and the Enlightenment political project that defined journalism, mainstream news media developed also as a "popular" platform of communicating news to the public (Conboy, 2006).

By being accessible to the broader masses, the news media also became part of a larger discursive project of populist politics. One that expanded its reach to the masses and that was driven by the market as an unspoken ideology. In doing so, it claimed for itself to be the genuine voices of "the people" and to be upholding the truths that are "universally" evident to "all" (Tumber & Prentoulis, 2005). Journalism was able to offer then an "alternative public sphere" (Örnebring & Jönsson, 2004) for people's "truth" in the words of common sense. This was not, however, the radical, rational and structured notion of "common sense" as presented by Thomas Paine (2004 [1776]) and others but instead, a very conservative form of framing news in terms of populist language.

Hence, the "industrial revolution" and the "communication revolution"—at least in relation to news—needs to be analyzed as to sides of the same coin (Briggs & Burke, 2002, p. 107) that claimed to bring about scientific reasoning into the public debate but that did so by fiercely defended private property as the cornerstone for free and independent journalism as part of an ideal of preserving the common sense upon which that reasoning was based. Over the subsequent centuries, this rationale became less about property and more about the Market Society to which Polanyi (2001 [1944]) referred to. As Armand Mattelart suggests, from then on, the market would become the matrix to cement the "general will" while constructing the nation's general bond (1996, p. 277) to which the news media still appeals to as a way of underpinning its own legitimacy in society. This is an arrangement that, despite being in crisis today, continues to lay the foundations of the way in which journalists produce their stories and how the audiences consume them.

ON COMMON SENSE

In light of the earlier given section, I would argue that one most enduring influences of Foreign Aid upon modern journalism in the Global South has been to underpin the establishment of the language of "common sense" as the hallmark for political discussion in the public sphere. Hence the importance of understanding not only how news language became to be common sense language, but also how common sense itself mutated from being a positivist way of using scientific reasoning to examine, explain, and transform the world to a populist simplification of the issues and problems of society; nowadays used as a rhetorical tool to mobilize the masses.

Indeed, the use of "common sense" by journalists reflected from the start a very long historical tradition of using the popular instinct for "truth." This tradition aimed at collapsing the difference between intellectual authority figures [what we today call experts] and "the people" as a whole. In so doing, this tradition has evolved first to award and then later on—in more recent times—to deny "experts" any special claim upon truth. This tradition—that started to spread in the mid-18th century hand in hand with the Enlightenment and the emergence of modern journalism—gave new validity to the judgment of the "everyman," the ordinary guy whose perception of the world is "unclouded" by the fancy dialectics or jargon used by the experts [philosophers] (Rosenfeld, 2011).

The "common sense" that I discuss here in the terms set by Antonio Gramsci (2003 [1935]) is present in contemporary journalism when reporting the outside world. Indeed, one glimpse at the front pages of the London-based newspapers such as *The Sun* or *The Daily Mail* or a brief encounter with Fox News in the United States is sufficient to see how common sense has become the defining feature in the news content produced by these and other news media outlets (as it is not restricted to right-wing outlets). The simplification and then exaggeration of reality—distorted or not, one could argue—that claims truthfulness on the basis of its own popular appeal among the masses, or part of them, became current currency a long time ago, way before the Trump administration came into power in the United States.

Consequently, political debate in the news media is simplified to intuitive narratives that allows for superficial explanations of society's wrongdoings—which often obviates structural causes and historical contexts—while displacing the blame to "the other" (Bailey & Harindranath, 2005). Hence, to give an example, instead of analyzing structural causes for poverty and social exclusion such as class, ownership, and property of the economic means of production, important segments of the media set instead a narrative tone where the problem becomes the responsibility of those who are the victims (Lugo-Ocando, 2014).

Let us remind ourselves that the explanation for the current state of the world economy, as most economists and experts today agree, is rather complex and it is not possible within the scope of the book to deconstruct such complex matter. However, it is important to provide perhaps an overview of what we have faced in the past twenty years of economic adjustment, austerity, and restructuring. It is a process that has translated into the dislocation of economic activities, jobs, and decimating local communities. Most economists today agree that one of the main reasons for increasing unemployment and subemployment in places such as the United States and Western Europe can be attributed to de-industrialization of large segments of their urban spaces (Emmenegger, H'Ausermann, Häusermann, Palier, & Seeleib-Kaiser, 2012; Kiesewetter, 1998).

This means that industries formally based in these countries have been displaced and relocated to places such as China, India and Vietnam, while owners have used the international copyrights regime under the World Trade

Organization to keep their profits from the use of their brands and giving them access to the global markets (Freyssinet, 2010). In addition, advances in technology have meant a reduction of the workforce in many areas, while de-regulation of the financial markets have facilitated the transfer of profits into offshore tax heavens (Holtzblatt, Jermakowicz, & Epstein, 2015; Palan, Murphy, & Chavagneux, 2013).

Trillions of US dollars, therefore, remain unused as capital by staying in the shadows of an increasingly globalized and opaque financial system, undermining the taxation capabilities of many nations. This in turn has translated into governments adopting neoliberal agendas and dismantling the welfare state. In this context, nations compete to the bottom against each other to see who can offer a better tax bargain for hyper-greedy corporations (Shaxson, 2011). All off this has been aggravated by anti-union policies that have crippled the ability of organized workers to fight back. This explains, at least partially, the increasing levels of inequality and poverty on a national and international scale. Yes, countries such as China have done well in this deal, but at the expense of entire continents, such as Africa, Latin America, and large sections of the populations of Europe and North America (Noble, 2017).

However, instead of presenting these complexities to the public, the news media tends to disseminate narratives that embrace a "common sense" explanation where jobs are lost to "immigrants" or "just stolen" by China. Hence, in a time when, for example, US and European workers have seen a long period of salary stagnation and fall in real terms (Bavier, 2014; Madrick & Papanikolaou, 2010), it is no wonder that many chose to vote for populist candidates that offered heaven and earth in the most simplistic—yet irresponsible—terms. For these voters, a wall in the border with Mexico or to stop a ship full of refugees from entering into their ports in order to deter "others" from coming appears to be a straight solution that resonates with their own experiences and common sense. This "common sense" explanation seem far more truthful and real to many on the ground than the complex explanations based on the counter-flows of migration from previous decades of colonial and interventionist history and the convoluted brutality of neoliberalism.

Another interesting example of this refers to reporting the politics of "choice." The politics of "choice" became extremely influential in mobilizing the right during the 1980s and 1990s, particularly in areas such as housing and education (although in health it had been present for a long time). This consisted of narratives that offer empowerment through choice and that are anchored in a sense of aspirational class progress by merit. In this sense, housing policy in the United Kingdom was perhaps seen as one of Margaret Thatcher's administration's most emblematic policies (1979–1990). One which privatized houses belonging to the city councils by giving tenants the "right to own" (Atkinson & Durden, 1990; Forrest & Murie, 2014). At the time, the policy and the news narratives provided an aspirational message of giving the people the possibility to become proprietors and get up the ladder of class, therefore changing the cultural politics of that time (Jensen & Tyler, 2015).

Neither one needs to reiterate, as most studies have suggested, that the main beneficiaries of the privatization of council houses were housing corporations and individuals who ended up grabbing a great deal of these properties after being resold in the market (Atkinson & Durden, 1990; Daly, Mooney, Poole, & Davis, 2005; Forrest & Murie, 2014; Whitehead, 1993). Neither do we have to remind ourselves that it is not surprising that current levels of homelessness are strongly associated with the fact that city councils in the United Kingdom no longer own enough facilities to accommodate those destitute and instead have to pay, at the market rates, for the accommodations that they once owned (Somerville, 1994; Willse, 2010).

However, perhaps even more widespread has been policies and narratives around school vouchers, which give parents the supposed ability to select the school "of their choice." This is in the background of a growing privatized education industry, which use flawed rankings to lure parents into private institutions in the belief that their children would have then a better chance to get into the ladder of success (Fuller & Elmore, 1996; Nechyba, 2000). Needless to say, these policies in reality give no choice to a single mother on a low income who lives in the other side of the city and holds down two jobs just to keep herself afloat, no matter how smart her kid is. They are fundamentally regressive and segregationist as they have meant on the ground a massive transfer of resources from the poor into the pockets of the well-off. However, thanks to the language of common sense, which proclaims "freedom of choice" in the school market, many remain convinced of its alleged merits.

INTERPRETING COMMON SENSE

Over the years, these ways of adopting "common sense" as the theoretical explanatory framework to interpret the world were also embraced by large segments of the news media in the Global South, which acted as "Maquilas of Power" (Lugo-Ocando, 2008) that reproduced and assemblage, locally, foreign ideologies that justified transnational axis of economic and political power. In so doing, professional mainstream journalism in the Global South was another postcolonial hegemonic institution in modern society that has been able to claim "truthfulness" while helping to set and protect the parameters of political engagement by linking them to the values of the superimposed Enlightenment as a political project, which turned over time into a positivist logics of interpreting facts as a way of achieving truth. In this manner, journalism as a professional mainstream body of knowledge production has for years underpinned the discourses of power, at least in relation to the issue of property, of the ruling elites (Harkins & Lugo-Ocando, 2016b, 2017) by claiming access to, and legitimacy over, truth.

This way of producing "truth" became a prevalent one thanks, at least partially, to embracing "common sense" as a discursive regime. Over the centuries, the commercial-mainstream paradigm of journalistic practice pushed other forms of journalistic practices to the margins while discrediting "structural analysis" as a legitimate discursive regime for being too "ideological" to be taken seriously and therefore restricting it to the periphery of the public debate.[3] To be sure, as a particular way of idealizing mainstream professional journalism as a "universal" (Randall, 2000) paradigm in the Global South, reporters and editors of the 20th century in that part of the world rushed to emulate those practices in the North, which they considered to be a "gold standard" for their practice.

In fact, in many newsrooms in the Global South, this approach became accepted as the only legitimate source to achieve truth in the news (Mujica, 1982; Wasserman, 2017), while other forms of journalism practices around news production and dissemination became increasingly downplayed and marginalized from the mainstream debates (Golding, 1977; Horne, 2017b). Therefore, labeling these other journalistic formats and practices as "non-scientific" became a way of de-legitimizing other forms of doing journalism while consolidating the commercial-factual model as the only credible source of news. Between 1840 and 1930, the Anglo-Saxon model of journalism consolidated as the prime hegemonic institution in providing news and setting the professional threshold across the globe. From there, it went on to become also the deontological reference to others around the world (Golding, 1977; Spurr, 1993).

However, the US news agencies were not alone in this transformation in the information markets. In countries such as Kenya and Tanzania, Reuters and other international news agencies adapted to decolonization and reinvent themselves as companies working to assist new nation-states. This is despite the fact that many new independent governments tried to secure informational sovereignty by placing international news agencies within their control. Ironically, decolonization enabled Reuters to gain greater control over information supply across Africa, because many African leaders viewed the capitalist model of news as better suited to their diplomatic goals and political views (Brennan, 2015).

In places such as Latin America, this rise of market-driven news provision coincided with the consolidation of AP in the United States as the main provider of international news, which rapidly set a process of standardization in terms of aesthetics and style as to how international news should be gathered and presented (Diaz-Rangel, 1976; Mujica, 2006 [1982]; Silberstein-Loeb, 2014). By the end of the 19th century, AP was already a key player in the world, capable of challenging its European counterparts, such as Havas (now Agence France-Presse), Reuters (now Thomson Reuters), and Wolff (Boyd-Barrett, 1980; Boyd-Barrett & Rantanen, 1998; Silberstein-Loeb, 2014). This rise, of course, coincided also with the United States becoming a world power and it says more about the geopolitics around the international flows of information (A. Smith, 1980) than about the ability of AP to produce, or not, "quality" news stories (Horne, 2017b; Silberstein-Loeb, 2014).

In a more contextual sense, the United States, as a new emerging power in the early 20th century, did not exert control in a traditional manner as the old Europeans empires did (Immerwahr, 2019). That is, it never claimed explicitly that it would pursue to be an empire as the Europeans did (their proclamation of "Manifest Destiny" only applied to the West of the US itself and territories stolen from Mexico). This despite the fact that it did so in practice, displaying overt imperialism practices in places, such as Cuba, Puerto Rico, and the Philippines (Go, 2008; Roman, 1997; Subervi-Vélez et. al., 2020). Instead, after World War II, the United States went to undermine European colonialism, in the understanding that its increasing dominant position relied more in the market expansion, military projection of power, and the ability to exert equal hegemonic power without traditional political direct control (Chambers, 2015; Reynolds, 2015).

From then on, and over the subsequent years, the more the United States was able to expand its markets through cultural hegemony and spread its own brand of political institutions as a way of incorporating the rest of the world into the market economy. In so doing, it went on to spread the "American Way of Life" as a cultural aspirational paradigm, which also meant reproducing a particular way of doing journalism in order to underpin liberal democracy and market-driven economy (Hagedorn, 2007; J. Hart, 2013; Horne, 2017a). This was by all means a nation-building exercise that required both effort inside the United States and abroad to standardize journalism practice and media content so as to expand cultural markets.

ASSOCIATED PRESS (AP) AND COMMON SENSE

It was in this context that AP played a pivotal role in setting canons for the gathering, production and dissemination of news, both nationally and internationally (Beard & Zoerner, 1969; González & Torres, 2011). It did so by facilitating the convergence of journalism practice toward the US model in many places in the Global South, where it rapidly displaced many of its European competitors as the main reference for journalists (Diaz-Rangel, 1976; Silberstein-Loeb, 2014). It is because of this that one can argue that the manner in which the US model of journalism was "exported" constituted both a way a postcolonial formation and—at the same time—a new way of exercising hegemony. Over the years to come, AP's news aesthetics and news culture—later on synthesized in its stylebook—became the norm in most newsrooms in the United States and was used as a key textbook in thousands of journalism schools from around the world, which saw it and other news agencies such as Reuters and the BBC as the "golden standard."

However, the rise of the US journalism commercial model as the dominant paradigm, to call it that, did not go unchallenged and in fact repeatedly clashed with competing notions of what journalism was and its role in society; particularly in relation to the late 19th-century workers' struggles and the rise of the Soviet Union as news media played a key role in mobilizing the masses. This tension between the different models of journalism would endure until Stalinism made it bluntly clear that what was done behind the Iron Curtin was mere propaganda to mobilize the revolution. In the Soviet Gulags, it became crystal obvious that freedom of speech had no place in the emerging totalitarian regime (M. E. Lenoe, 2004; Powers, 1998). However, the initial Soviet model was not the only alternative form of journalism. Several manifestations were also present throughout the 20th century (González & Torres, 2011; Harcup, 2011; Urribarrí, 2011), but they were never as prominent as the prevalent commercial paradigm and most never survived beyond a few decades or so.

Moreover, the tensions and fears around the Red Scare were used to obscure and discredit these alternative practices. Under the wider dichotomy of free Western press against Soviet/Communist propaganda (Defty, 2004; Siebert & Schramm, 1956)—as highlighted by Walter Lippmann (2010 [1920])—no undertones were possible and all got essentialized in two conflicting sides with nothing in-between in the world of journalism.

It was in this way that mainstream commercial journalism became part of what Antonio Gramsci (Gramsci, 2003 [1935]) called the "intellectuals" who underpinned the "Modern Prince." As he saw it, this was at the center of class struggle and capitalism's attempts to forge a proletarian counter-hegemony, which he claimed was a contest of intellectuals versus intellectuals (Claeys, 2018). This explanation, I believe, is still relevant today as the traditional media becomes increasingly concentrated and large oligopolies in social media now control people's free time.

Consequently, traditional historical narratives about news reporting and society were able to portray a "legitimate" type of journalistic practice that saw itself as a product of the Enlightenment, making constant references to ancient Greece, Roman, and Judeo-Christian traditions and the values associated with those civilizations such as freedom and democracy (Barrera, 2004; McNair, 2000). Meanwhile, other very important discussions that were taking place in other parts of the world about how to achieve truth and what truth itself was in the public domain have been altogether ignored or made invisible in many Western debates and accounts about the history of journalism. These multiple conversations included many taking place in the Global South that saw journalism as a social practice with the quest for social justice and decolonization (Alonso, 2004; Bamba, 2013; Horne, 2017b; Peycam, 2012).

These exchanges also included the debates within radical journalism in the light of the Russian Revolution of 1917, which actively engaged with the notions of scientific objectivity in their own press. Indeed, and contrary to many of the prevalent accounts, many of these transatlantic conversations were closely interlinked and informing each other. For example, John Reed's work on the Mexican Revolution (2009 [1914]) was not only influential among the public but particularly with journalists in the United States (Álvares, 2017; Sims, 2007). Moreover, Reed acted as a bridge between journalists from other parts of the world and newsrooms in the United States, particularly after witnessing the Mexican Revolution, which in itself generated a very distinctive debate among reporters and editors in Latin America (Serna Rodríguez, 2014).

The conversations between the periphery and the center in relation to the formation of journalism as a professional entity have not been fully documented and there is a particular gap in our knowledge about how the periphery influenced and help shape news reporting in the United States and Europe over the years (as it was by no means a one directional imposition, as suggested by some authors). In fact, there is sufficient evidence to suggest that these connections and flows happened both ways.[4] For example, studying the interrelations of the news media outlets and journalists within the Portuguese empire, some authors have highlighted the flow of ideas between newsrooms and the creation of joint guilds of professional journalists in distant parts of that empire (Lima, Hohlfeldt, Sousa, & Barbosa, 2014). In any case and in relation to how journalists and media from all over the world appropriated and exchanged approaches and practices, certainly the late 19th century and beginning of the 20th century was in fact a far more globalized and interconnected period than we give it credit for. Marcel Broersma (2004, 2019), as part of his remarkable research network project on Transnational Journalism History, one which incorporates Professor Michael Schudson himself, has done an extraordinary and very valuable contribution in highlighting and substantiating this argument. In his work, he has explained how European journalism was "Americanized" as it embraced modernity and mass society and how this, in turn, shaped the development of journalism in terms of professionalization and its modernization. In so doing, he also remarks the need to recognize European traditions of journalism in their own right.

In addition, one must highlight that if well, at the end, "journalistic objectivity" in the West developed as a quest for credibility and authorial control over "truth," this did not happen in isolation. This, since its deontology was also shaped by the efforts to confront the more explicit propaganda threats from the USSR and the tensions created by the exclusion of the other discussions and dynamics around journalism that directly linked to workers' struggles.[5] As part of the hegemonic effort, mainstream journalism was broadly critical of workers' movements and trade unions because of its own dependency to private/commercial media organizations in order to guarantee its independence from the state. John Nerone (2013a) succinctly explained this when describing the historical roots of the normative model of journalism. For him, the hegemonic Western model of journalism derives from a set of relationships and practices formed around relatively monopolistic daily newspapers and wire services at the end of the 19th century. Hence, the model assumes that journalists' capacity for independence is provided by the media organizations that employ them. However, as he also argues, this model of journalism never described more than a sector of the news environment in the West.

To describe other segments of the news media environment, we have instead to start first by acknowledging that many of the current aspects of US journalistic deontology were developed in opposition to those trends and ideas that stand at the other side of liberal democracy and the market economy. In this sense, the confrontation between liberal democracy and Soviet socialism helps explain, at least partially, why in the Global South notions such as "journalistic objectivity" became historically intertwined in the public imagination—and among journalistic values—with freedom and democracy while "structural analysis" and "dialectical materialism" became associated with propaganda, ideology, and totalitarianism.

For many still living then under colonial rule or just awakening to independence in the early 20th century, the United States seemed then to be a beacon to follow and its institutions ones to be emulated; including its model of journalism.[6] To be sure, the US model of journalism was not exported in isolation but as part of a wider construct that included liberal democracy and the market-driven economy and that was designed to underpin US hegemony by replicating its model in the Global South. Karl Polanyi would call this setting "the Great Transformation," which saw the convergence of the modern market economy and the nation-state into a single entity. He called this the "Market Society" and argued that it gave way to a "market utopia" (2001 [1944], p. 267), one that would go on to dominate discourses of power for the next century. Indeed, despite the Welfare Consensus—that dominated the postwar period (1945-1980)—the market utopia would continue to influence and define the political imagination while shaping the key institutions in Western society, including mainstream journalism.

It is within this construct that we find the notion according to which journalism can only operate fully in a system that gives it the freedom to present the "facts" beyond and despite of any ideological consideration (Gauthier, 1993; McNair, 2000; D. Mindich, 2000). According to this ideological layout, journalism needs to be objective and this can only happen, arguably, in the context of a liberal system in which individuals can make rational and free political choices (McNair, 2000; Overholser & Jamieson, 2005) as they do in the market place. In fact, the notions of journalism and liberal democracy are not only historically intertwined in both the public imagination and professional practice but also, they are equally underpinned by the commercial and market economy (Mujica, 2006 [1982]; Steel, 2013). For Michael Schudson (1976), the idea of "objectivity" prevailed as a dominant discourse among journalists since the appearance of modern newspapers in the Jacksonian Era of the 1830s in the backdrop of the democratization of politics, the expansion of a market economy, and the growing authority of an entrepreneurial, urban middle class.

Over the years, many historians have agreed upon an explanation that sees the process of commercialization as the key driver for the emergence of this particular model of the press and its consolidation as the archetypical type in modern society (Conboy, 2004, 2006). In this context, one of the key notions in journalism theory and practice, that of journalistic objectivity—that arguably brought about reason and common sense to the public debate—has been interpreted to be a by-product of commercialization, political changes, and technological advances that somehow emerged in the Anglo-Saxon world as a guiding principle between the 1890s and 1930s, which was closely associated with the rise of the mass audiences for newspapers (Muhlmann, 2008, p. 2). Accordingly, journalistic objectivity is seen as a universal and core value in the mainstream newsrooms that somehow "happened" as a derivate phenomenon from particular events and circumstances.

This view has been adopted as the most important explanatory theoretical framework within debates around professionalization (Banning, 1999; Waisbord, 2013) and Freedom of Expression (Osiel, 1986; Steel, 2013) as to why it became the dominant form of journalism around the world. Accordingly, one of the reasons as to why there seems to be such a remarkable convergence of values and professional aspirations across practitioners from so many journalists operating in different societies is because these values were seemingly developed as historical formation, underpinned by the political economy of the press operating within the confines of capitalism.

To be sure, as the data collected by the Worlds of Journalism Study (2016) has gone to show, the idea of professional autonomy is closely connected to the notion of objectivity (Hanitzsch et al., 2011; Hanusch & Hanitzsch, 2017), which despite criticism continues to be paramount in the conceptualization of journalism as a professional and independent field. Thanks to this prevalent interpretation, we have come to accept the official history of journalism as we know it today. One that proclaims that the current news cultures and practices that have so far characterized professional journalism somehow emerged "naturally" from the process of industrialization and commercialization of the press and that it then became adopted as a universal notion by other societies around the globe.

Contrary to this almost homogenous view, however, I would ask why do we have to interpret the emergence of "professional journalism" as a natural derivation of the marketization of the press rather than as an orchestrated political reaction to the increasing mediatization of society and the rise of forces that threaten the past and current order of power? I would also ask, who says that the spreading of the normative values that today characterize journalism happened without agency or even intentionality in the Global South in the midst of the Cold War? Moreover, why shouldn't we think also of journalism as a US "national enterprise" deeply shaped by the Red Scares (Kathryn, 2017) aimed at building an imagined community around culture and the market? After all, this has been exactly how many historians have interpreted the role of the media in the formation of Soviet nationhood[7] during the Stalin era (Brandenberger, 2014; M. E. Lenoe, 2004). In this sense, it is important to recognize that journalism has played in the United States equally a decisive role in the formation of its sense of nationhood (Zelizer, 2017) as an imagined community, which proclaims to be politically free and market-driven economically.

DISSEMINATING COMMON SENSE

Therefore, as an enterprise commissioned to underpin and promote a specific political ideal, that of the US liberal democratic model, journalism in the United States embraced news values such as objectivity, balance, and fairness, which remained interlocked with those of freedom of expression, market society, and private property. Consequently, journalism as we know it today became closely associated with the notion of the private and independent media. This blatantly became clear during the First and Second Red Scares—and particularly during the initial stages of the Cold War—when this historical formation meant the use of journalistic objectivity as an attack against communism and moreover during the McCarthyism era in which journalism objectivity was presented as a virulent anti-communist exercise in defense of freedom (Maras, 2013, p. 130). It was from this historical context that the tone was set in relation to how world politics should be covered by the Great Press in the United States as well as in many newsrooms in developing countries that aimed at emulating them (Alvear & Lugo-Ocando, 2016, p. 4).

The wave of de-colonization movements in the aftermath of World War II brought a degree of contestation to prevalent political forms in the Global South. This was accompanied by the emergence of a whole critical school of communication in the West, epitomized in the Frankfurt School in Europe, that came to question not only the Western premises of communication in general but to also challenge the conceptual foundation of the Enlightenment (Claeys, 2018; Connerton, 1980; Slater & Connerton, 1981). This opened up an intellectual space for new demands, which included a New Communication Order that provided better balance in the exchange of knowledge and information between the North and South (Lugo-Ocando & Nguyen, 2017; Roach, 1990).

In places such as Latin America, this would go on to have a profound effect in the way that journalism was thought and taught, where journalism schools were transformed into schools and faculties of social communication. During these period, research agendas and academic degrees witness a profoundly transformation that incorporated far more critical approaches that embraced sociological and anthropological elements (Barbero, 1981; Fuentes-Navarro, 1992). These critical intellectual movements, approaches, and demands crystallized in the UNESCO (United Nations Educational, Scientific, and Cultural Organization) McBride Report of 1980 (MacBride-Commission, 2003 [1980]), which proposed a new information order.

However, these demands met with staunch opposition and the idea that "facts are sacred" and the political push for the free flow of information would be used to counter international demands for a new information order (Lemberg, 2019; Pasquali, 2005; Schiller, 1977; Stevenson, 1988). Indeed, these counterarguments were both academic and political but they all had the common element of arguing from the point of view of liberal democracy and a market—driven economy (Mehan, 1981; Singh & Gross, 1981; Thussu, 2005). Hence, it is important to remind ourselves that the belief systems behind the idea of journalistic objectivity and other associated values such as fairness, balance, as logical and rational as they sound and as practical and useful as they might be to society today, were above all ideological discursive regimes that helped construct knowledge in the terms of the centers of power at that time.

As key Western ideas and notions about journalism were disseminated across the globe and practices became standardized, these professional ideologies foster core values and normative aspirations among journalists in different parts of the world. Fundamental in these efforts of dissemination was the training and education of journalists in the Third World. In regions such as Latin America, this included both programs deployed directly by the United States and also through multilateral institutions such as the Organization of American States (OAS)—which launched in the early 1960s as a program to train science journalists—and, training in more general terms delivered by the Centro Internacional de Estudios Superiores de Comunicación para América Latina (CIESPAL) in Ecuador, which was financially backed by UNESCO in times in which its own policies and approaches were driven by the United States as its main donor (Dellamea, 1996; Mellado Ruiz, 2010).

All over the developing countries, there were efforts to disseminate Western journalistic values and models. In the African continent, efforts to standardize journalism education in Sub-Sahara Africa were led by UNESCO in the 1960s and 1970s (Murphy & Scotton, 1987) and in Asia by means of the support, training and resources given by national radio networks (i.e., Radio France and Radio Netherlands) to train journalists in Asia. In addition to journalism education and training, donor governments and private foundations supported throughout the Cold War the implementation of Western models of journalism in other forms and was one of the foreign policy priorities (Saunders, 2000; Schiller, 1977; Statler & Johns, 2006). These diplomatic efforts include NGOs, private foundations and other players in the Third Sector, which also take part in the process of disseminating current prevalent models of journalism in the Global South. All this in the context of NGOs and foundations being historically part of Western efforts to project soft power (Betsill, Corell, Burgiel, & Andresen, 2008; Sanborn, Portocarrero, Coatsworth, Aguero, & Arrom, 2005).

Therefore, one can argue that far from being a "natural occurrence," notions such as objectivity, fairness, and balance—now so central in our definition of professional journalism in the Global South—were spread through orchestrated efforts disguised as "media development" efforts and policies, which ultimately were underpinned by foreign aid (Alvear & Lugo-Ocando, 2016; Lemberg, 2019; Mattelart, 2002; Saunders, 2000). In so doing, US and European policy-makers had the intention of promoting models of journalism that reflected the type of liberal values in their own societies; all this as part of ideological, geopolitical, and strategic efforts to replicate similar models of liberal democracy around the world while containing the spread of communism (Appy, 2000; Roth-Ey, 2011).

Finally, it is also important to highlight that despite the normative claims of pushing for liberal democracy, these efforts of disseminating particular models of Western journalism nevertheless ended up colluding at times with dictatorships and authoritarian regimes in order to protect US strategic interests in subservient markets (Conaghan, 2002; Straubhaar, 1989). This paradox is perhaps one of the key characteristics of Foreign Aid for Media Development during most of the Cold War. This, given the fact that it predicated freedom on the basis of liberal democracy but was willing to subordinate that in order to guarantee free market and alignment toward the US orbit.[8]

In this context, one of the most important vessels in connecting the North with the South and facilitating the transfer of particular cultural news values and reporting approaches was the use of foreign aid toward media development. Hence, examining this relationship is key in understanding the reproduction of hegemonic news cultures in the Global South and central to explaining how it was pivotal in setting a particular discursive regime; that of common sense.

In this sense, the role of foreign aid in media development has been to help spread notion of "common sense" as a core value in the newsroom across the globe at times under the metaphor of "objectivity." It is because of this that "objectivity" got translated and then transplanted into the Global South as part of an orchestrated effort to "modernize" newsrooms in these societies. This transplantation of values became entwined with the establishment of the parameters of news discourses that were delimited by the general notion of "common sense," which limited news narrative to what was accepted by the general consensus while excluding structural analysis.

To be sure, the spreading of common sense as part of a "universal" journalistic paradigm meant that "truth" was considered something that derives from the collective understanding of the world. As such, the personal-collective experience superseded the complexity of counterintuitive interpretations of the world (something that even today explains why some many people have very conservative attitudes toward prison and justice reform, welfare, immigration, and government expenditure). This is something that Immanuel Kant (1724–1804) foresaw in his time in his scathing indictment by saying that this "convenient" talk on "common sense" was nothing but a perverse and philistine form of anti-intellectualism, an endorsement of the opinion of the multitude, of whose applause the philosopher is ashamed, while the charlatan glories and boasts in it (Kant, 1985 [1783], p. 7). For philosophers such as Kant and Joseph Priestley, this was indeed a dangerous precedent in terms of how, and on whose behalf, political claims might be issued in the future (Rosenfeld, 2011, p. 89), something that we witnessed centuries later with the rise of "alternative facts" and "post-truth" in the United States under President Donald Trump and in the Global South with the administrations of Narendra Modi in India, and Rodrigo Duterte and Jairo Bolsonaro in Brazil (Gross, 2017; Lugo-Ocando, 2020; Rich, 2018).

NOTES

1. Not that that I am ascribing the agency to the media as such. Instead, I am trying to reiterate the notion of the media as a space in which a set of human actors converge to exercise hegemony by articulating and imposing discourses and narratives of power upon the masses. This is expressed already by authors such as Castells (2011) when referring to the notion of "media space."

2. In a way, journalism never made the Copernican jump of allowing counterintuitive logics within its examination of the world, hence it remains truly nonscientific in that sense. Instead, it remained in the realm of what people could experience through their senses, given its fundamental nature as a storytelling activity that needs its audiences.

3. Let us not forget that these debates around scientific/rational approaches against irrational/ideological did not only happen in the West. In the Soviet Union, they were also a motive of discussion and ample debate (Ings, 2017; Pollock, 2006).

4. Veteran journalist and journalism professor Mort Rosenblum (1977) has said that this is particularly the case of journalists who get deployed and work in the Third World and who later return to work in the United States.

5. It is well documented how the BBC implemented its own journalistic ethos in the aftermath of the General Strike of 1926 (Pegg, 1983; Symons, 2014).

6. Not all, of course, were on board with these perceptions. Many leaders in Latin America from Simón Bolívar in Venezuela to Augusto César Sandino in Nicaragua expressed their distrust about the increasing hegemonic role of the United States in the continent.

7. I am perfectly aware of the fact that the creation of the USSR was initially an attempt to transcend the notion of nation and that dynamic debates took place at the time about the international character of the workers' struggle. However, as most historians today acknowledge, the rise of Stalin to power marked a departure from this and meant instead the revival of nationalism as a framework defining the USSR (Brandenberger, 2002; Lenoe, 2004).

8. The Soviet foreign aid toward media development never had such pretensions or made such normative claims as can be seen in the case of Afghanistan, Angola, and Cuba, where support for media and journalists was openly conditioned to them committing to the "revolution" (Barghoorn, 2015; Garcia-Santamaria, 2018; Radosh, 2012).

Chapter 3

How Journalism Came to Be in the South

On December 15, 1815, after suffering defeat at the hands of the Royal Spanish forces in Cartagena de Indias in what today is Colombia, Simón Bolívar (1783–1830) arrived in Aux Cayes, Haiti. Having lost many his supporters and deprived of resources, he went to the only place on Earth that still seemed to have hope for Venezuela's independence; the newly created Black Republic of Haiti. There, he sought the aid of General Alexandre Pétion (1770–1818), one of the founding fathers of Haiti and the first president of the newly liberated Black Republic. In response to Bolívar's request, Pétion provided shelter and food for him, his remaining soldiers, and their families. As narrated by Marion Ainé (Fischer, 2013; Wesley, 1917), Pétion not only provided Bolívar with supplies, 4,000 rifles, gunpowder, food, military strategists, and veterans from the Caribbean nation's revolution to accompany him on his April 1816 expedition back to Venezuela but also, and perhaps more importantly, a printing press.[1]

Initial attempts by private individuals to import a printing press into Venezuela had been denied by the Spanish colonial authorities, who allowed it afterward but only in order to print pro-colonial newspapers (Earle, 1997).[2] One of the main reasons to deny it was the authorities' fears of the print being used to promote uprisings led by black slaves and mulatos such as that of José Leonardo Chirinos and José Caridad González in 1795 to end slavery and establish a free republic. The rebellion was inspired by the events in Haiti and proclaimed to defend universal human rights for people of all colors. The insurgents had received news about what had happened in the French colony and intended to repeat the experiment in the Spanish colony.

It was because of these first attempts to end slavery and declare a republic that the Haitian generals decided to provide Foreign Aid for Media Development (even though never called it that) to Bolívar's enterprise, which, in turn, would support the spread of the Haitian ideal (Aizpurua, 2011; Ruette-Orihuela & Soriano, 2016). The expedition failed but would encourage the British to also provide later Bolívar with a printing press. However, they did not have the same altruistic purposes as those of the Haitians. Their aim was instead to destabilize the Spanish empire and to gain influence and access to lucrative commercial routes, although to be fair some within the civil service were strongly committed to abolitionism (Barea, 2016; Ogelsby, 1969).

Even then, foreign aid showed to have intrinsic ideology and represent geostrategic interests as these set of foreign interventions were perhaps one of the earliest examples of foreign aid toward media development to be recorded. Both the Haitian aid to Bolívar and the British and Spanish resources allocated to establish printing machines in Venezuela, such as La Gazeta de Caracas and several pro-colonial newspapers, where efforts of public diplomacy and examples of foreign intervention.

This case offers also a variety of lessons for the present. To start with, it is important to notice how geopolitical struggles and ideology were central drivers for allocating resources and who got them, something that is still relevant to ask in our times. In addition, foreign aid toward media development has also been key in the spread of ideologies. In relation to this, two fundamental questions need to be asked about the Haitian aid. On the one hand, what did Simón Bolívar wanted to do with the press and resources he was given by the Haitian generals? The second, what did the Haitian generals ask Bolívar for in exchange? Both, I argue, are not only historical questions but very current ones too.

In a way, the first question is answered mostly above. After two unsuccessful attempts to establish an independent Venezuelan republic, Bolívar came to understand—particularly after the confrontation with the pro-Spanish Church—the importance of propaganda. He understood, based on his experience in France, the power of news and why he had to counter the Spanish influence, not only by selling the idea of a free and independent nation from colonial domination but also reinforcing the aspiration of nationhood as a distinctive construction in the public imagination. Indeed, there is probably no single institution that so clearly reflects the changing conditions of Latin American life in the years during and immediately following the War of Independence as the periodical press (Bushnell, 1950).

However, the other question is perhaps more interesting for the purposes of this book. The Haitian generals not only were looking to create allies in the international geopolitical landscape and spread the anti-slavery cause to Spanish colonies, but perhaps and even more importantly, change the way Europeans thought about Africans and to make them accept them as human beings of equal standing. This last point was a fundamental attempt to change the "common sense" discursive regime of the time for which the idea of "negroes" as merchandise (private property) was widely accepted as a given truth; a notion that would survive even after abolition in the face of the reparations paid to the former slave owners in Britain, France, and the United States, among others.

The Foreign Aid for Media Development given by the Haitian generals to Bolívar is a key case of study in history. For once, we should ask: What type of journalism were both the Haitian generals and Bolívar expecting to happen? Certainly, as one could argue, the expectation was in no lesser degree that the newspaper performed advocacy and campaigning in favor of independence while helping to support new republics that would be far friendlier toward Haiti (Fischer, 2013; J. Popkin, 2010). Perhaps less understood was the expectation that this newspaper would also advocate for a new common sense, one that gave humanity to all individuals, not just the white, and that challenged the type of liberalism emerging in France and the United States that saw somehow compatibility between universal rights and slave ownership. Indeed, by promoting a universal sense of human rights, truly universal, for the first time in history acknowledging the humanity of Africans, its aim was to set in motion different dynamics in the public sphere in which all voices were equally heard (Losurdo, 2014).

As I mentioned earlier, his was not to be the case and the press supplied by Haiti would be sized and destroyed by the Spaniards. Nor would Bolívar go on to write his liberating history with Haiti at the center of the narrative despite the fact that Venezuela's independence would not be possible without it. In the face of internal struggles with many of his own generals—who were landowners that possessed slaves—and the fall of the Gran Colombia project, his promises to liberate the black would fade with his own political power (Blanchard, 2008; Bushnell, 2003). It would instead be the British who would provide aid and resources for Bolívar's newspaper. El Correo del Orinoco and other pro-republican publications would go on to inspire a series of subsequent newspapers while setting the basis of a very liberal type of journalism in Venezuela, which thrived and spread despite successive dictatorships and that continues to reverberate nowadays in that country's newsrooms (Ratto Ciarlo, 1971, 1977). Journalism in that country never became the radical abolitionist press that the Haitians perhaps aspired to; one that would agitate for the liberation of the slaves. Instead, the Venezuelan press, with some exceptions, embraced the type of "common sense" already predominant in Europe and that served well the new ruling elites of that country who were slave owners themselves (Lombardi, 2012). One that helped to preserved slavery for years to come and that promoted property and conservative values. In other words, what was imported from Britain was a type of journalism that embraced ideas of common sense that were underpinned by the Malthusian logics of private property. The new postcolonial setting in that part of the New

World was more an emulation of a liberal Europe (that still embraced slavery, while protecting elites and existing property structures as they were) than an experimentation of new ways of allowing society to communicate with itself.

IN THE GLOBAL SOUTH

Although the case of Bolívar and Haiti was by no means unique regarding the use of foreign aid to support media outlets in the colonies, it was different in the sense that aid was allocated on a South-South aid direction, something unusual then (and still now). This contrary to most foreign aid toward journalism, which has been allocated from the North to the South and that consequently have been defined by colonial and then postcolonial exercises and projection of hegemonic power. More generally speaking, aid toward supporting journalism to develop as a political institution has been marked by modernization efforts, which was a mutation of the old empire's normative quest to spread "civilization" (Gilmartin, 2015; Lugo-Ocando & Nguyen, 2017; J. Smith, 2006). In this sense, European empires, and subsequently the United States, created standards through their own news agencies that imposed specific types of news cultures in their colonies and new markets. The key disseminators, as Startt (1991) points out, were the "imperial journalists" who

> were of one mind when it came to the more neutral aspects of unity [of the Empire]. On these points their differences, when they appeared, were minor. They all professed to see a common stick of British ideas and ideals of Empire. They supported imperial education, a term by which they meant mutual understanding by the British and the people of the dominions of one's and another's history, politics and common concerns. Improving imperial communications and, in large measure, imperial security received their broad endorsement. Moreover, they all agreed that imperial relations were evolving into a type of partnership.

These individuals and their media organizations operating in a colonial and then postcolonial setting were pivotal in the spread of the news cultures that today are prevalent in the Global South. This as they served as ideological blood vessels, disseminating particular worldviews and cultural values relating to journalism practices and approaches. They were particularly key in determining news values both within newsrooms and among the public. The question, nevertheless, remains as to how much agency they actually exercised in the definition of a broader and more universal form of journalism as an apolitical institution.

Indeed, far from being only a Western "occurrence" that resulted as a byproduct of commercialization, political changes and technological advances that somehow emerged in the Anglo-Saxon world between the 1890s and 1930s (Carey, 2007), news cultures and values in the Global South were also forged by targeted interventions across history. While it is true that the emergence of journalism objectivity was closely associated with the rise of the mass audiences for newspapers (Muhlmann, 2008, p. 2), agency from specific political actors in the South also played a role in shaping and spreading these values given the particular colonial and postcolonial settings that governed North-South relationships.

In addition, there were important dynamics, both materialistic and ideological, that surround the way news values, professional ideologies and journalistic practices were embraced as core universal values across the world newsrooms. For example, political and ideological responses to the workers' struggles during the 19th and early 20th centuries, especially those that took place in the aftermath of the Soviet Revolution of 1917 (Carroll, 1919; Hagedorn, 2007; Read, 2008), played an important role in shaping and defining journalistic objectivity as way of subduing the role of the media in relation to political mobilization of the proletariat. These events produced dynamics exchanges that flow in several directions across the globe. In the backdrop of these conversations, there was the historical role that the media had in advocacy and political mobilization in the workers' struggles (Feuer, 1962; Lehman, 2002). The formation of journalism owes in fact a lot to the multiple conversations, including those reporters had during a brief period of the Russian Revolution about scientific objectivity in their own press, which were closely interlinked, informing each other. It is because these conversations—not always directed at engaging with the ideological opponents but also listening closely to what they said in order to produce a counterargument—that we can suggest that the norm of journalistic objectivity as we know it today in the West owes more to the workers' struggles and political mobilization in Russia and Eastern Europe that what it is often acknowledged.

The aim of this initial discussion is not to provide a historical account of the formation of journalism as a cultural practice and political institution of liberal democracy—a task for which there are far better researchers than myself—but to contextualize the model of journalism that was exported to the Global South using foreign aid for both media development and media assistance. My intention is to offer a specific frame that helps us understand better the formation of news reporting in the Global South. However, it would be impossible to examine that without providing the necessary historical context and recognizing the multiple interventions that took place from around the globe and acknowledging the role that journalism had in nation building in the United States in the face of a market-driven economy and the installation of a liberal democracy.

THE FEAR OF THE MASSES

For this analysis, let us start by pinpointing that the period between the end of the 19th century and until the 1930s was crucial in the formation of modern journalism as a political institution in the West (Schudson, 2001; S. J. Ward, 2015). Not only because of the way the market of readers had exploded and became industrialized or because of the development of a new media commercial model based on advertisement but also because of the way the people on the ground in urban spaces had started to organize themselves against those in power. Some authors had by then sounded the alarms about the rise of the "masses" (Le Bon, 2010 [1897]; Ortega y Gasset, 1983 [1930]; Tarde, 2010 [1895]). Their work reflected the elites' misgivings and fears toward the rapid urbanization of society in the light of the aftermath of the Industrial Revolution. Their writings broadly reflected the most conservative fears of that time; that the crowds would take over followed by anarchy and chaos. These fears were not completely unfounded as several uprisings had characterized the preceding period, which saw the Paris Commune and overall the working class at the center of new political struggles (Rapport, 2009; Read, 2008).

One of these key fears centered around the role of the newspapers in stirring the masses and contributing to political uprisings (Eley, 2002; J. D. Popkin, 1990). This sort of elite moral panic around the press saw it as having a potential role in agitating workers in many parts of the world (M. E. Lenoe, 2004; Read, 2008). As many newspaper owners in the US and Europe became part of the new industrial status quo, they also started to express their own reservations against that part of the press that remained vociferous and politically militant (Brendon, 1983; Seldes, 1938). It was a concern that dated back in time, when authorities in the United Kingdom had imposed the first newspaper tax in 1712, one that was intended to place limits on newspapers' readership and curb radicalism (Oats & Sadler, 2007; Sadler & Oats, 2002).

In the United States, similar concerns were raised by editors and newspaper proprietors some of who had supported radicalism in the past to only later, in the new republic, call for limits upon the populist and pro-negro press (Hogan, 1984; Horne, 2017b). In fact, one could argue that from the 19th century onward, there were orchestrated efforts to limit public access to the press and place constraints on its ability to mobilize the public. However, for those making these calls, it was almost impossible to counter the growing popularity of the press. Hence, the control efforts shifted toward an attempt to de-ideologize its role in society. To be sure, by the second half of the 19th century, in places such as the United States, these efforts became progressively less coercive and far subtler. The appropriation and co-option of the news media by commercial enterprises proved to be far more effective in depoliticizing the news. This by converting the press into a commercial enterprise and attempting to convert journalism in to an innocuous practice that embraced a deontological approach that detached itself from the events that it covered and that proclaimed its neutrality as a pre-condition to make claims of scientific truth.

This became over the years the US journalistic model that would be transferred to the Global South. One that was historically a by-product of a nation-building exercise and the efforts to confront the rise of Communism at home and abroad (Haynes, 2000; Theoharis, 1977). To be sure, the development of modern journalism deontology and its associated news cultures did not happen in a vacuum but as part of series of historical dynamics that were taking place at the time and that are rooted in the ideological struggle that would characterize most of the 20th century between a free market economy and its liberal democratic paradigm against the socialist utopia that led to the totalitarian Soviet state and its satellites (Knock, 1992; Lugo-Ocando, 2018). In this sense, Adam Hochschild reminds us that as soon as the United States entered the First World War in 1917 there was an

> assault on the media unmatched in American history or—so far—since. Its commander was [Woodrow] Wilson's postmaster general. Albert Sidney Burleson, a pompous former prosecutor and congressman. On June 16, 1917 he sent sweeping instructions to local postmasters ordering them to "keep a close watch on unsealed matters, newspapers, etc." for anything "calculated to . . . cause insubordination, disloyalty, mutiny . . . or otherwise embarrass or hamper the Government in conducting the war." What did "embarrass" mean? . . . One after another, Burleson went after newspapers and magazines, many affiliated with the Socialist Party. (Hochschild, 2017b, p. 82)

Using his discretional power, Burleson bypassed the First Amendment and went effectively to censor many newspapers. He used the post office as a weapon to limit and ban the distribution of many other publications and literature in what was effectively the first anti-communist crusade of the 20th century. Although Burleson initially justified his crusade referring to nationalism as a way of preventing foreign agents of the Axis Powers from using the media against the US government, it soon evolved into an effort to undermine any pacifist and socialist media in that country.

From the start, it became clear that one of the most important discursive tools used against militant, revolutionary, and pro-soviet tendencies within the

US and UK journalism was that of nationalism. Indeed, as Bertrand Russell pointed out, one of the key mistakes of the Marxists was to underestimate the most obvious of the non-economic factors—he previously criticized the fixation with economic materialism as if this were the only materialism that explained history and society—and that ultimately left socialism in disarray, was that of "nationalism" (Russell, 1969 [1920; 1948], p. 105). For Russell, even if the capitalist elites of Europe and the United States had been caught off guard by the 1917 Soviet Revolution, later they read and understood all too well Marxist theory and Bolshevik practice in general and designed important counterreforms and actions.

This was no less than a nation-building exercise that used anti-communism to create dichotomies between "them" and "us" that obliged all to take sides. Even relatively moderate officials such as former secretary of war Elihu Root would go on to say,

> There are men walking about in the streets of this city tonight who ought to be taken out at sunrise tomorrow and shot. . . . There are some newspapers published in this city every day the editors of which deserve conviction and execution for treason. (Hochschild, 2017b, p. 82)

These officials became totally focused on eradicating what they saw as the spread of the communist threat from Russia and who were influenced by Lenin's retreat from the Eastern front in World War I. In fact, on June 1917, aged seventy-two, Root himself had gone to Russia, which had just overthrown the czar. He headed a mission sent by President Wilson, the Root Commission, to arrange American co-operation with the new revolutionary government. Root remained in Petrograd for close to a month, and was not much impressed by what he saw. American financial aid to the new regime was possible only if the Russians would fight on the Allied side. The Russians, he said, "are sincerely, kindly, good people but confused and dazed." Root would became later the founding chairman of the Council on Foreign Relations—referred to as the brain trust for the US geopolitics expansion at the beginning of the century (Shoup & Minter, 2004) and established in 1918 in New York. He would go on to have a profound influence among the national newspapers and editors in the United States in the way they set the new standards and news vales.

In the United States, the task of de-politicizing journalism practice was advanced thanks to the standardization imposed by the post office and AP to its members, which demanded the type of neutrality and detachment that today is seen as the core effort to underline the norm of objectivity. AP then became the "de facto" power cartel that helps refine the character of news as a commercial and exchangeable commodity. Certainly, although AP was not alone in the market other news agencies such as United Press (later UPI), quickly adapted their own codes of practice and styles to the standards set by AP. This process of standardization occurred in the backdrop of the historical monopolization of international news content by the news agencies (Boyd-Barrett, 1980; Boyd-Barrett & Rantanen, 1998; Diaz-Rangel, 1976). Nevertheless, for this to happen, it was also pivotal advancing new copyright laws, which made the exchange of material and news by local newspapers almost impossible (Baird, 1983; Epstein, 1992).

Additionally, the US Postal Service was also used to encroach upon dissident news media outlets. This was done by rolling back on a preference treatment that the postal services in the United States had given to all newspapers since the foundation of the country. This consisted in the almost free delivery of newspapers by post across the United States, which had allowed news editors and the public in the United States to enjoy a remarkable and unprecedented access to the news (González & Torres, 2011; Machlup, 1962). In fact, from the start of the postal services in the United States, editors and journalists could subscribe (mostly through exchanges) to any newspaper in the country and then lift and copy any content into their own newspapers. These newspapers had then been able to reproduce and share stories from all over the country and the world without intermediaries and at almost no cost, except for the value of the copies they bought from their competitors.

New copyright laws and other limitations imposed by the postal services (e.g., requiring newspapers in other languages to be translated before distribution, which was effectively a taxation on non-English-speaking newspapers), added an unreasonable burden to independent outlets. This facilitated the expansion of AP and its affiliated newspapers that would go on to dominate and almost monopolize the distribution of news in the United States. AP became effectively a closed-club in which only newspapers from the establishment were admitted, which then were able to determine the news agenda, content, and editorial style of the news. This also meant that smaller outlets that wanted to become part of this national circuit of news distribution had to adhere to AP standards, principles, and norms.

It was in this way that journalists and editors in the United States were systematically driven toward a "professional standardized" model, which soon became the dominant ideological paradigm of what reporters wrote. Journalism Schools then adopted the AP Stylebook and this meant also, in turn, setting the parameters in the way language in reporting would be shaped for future generations. Overall, the AP Stylebook introduced specific conditions and rules that aim to reassert objectivity and detachment. This was crucial in making "journalistic objectivity" a core feature in the quest for professionalization. This not only as a way to underpin credibility but also—and mostly—as a way of exercising authorial control over what can be considered to be "truth," as the style consolidates across the newsrooms and became the central paradigm on how to present news stories (DiNicola, 1994; Silberstein-Loeb, 2014).

This control over what is "truth" in the public domain was defined—as already argued—by a language of "common sense," which in itself was framed by nationalism as a counter-narrative to militant and revolutionary journalism. However, it was the response to the "First Red Scare" that partially reinforce the notion of objectivity as a normative ethical claim that could help make US journalism a distinctive political institution (Streckfuss, 1990; Wilson, 2015). Therefore, objectivity cannot be seen simply as an historical effort to detach journalism from opinion but should also be understood as an effort to articulate a response to the use of the news media for workers' struggles, activism, and mobilization in general and particularly as a response to the emergence of the Soviet Union and the menace it posed in ideological and political terms. This is, of course, not to say that objectivity was just a by-product of the modern anti-communism, but also to emphasize that it is also linked to it.

In truth, the Soviet model of journalism never was an alternative as such and less so as it descended into Stalinist propaganda over the subsequent years. However, this should not prevent us from acknowledging the powerful inspiration it generated at the time upon many journalists in the United States. In his piece on Lenin and Freedom of Speech, Albert Resis (1977) accounts for how the Soviet Revolution initially rises hopes for journalism, which would be later crushed when Lenin himself became convinced of the inviable nature of the bourgeois press within a worker's revolutionary project as he fear since had the capacity of winning over the masses. Nevertheless, the critique from Lenin and others stood in the light of the subsequent attacks against the Bolsheviks during the counter-revolution. It resonated all over the world as a demonstration that the workers needed their own press. This would be the case for many of the Muckrakers, the reform-minded journalists in the Progressive Era in the United States, many of whom proclaimed to be socialists and admire the Soviet Revolution, as well as the news reporters in the colonies whose pro-independence views would be deeply influenced by Marxism-Leninism.

In counter-position to the aforementioned, the experience of World War I and the Soviet Revolution would bring about an increase in urgency to deploy national propaganda in the West. One that would change the course of journalism history and the way in which news reporting is defined as a political institution. What came after was an effort from each side to shaped journalism in their own terms and to turn journalism from a social practice into an organized and bureaucratized institution that could help support, rather than hinder, their own hegemonic power structures. To be sure, over this period of time, important efforts were made to use the media as a way to control the masses—or as Lippmann (2017 [1922]) wrote to "manufacture consent." This aim to engineer communication to control the masses was predominantly a national project that had also a transnational one.

This in times of the European empires, which were still relatively powerful—although in decline—and an emerging United States that intended to expand its markets by means of establishing a more hegemonic market for culture and ideology. While the new Soviet world insisted on an advocacy press that suited the objective and goals of the workers' struggle, the United States and the United Kingdom instead promoted a press that claimed to be truthful, objective, and impartial but that equally was part of an exercise to reiterate their own political and economic model of liberal democracy and mark-driven economy. This translated into specific values such as those of objective and impartial reporting, which over the subsequent years would be also adopted by the media in the Global South as a way of extending and projecting soft power from the center to the periphery.

THE SCIENCE OF TRUTH

It was in this context in which the theory of journalism objectivity was rationalized as such within the professional guild of newspapers and became, over the years, the key paradigm in the West. In the United States, its adoption by the journalism guild was a tacit form of accepting that humans could not be objective and that there was the need to impose, upon news reporters, the norms and procedures that could guarantee a degree of impartiality and detachment (Streckfuss, 1990). Thereafter, this deontological aspiration of objectivity soon reached the status of professional ideology (Deuze, 2005; D. T. Mindich, 2000) and went on to dominate news reporting practices in the 20th century. Today, the aspirations of "objectivity" and "impartiality" continue to form a cornerstone of the cultural authority of journalism, although in a more critical fashion; one that spills over a lasting shadow into the new millennium and that went on to be disseminated across the globe and particularly be embraced in many places in the Global South.

One can argue then that journalistic objectivity was, on the one side, an effort to develop ethical standards that brought truth but also turned out to be, on the other hand, a way of producing news content as a commodity, one that could be easily exchanged and sold to standardized and universally accessible markets. Hence, allowing the elites who owned the media to influence also all types of cultural practices and products (Horkheimer & Adorno, 2001; Sommerville, 1996). However, to do so in a way that it was seen and accepted as legitimate practice, objectivity had to be given the same type of "naturalization" historical narrative that embraces the positivist instrumentalization of science, one that anchors itself in the Enlightenment as a political project and that was linked to the quest for knowledge.

The current journalistic conceptualization of objectivity can be traced back to the 19th century to the "scientific rationalism," which justified a particular type of news reporting paradigm (Lippmann, 2010 [1920]; Wien, 2005). This despite the fact that the term itself would not be widely used by news reporters until after the 1920s in the United States (Streckfuss, 1990). Consequently, objectivity is a "product of history, linked to particular cultural formations, as well as the professional aspirations of journalists themselves" (Maras, 2013, p. 2).

In places such as the United Kingdom, journalistic objectivity appears closely tied to the public service broadcasting regulation system but expressed distinctively in the notion of "impartiality," which dominates the regulative framework (BBC, 2016; Secretary of State, 2006)[3] and that is anchored in the Royal Charter and Ofcom regulations (Hampton, 2008; Sambrook, 2012). The United Kingdom rather adopted the principle of "impartiality" in the context of its transformation from a private organization into a public corporation (Curran & Seaton, 2002 [1981]; Easthope, 1990; H. Smith, 1993). All this in the face of the General Strike of 1926. For nine days in May 1926, the United Kingdom's industry was at a standstill as a consequence of workers demanding better conditions and pay. In support for other workers, newspaper employees also stopped printing, so there were few means of communication between authorities and the populace. However, by then the British Broadcasting Company, forerunner to the BBC, had already started to broadcast under its then founding Director-General John Reith.

The Conservative government had its own British Gazette, launched and edited by the Chancellor, Winston Churchill, who nevertheless saw radio as a more immediate and versatile medium in the chaos of the strike tried to lobby Prime Minister Stanley Baldwin into commandeer the Company. Reith, just thirty-seven years old, but remarkably acute, lobbied back. He convincingly argued, in a series of exchanges with Baldwin, that such a move would destroy the Company's reputation for independence and impartiality. Baldwin ruled, the day before the strike ended, that the BBC should remain independent (Hajkowski, 2013; Seaton, 2007).

It is important to highlight that the notion of impartiality not only derived from the British nation-building project seeking social cohesion but also that it was closely related to the emerging welfare state in Europe (Burns, 2016 [1977]; Hajkowski, 2013; Potter, 2012). In fact, it is impossible to understand the role of public service broadcasting without considering the policies undertaken by European governments after World War I and the Soviet Revolution to redistribute wealth as part of wider efforts to appease workers' movements and actions. Public service broadcasting (PSB) across Europe was both an attempt of enforcing national unity—against the idea of internationalization of workers' struggles led by the Soviets—and the articulation of a wider welfare state that enabled greater hegemony and the survival of the market economy (Calabrese & Burgelman, 1999; Scannell, 2005; Syvertsen, Mjøs, Enli, & Moe, 2014).

In the United States, on the other hand, the concept of "objectivity" had a different historical development as it was mostly linked to the private media. Hence, its procedures to guarantee fairness and balance derived from the opposite idea; one that envisaged that only by being privately owned and detached from the state could the media sector have the freedom to provide detached accounts of truth. This is something that I have already discussed when discussing the imposition of "common sense" in journalistic discourses and narratives. This link between media ownership, market and private property as a sustaining basis for press freedom is ingrained in the news media's psyche and in the philosophical framework that justifies it (McNally, 1989; Wellington, 1978).

This contextual framework discussed earlier is key to explaining the type of journalistic paradigm that was exported to the Global South. It also allows us to understand better as to why this news gathering and dissemination paradigm continues to dominate the public imagination and, most important, the deontological aspirations of many professional journalists from around the world in multiple forms (Hanitzsch et al., 2011; McNair, 1998). From Venezuela and Colombia to India and South Africa, objectivity has been commonly associated with neutrality, balance, and facticity (see Yadav, 2011, S. 6). Moreover, specific normative professional aspirations and general perceptions around objective reporting and impartiality are not exclusively related to journalism practice but also to media audiences.

Indeed, several studies have suggested that perceptions about the ability of a particular media outlet to remain detached, impartial, and objective are crucial in defining the size, nature, and trust of its audience. However, the same studies also point out that the perception of which outlet is truly objective and provide impartial content remains a subjective matter. In other words, in the public's imagination the question of who is objective or not depends on the ability of the particular media outlet to reflect or not the ideology and worldviews of the audience (Feldman, 2011; Morris, 2007). Indeed, decades of intense rhetoric regarding bias in the media have taken their toll on the mass public. The public is leery of trusting the mainstream media. The evidence indicates that different news audiences have different attitudes toward the media and the political world and consequently determines the degree of objectivity by the ability of the media to reflect people's own political beliefs and views (Morris, 2007; Rouner, Slater, & Buddenbaum, 1999).

In all of these cases, the common denominator is that news that is truthful presents somehow universal characteristics in that it centers around facts and is detached from opinions. This is, for our analysis, the most important aspect of this interpretation of how journalistic objectivity came about. In other words, the intrinsic connection between its use to "standardize" journalistic practice and the need to de-politicize the media landscape, foremost in relation to workers' struggles. Michael Schudson (2001) is right when he points out that in the United States, objectivity was the product of the self-conscious pursuit of internal group solidarity together with the need to articulate the ideals of social practice in a group in order to exercise control over subordinates and to pass on group culture to the next generation, all of which was underpinned by alternative technological and economic factors. However, I would add, not that there was just agency by means of a more corporate efforts by the press to set standards that excluded potential commercial and ideological competitors but that this happened also in a context of US nation building in which the United States and other European countries saw the propaganda and ideological challenge coming from the Soviet Union.

DE-POLITICIZING THE WORKERS

The type of journalistic models that were exported to the Global South mostly reflected these nation-building efforts that were linked to expanding geopolitical aspirations of the market economy and the tensions created by the struggles between the ruling elites and the workers during the late 19th and early 20th centuries. The creation of the Soviet Union was in fact central in the articulation of the notion of a journalistic deontology as we know it today as this was set partially in contraposition to the Russian social experiment. This was not only from the perspective of the US model as an emerging paradigm but also from the point of view of the cross conversations and dynamics among journalists from around the world.

So, let me start by reiterating once more that, contrary to some common views around the Marxist stance on journalism—which reduces Marxist theory on the press to pure organization, agitation and mobilization propaganda—many Marxists did try—as did their Western counterparts—to conceptualize and rationalize freedom of expression. Rosa Luxemburg, for example, spoke in favor of it when she stated that

> it is a well-known and indisputable fact that without a free and untrammelled press, without the unlimited right of association and assemblage, the rule of the broad masses of the people is entirely unthinkable. (2017 [1922], p. 113)

This was not, of course, the view of Lenin himself, who was no advocate of free press,

> Freedom of the press is another of the principal slogans of pure democracy. And here, too, the workers know—and socialists everywhere have admitted it millions of times—that this freedom is a deception while the best printing presses and the biggest stocks of paper are appropriated by the capitalists and while capitalist rule over the press remains, a rule that is manifested throughout the world all the more strikingly, sharply, and cynically, the more democracy and the republican system are developed, as in America for example. The first thing to do to win real equality and genuine democracy for the working people, for the workers and peasants, is to deprive capital of the possibility of hiring writers, buying up publishing houses, and hiring newspapers. And to do that the capitalists and exploiters have to be overthrown and their resistance suppressed. (Lenin, 1919)

Lenin's position was critical to what he saw as the real limitations the right to that freedom, which under existing material conditions and ownership of the means of production gave all the privileges to the ruling elites. For him:

> Genuine freedom and equality will be embodied in the system which the communists are building and in which there will be no opportunity for amassing wealth at the expense of others, no objective opportunities for putting the press under the direct or indirect power of money, and no impediments in the way of any workingman (or groups of workingmen, in any numbers) for enjoying and practising equal rights in the use of public printing presses and public stocks of paper. (Lenin, 1919)

Equally important is to highlight that Lenin did seem to believe, at least at the start of the revolution, in a type of journalism that was "scientific." For him, "scientific journalism," carrying out structural analysis using dialectics, would inevitably lend support to workers' struggles as this, he would argue, would be the logical conclusion from its scientific and structural analysis of society (Hopkins, 1965; Kenez, 1981). However, to achieve this "scientific character" in journalism practice did not necessarily mean that it had to be "objective" in the sense of detachment but in relation instead to scientific objectivity; that is, in its capacity to understand the world through structural analysis. In other words, if the key issue is inequality and social justice, then the role of journalism is to uncover those issues and point them out as the culprits of society's malaise.

It is now very easy to forget, in the light of what happened next under the later years of Lenin and subsequent Stalinism, that there was a short but vivid period of Soviet Enlightenment that saw the flourishing of the popular press and active engagement of journalists with people's issues and problems using a more structuralist and interpretative approach. This period provided a variety of examples and ample debates around the question of what is proletarian culture and what is the relationship of the proletariat to the bourgeois knowledge (Chehonadskih, 2017) as stated in records of the discussions between Vladimir Lenin and Alexander Bogdanov (1873–1928). Particularly, in relation to the debates around the Metaphysics of Positivism that took place between Lenin and Plekhanov, on the one side, and Bogdanov, Lunacharsky, Yushkevich, and other Machists on the other. This would have long-standing effects on the approaches toward journalism in the Soviet sphere given the fact that many of Lenin's doctrines—even through the Stalin era—became ideological doctrines to be followed. Lenin

> saw the full danger which was present for the fate of the revolution in Russia—and not only in Russia—in the Russian variation of the positivist revision of the philosophical foundations of revolutionary Marxism. The philosophy of dialectical materialism, materialist dialectics, the logic of the development of the entire Marxist world outlook, the logic of cognition by virtue of which Capital had been written, and finally the strategy based on Capital of the political struggle of the revolutionary movement of the international working class—that is what this revisionism was directed against. So, the discussion was not at all about abstract "epistemological research," but about that "aspect of the matter" upon which, in essence, depended all the remaining "aspects" of the Marxist world view, the direction and paths of development of all its remaining component parts. And such an "aspect of the matter" is called, in competent philosophical language, the essence of the matter. (Ilyenkov, 2001 [1979])

For Lenin, it was essential to reject the type of positivism enunciated by Ernst Mach (1838–1916) and Alexander Bogdanov (1873–1928) and to superimpose materialist dialectics as the logic and theory of scientific cognition, and, consequently, who had not mastered the ability to think in a scientific manner about contemporary reality, and who were unable to resolve the enormous and difficult problems of the century in a scientific way, on the level of real science of the 20th century (Ilyenkov, 2001 [1979]).

By doing this, Lenin was challenging the type of phenomenological objectivity that still underpins the deontology of modern journalism in the West and that prioritizes factual analysis over structural analysis. Consequently, for Lenin and his followers, a type of journalistic practice that advocated for revolution and that set itself to mobilize the workers against the ruling class was not, in his view, incompatible at all with being scientific. To be sure, in the broad understanding of journalism, Marxists behind the Soviet Union created a tradition that claimed to be objective and based on scientific inquisitorial approaches. In the sense, news was intrinsically linked to class interest and concerns, which to them was the truth. The difference between socialist and bourgeois was that the latter attempted to cover up this bias through claims of objectivity while the former uncovered these truths. Consequently, in their own words, socialist journalism was more frank and honest, as it acknowledged the role that class interests played in shaping news and information (Schlosser, 2015, p. 56).

Therefore, as in the case of the United States, the Soviet Union also tried to create a model of journalism that helped it underpin the public imaginary around their own national ideological project; one that was epitomized by the emerging model of real (scientific) socialism that had to be exported and internationalized. It was part of the Bolshevik leadership's efforts to make "the new Soviet Men" in Russia and beyond its borders; one that started under Lenin as part of the push for "Soviet Enlightenment" but that tragically ended in the travesty of Leninist and Stalinist propaganda.

The Soviet Union rapidly moved also toward a model for which the media's role was to underpin ideology and foster nationalism (as well as geopolitical ambitions). This meant a push for a "National Bolshevism" (Brandenberger, 2002), particularly after the Great Break, which meant acceleration of collectivization and industrialization. Consequently, there was a transition in the media layout, style, and content from fostering enlightenment to pushing for mass mobilization. As Matthew Lenoe (2004) has argued, this shift was not one of rhetoric, but one of practice. It was part of the greater efforts under Stalinism that meant consolidating power and rapid industrialization (M. Lenoe, 2004, p. 3).

It was within this context that journalism in the USSR transitioned from a quest for alternative rationales about searching for truth in news reporting, although distinctive from the US model as it incorporated structural analysis, to blunt propaganda under the Stalin era. Indeed,

> Between 1925 and 1933 the layout and the tone of the Soviet central press underwent an obvious change. Issues of Pravda and Izvestia from the period of the New Economic Policy (1921–1927) contain journalistic genres familiar to today's Western reader: the papers feature wire service reports written in an "objective" style, editorial commentaries, economic analysis, and short satirical pieces about everyday life. The shrill declamation of the same newspapers in the early 1930s, by contrast, seems alien and bizarre. Exclamation points, commands, military metaphors, and congratulations from the party leaders to factories for surpassing their production plans dominate. (M. Lenoe, 2004, p. 11)

These debates taking place in the United States and the Soviet Union would come to be central in defining the "models" of press that would be exported to the Global South using Foreign Aid during both of the World Wars and the Cold War. Hence, the need to recognize the modern concept of "journalism objectivity" as also a collateral output of the tensions between workers' struggles in the 19th and 20th centuries and the effort to create a liberal democracy that could retain preexisting power structures. These ideological and political tensions, which ran until the end of the Cold War, created important dynamics that shaped the efforts and resources allocated toward the Global South. This is in materialistic and ideological terms and it would go on to shape the policies and approaches toward Foreign Aid for Media Development and media assistance in the subsequent years. More important, this was the context that surrounded the emergence and consolidation of the notion "journalism objectivity" as a universal and core value among prevalent news cultures.

THE FEAR TO THE MASSES

Therefore, it is important to review and complement interpretations around the way in which journalistic objectivity "just happen" in the West—or the United States for that matter—or about how it went on to shape the values and cultures of journalism around the world only as a consequence of the expansion of the market economy. As we seen here, there was nothing "natural" or "inevitable" about the expansion of this journalistic paradigm that came to dominate the 20th century. In fact, journalism became part of an orchestrated effort to articulate particular ideologies by standardizing professional practices.

The dynamic and fluid conversations that flowed in several directions across the globe went to shape these practices. These multiple conversations—including the one Soviet journalists were having about scientific objectivity in their own press—were closely interlinked, informing each other, and also transcending into alternative journalistic traditions such as the Muckrakers in the United States (Filler, 1993; Wilson, 2015). It is because of these direct and indirect conversations, which not always engaged with the ideological opponents but definitively listened closely to what they said in order to produce a counterargument, which we can suggest that the norm of journalistic objectivity as we know it today in the West owes more to the fear to workers' struggles and political mobilization that what is often acknowledged.

The Muckrakers, as mentioned before, were influential over the years for the rest of the professionals in the mainstream media (Filler, 1993; Schiffrin, 2014; Wilson, 2015). Interestingly, Chris W. Anderson's account of the rise of interpretative journalism in the United States sees it as a series of intellectual formulations. He suggest that there was an interpretative and explanatory turn that had been percolating through journalism since at least the 1930s (2018, p. 113). Anderson himself acknowledges the profound indebtedness of that new trend from the more radical forms of journalism (e.g., the Muckrakers], many of whom not only were openly self-declared socialists due to their pro-workers' movement views (Reynolds Jr, 1979). If what would follow within the mainstream newsrooms in the form of McCarthyism would be an equivalent to the Christian counterreform, the overwhelming liberal characteristic of journalism in the United States would be forever indebted to this initial link to the workers' struggle.

COUNTERREFORM IN THE UNITED STATES

It was precisely in confrontation to the Russian Revolution that the standardization of journalism in the United States came to be—starting with President Wilson's administration, when it became a national project. One that was profoundly defined by the US self-view that it was somehow different to the old European empires—which also developed their own models of journalism, such as Britain, Portugal, and Spain—but that somehow would also have to play a role in reaffirming the new hegemonic role of liberal democracy and the market-driven economy. Particularly important to this endeavor would be the self-ascribed role of defender of the market economy and liberal democracy, reflected in Wilson's own personal project of supporting the creation of the League of Nations (Knock, 1992).

Crucially important to these efforts was the role of Albert S. Burleson (1863–1937) as US Postmaster General, who implemented a series of measures to restrict the distribution of non-mainstream newspapers (Gallagher, 2016; González & Torres, 2011). This and a series of legal actions from AP created the perfect context for mainstream journalism to be standardized. From there, the US model of journalism would go on to try to present itself as one that emphasizes "liberty and freedom" over "justice" and in that, it wanted to distinguish itself from the Soviet journalistic proposal.

US journalism went on to define itself in opposition to the Soviet imaginary and against what the Soviet Revolution seem to offer to its own workers. This meant that the ethos of journalism in the US became a model that catered for all classes. Moreover, it became one that did not mention class and that was arguably both de-politicized (non-ideological) yet explicitly supportive of liberal democracy and the market economy. These were the seeds of what would become the norm of deontology of journalism, one that would dominate all through the 20th century.

One of the key aspects to highlight, as explained in previous sections, is that the shaping of the current US journalistic model was, historically speaking, part of a nation-building exercise, which in itself was deeply influenced and defined by the rise of anti-communism in the United States. By this, I mean that the developing of modern journalism deontology and its associated news cultures did not happen in a vacuum but as part of a series of historical dynamics that were taking place at the time and that are rooted in the ideological struggle that would characterize most of the 20th century; one that oscillated between a free market economy and its liberal democratic paradigm against the socialist utopia that led to the totalitarian Soviet state and its satellites.

In this context, Adam Hochschild (2017a) reminded us that as soon as the United States entered the First World War in 1917, there was an

> assault on the media unmatched in American history or—so far—since. Its commander was [Woodrow] Wilson's postmaster general. Albert Sidney Burleson, a pompous former prosecutor and congressman. On June 16, 1917 he sent sweeping instructions to local postmasters ordering them to "keep a close watch on unsealed matters, newspapers, etc." for anything "calculated to . . . cause insubordination, disloyalty, mutiny . . . or otherwise embarrass or hamper the Government in conducting the war". What did "embarrass" mean? . . . One after another, Burleson went after newspapers and magazines, many affiliated with the Socialist Party. (Hochschild, 2017a, p. 82)

Using his discretional power, Burleson went to bypass the First Amendment of the US Constitution and went effectively to censor many newspapers using the post office as a weapon to limit and ban distribution of many other publications and literature in what was effectively the first anti-communist crusade of the 20th century. Although Burleson's crusade initially was justified by nationalism as a way of preventing foreign agents of the Axis Powers from using the media against the US government, it soon evolved into an effort to undermine any media outlets in that country that were either foreign or had a pro-socialist or pro-pacifist stance.

Overall, the First World War served as a perfect excuse for an unprecedented use of censorship, dissemination of propaganda and the effective co-option of the news media in ways not seen before in the United States. However, this did not happen only in relation to external threats but also against what were seen as internal ones, such as the unionization of workers. The targeting of pro-socialist publications included those such as The Masses,[4] which was forced by the US federal government to cease publication in the fall of 1917 after the magazine refused to change its policy against the war. This was a direct result of the passing of the Espionage Act—approved on June 15, 1917—that set fines and imprisonment terms to anyone who interfered with the recruiting of soldiers while prohibiting the mailing of any newspaper or magazine that promoted such sentiments.

Again, it was thanks to the US Postal Service that the US government and elites were able to enforce a particular model of journalism as a hegemonic one by giving leave to deny any mailing that fitted these standards from further postal delivery, and then to disqualify a magazine because it had missed a mailing and hence was no longer considered a regular publication (Mott, 1941; Schudson & Tifft, 2005). This systematic elimination of news media outlets translated in an increasing homogenization of the media ecology in that country and the consolidation of a particular style of gathering, producing, and disseminating news, which gravitated toward the normative aspiration of journalism objectivity; one that claimed to be non-ideological and politically neutral but that supported liberal democracy, the private ownership of property, and the free market.

However, this model needed to be legitimized by more hegemonic means in order to become an accepted standard. This included not only the early setting of journalism schools across the United States (Stephen A Banning, 1998; Carey, 2000; Folkerts, 2014) but also the cartelization of news exchange through the news agencies. On the one hand, one can suggest that the creation of journalism schools was both an attempt to standardize conceptualization and practice of journalism as a professional guild and, at the same time, a reactionary effort to control and engineer future normative aspiration and practice (let us not forget that the first journalism school in the United States was set by the confederate states in the South). On the other, the increasing cartelization of international and national distribution and exchange of news content through the news agencies (Boyd-Barrett, 1980) in what Federico Álvarez called the spreading of "industrial journalism" (Álvarez, 2010 [1978], p. 72). This meant that while the exchanges of newspapers through the postal services decreased, news agencies such as AP were able to establish a firm grip upon the distribution of news content. This in turned allowed the AP to define the aesthetics of the format, structure, and language as well the deontological procedures to follow. This was achieved namely by complying with its style—later turned into manuals. In addition, news agencies went further to use the new copyright law to strengthen their dominant position as intermediaries in the exchange of news content in what is often referred to as the "Associated Press Doctrine" (Baird, 1983; Epstein, 1992; Sell, 1957).

Over the years, AP consolidated its position as the main provider and mediator of news in the United States thanks to an unholy alliance with Western Union, which monopolized the telegraph in that country and the post office, which by now imposed restrictions on the distribution of newspapers. In doing so, AP was able to set the parameters for style and make sure that any newspaper or publication that deviated from its norm was automatically excluded from its circuit of content distribution (González & Torres, 2011, p. 141). This to the point that a US Senate Report of 1875 would point out:

> The news furnished to every leading citizen and almost every other daily paper comes from one source, and its preparation, wherever it is collected, is under the supervision of the agent of the seven associated papers in New York. It is inevitable that the views, opinions, and interests of these seven papers should be expressed through this channel, especially by the full or short reports upon topics they favour or oppose and by the bias of the writer's mind. (Cited by González & Torres, 2011, p. 137)

Later on, Walter Lippmann, one of the intellectual architects of journalism objectivity as a fully developed ideological doctrine, would go on to write, in the aftermath of World War I and the Soviet Revolution, his book *Liberty and the News* (1920) in which he denounced the wartime misinformation and propaganda fed to the public and called journalists to focus on the facts. By examining the tenuous relationship between facts and news and the consequences of media distortion, he elaborated a crafted argument in favor of objectivity, which helped establish the standards of objective reporting that were subsequently embraced by the rest of the media landscape.

In this book, Lippmann focused not only on war but clearly referred to "revolution" (aka the Soviet Revolution and other workers' struggles) as the main source of propaganda and manipulation (1920, p. 56). In his defense of objectivity and freedom, he criticized those who condemned the censorship imposed by the Postmaster General Albert S. Burleson but that then let off the hook the censorship imposed by the Soviet leader Vladimir Lenin (1920, p. 24).

It was clear that Lippmann was aware of the discussions that were taking place in the Soviet Union around what journalism ought to be. He was also familiar with the work of pro-socialist reporters in the United States and with the debates influencing views in his own country. Lippmann saw the Russian Revolution as a once-in-a-lifetime test for professional journalism standards. In this respect, he would write,

> The professional standards of journalism are not high enough and the discipline by which standards are maintained not strong enough, to carry out the press triumphantly through a test so severe as that provided by the Russian Revolution . . . the analysis show that certain correspondents are totally untrustworthy because their sympathies are too deeply engaged. (Lippmann, 1920, p. 144)

It is important also to notice that Lippmann used the Russian and not Mexican Revolution as an example to make his argument. This is because the earlier posed less of an ideological challenge to the US model despite the geographical proximity of the latter. Hence, as an oppositional definer for journalism objectivity and identity, the case of Soviet propaganda allowed him to consolidate a view of journalism that operated in privately owned and self-regulated media. He and others like him would become influential voices in shaping the theory of journalism ethics in the United States and beyond, helping to define the professional guild through a specific imaginary that was deeply influenced by both US liberal democracy and the Soviet Revolution.

This because, the 1920s popular anti-radicalism had not been until then anti-communist per se. Nevertheless, it did became so in the face of growing fear of domestic revolution agitated by the supposed alien-subversive character of immigrants who where seen as being influenced by European anarchism and socialist ideas. The main concern focused on some major groups such as what was left of the Populists, the growing Industrial Workers of the World (IWW), most labor unions, and, of course, the socialists and communists parties (Athan, 1971, p. 6). Indeed, the Soviet Revolution, with its proclamation of a permanent and international proletariat revolution, would shift the attention from the domestic front to the international threat posed by Lenin and his followers and create in the public imagination a link between Lenin's movements and the homegrown radicals. The response was to reinforce the imaginary of a United States that was the guarantor and protector of freedom and Western civilization and to make sure that each and every one of its key institutions would embrace this imaginary. Journalism, by then one of its key political institutions in liberal democracy, meant that it would also fall in line for the rest of the century with this imaginary that says any call for structural analysis and socialism is "un-American."

Contrary to the common narrative, there was no interim between the First and Second Scares. If anything, the Allied intervention in the Russian Civil War (1918–1925) and the protests derived from the Great Depression (1929–1939) that marked those years making the US political elites ever-more anti-communist and suspicious of the Soviet threat during that whole period. During the inter-war era and after World War II, this was clear for US officials who never stopped expressing their concern about the Soviet threat. Gordon Grey (1909–1982), appointed by Truman as head of the Psychological Strategy Board, would summarize the feelings when writing,

> Towards the end of the First World Warm a Russian revolutionary leader conceived the idea of a kind of a struggle which would be "neither war nor peace." That leader was later disposed of by his less inventive comrades, but they eventually found merit in his idea and resolved to adapt it to the convulsive situation which would follow the Second World War. Today the world knows the meaning

of their choice—an assault which stops short of general war, carried out under the cloak of a natural peace. The assault began in fact before the Second World War was over. As the armies of the Western Allies advanced, the forces of international Communism set to work in their rear to poison the minds of the liberated against the liberators, to turn the free nations against each other, to seize position of power, and to break down the prestige of the United States. And while the victorious nations of the West were disbanding their armed forces, the Kremlin's men in every country were moving to battle stations in preparation for the "final struggle" so long foretold in Communist song and fable. (Grey, 1952b, p. 3)

Grey (1952a) would go on to call for a set of "New Cold War Instruments" that he defined as a set of approaches and policies to bring about a relative reduction of Soviet power and influence across the globe.

It is also true that there was also a more cynical side to the Red Scares and that anti-communism was used in fact to facilitate anti-workers' actions and legislations, undermining Franklin Delano Roosevelt's New Deal and undercutting any other progressive movements and actions including racial and gender equality (Storrs, 2013; Woods, 2003). Consequently, efforts to standardize journalism practice were also defined by the attempts to turn it into a rhetorical effort to disseminate and underpin ideas about free market and liberal democracy by confining journalism to the narrow spectrum given by "objective" reporting.

THE SCIENCE OF TRUTH

From a materialistic point of view, one could argue that the adoption of journalistic objectivity was by all means an effort to turn the content produced by the Western mainstream news media into a commercial commodity, one that could be easily exchanged but that at the same time did not pose a danger to the status quo (Brovkin, 1998; Fitzpatrick, 2002; Lenoe, 2004). The most important aspect, for our analysis, of this dialectical interpretation of how journalistic objectivity came about is the intrinsic connection between its use to "standardize" journalistic practice and the need to de-politicize the media landscape, foremost in relation to workers' struggles. Indeed, if "journalistic objectivity" in the West, particularly in the United States and the United Kingdom, developed as a quest for professionalization—ergo underpinning credibility and authorial control over "truth"—this was done to confront what the emerging bourgeoisie saw at the time as the danger of agitating the masses into revolutionary mode.

News reporting practices became increasingly standardized as they took an "industrial" form (Álvarez, 2010 [1978]) as they emulated the modernization process that took place in the industry, which incorporated Taylorism. This was a system of scientific management named after Frederick W. Taylor (1856–1915) that advocated that management was to determine the best way for the worker to do the job and provide tools to improve performance such as setting functions and routine (Littler, 1978). Let us not forget that by the end of the 19th century, newspapers had become already massive industrial operations, which would be increasingly driven by commercial prerogatives (Sotiron, 1997). This was a trend that would intensify over the years and reach a climax after World War II.

From an international perspective, standardization was at every level a key concept of the postwar US efforts to establish its own international hegemony over the markets. It was originally linked to the military and the pursuit of a standardized arms program for the Western hemisphere in a way that could guarantee the supply of US weapons to all its allies (CIA, 1949). This concept transcended into several other spheres, including journalism and mass communication. In this respect, some authors have drawn attention to the link between efforts to standardize professional communication practices and exercising communication hegemony (Gregory & Halff, 2013, p. 417). The broad agreement around standardizing journalism ethics was that news reporting had to be objectively scientific; that is, to tell the truth as it is by focusing on the facts.

To accomplish a standardized type of objectivity, it was argued then (Carroll, 1919; Duniway, 1906; F. B. Hart, 1919), journalists had to enjoy "independence" and "freedom" to say what they needed to report, which was seen as an essential condition that distinguished United States from Soviet journalism and free press from propaganda. Consequently, it was argued, true journalism could only take place in democratic societies rather than be, as it actually was, a social practice that happened on its own terms in every country (Lippmann, 2010 [1920]).

Moreover, contrary to common assumptions about journalism practice in socialist societies—according to which they were pure propaganda—many Marxists tended instead to coincide with their Western counterparts in relation to the need for freedom of expression as we discussed earlier. It is easy nowadays to dismiss the initial Soviet efforts to construct its own way of doing journalism as pure propaganda. Nevertheless, reading what they produced at the start of the revolution one can argue that in many ways, it was a genuine debate around the aspiration of Soviet journalism to be truly scientific. More importantly, these discussions in the former USSR about how to do more scientific news reporting were shared among supporters and admirers in the USA.

In this context, it would not only have particular repercussions among a group of US-based journalists known as "Muckrakers"[5]—many of whom identified themselves as "socialists"—but also foster dynamic and fluid conversations that would go on to influence too the way mainstream commercial journalism was conducted in the United States. All this despite the fact that mainstream journalism had clearly defined itself in opposition to the Soviet imaginary and against what the Soviet Revolution seemed to offer to its own workers. This was a model of news making that catered for all classes but without mentioning class and that was both politicized but claiming to be non-ideological and yet openly supportive of liberal democracy and the market economy. These were the seeds of what would become the norm of objectivity in journalism. A point robustly argued by John Dewey (1991 [1927]), who not only recognized the limitations of the "pursuit of facts" but also highlighted the problems associated with the "ideology of objectivity" itself.

Between World War I and World War II, there were particular and very important laboratories for what would become, in the future, a set of more structured policies around foreign aid for media assistance and media development. One of the key scenarios was the Spanish Civil War (1936–1939) where both Nazi Germany and the Soviet Union experimented, not only with military weapons, but also with winning the hearts and minds of the population. To be sure, both countries helped to set up and operate radio stations in that country to support both sides of the conflict. One of the most interesting developments of that intervention was the setting up of a radio station in Morocco to broadcast from there in support of General Francisco Franco's (1892–1975) troops going to Spain (Arasa, 2015).

This last one was not the only case. Across the European empires in Africa and Asia, there was a multiplicity of media outlets that dated from early colonial times, which were examples of early foreign aid interventions. Over time, many of these efforts increasingly turned to radio as one of the most cost-effective ways of developing and assisting new media outlets. These outlets were funded by the colonial powers or were at least linked to larger colonial radio networks such as the BBC, Poste Colonial created in 1931 (later renamed as Radio France Internationale), Philips Radio (which preceded the Dutch Radio Netherlands Worldwide) broadcasting to Batavia—now Indonesia—among other radio stations in Africa and Oceania. In fact, over the next few decades, radio would become one of the biggest recipients of foreign aid in Africa, Asia, and Latin America (Bustamante et al., 2008; Tarnoff, 2005). This is an area that we will explore in greater depth in subsequent chapters.

During the inter-war period, the world not only would face the Great Depression of the 1930s and the rise of Fascism but also a series of initial uprisings in the Global South that germinated into what later became the seeds for many of the independentist movements (Haithcox, 2015; Scotton, 1973). During this period, journalism in the West would become increasingly defined by these tensions. However, in the Global South in addition these tensions, the development of a journalism culture would also shape the clash between the fact that many media outlets were originally created by agents of the colonial powers and that their journalists were nevertheless strong advocates for independence in a time in which many European empires started to agonize (Scotton, 1973).

The end of World War II in 1945 marked the expansion of both United States and Soviet influence around the world and the retreat of the old European empires. Orchestrated efforts by both sides were made to incorporate new independent countries into their own orbits of influence and develop new markets. To achieve this, there was an important effort to gain the hearts and minds of the people in the Global South. This included making sure to have control over the media, the narratives it disseminated and the content that it created. However, in doing so, they took very different approaches. The United States, during the Truman administration, placed emphasis on exporting the idea of a "free press" to the Global South and Western Europe, which became a priority in the struggle against Soviet propaganda.

The Soviet Union embraced instead the idea of using the media to agitate and mobilize. Truth, for the Soviets, was not about fact but about achieving social justice. This was a model that was inspirational to many in the newsrooms around the world. Although today, after knowing about all of its excess and the gulags, it is easy to dismiss Stalinism as a model—back then it was certainly a source of inspiration. Whatever the cost, Joseph Stalin had transformed the USSR from an agrarian backward society into one of the top industrial powers of the world in a very short period of time. Real Socialism presented itself as model to be replicated across the Global South.

As European decaying empires retreated from the world stage, many former colonies started to look for alternative models for their own future. In many of these uprisings, the Soviets offered help and support for development. In North Korea, North Vietnam, Cuba, Angola, and many other countries, the formula was the same—appropriation of the "bourgeois" press and then setting up a news media system to mobilize the people toward industrialization. The Soviet Union assisted these attempts with ample funding, which included not only financial support for media development in those countries (Barghoorn, 2015; Radosh, 2012) but also the training of journalists. Even today in Vietnam, to cite an example, an important proportion of the news editors went to study or train in the Soviet Union and new generations still go to Russia.

Hence, it is important to remark that the Soviet news media system was characterized by a different balance between official and civilian views. Despite a near-universal assumption that the Soviet press was elitist and propaganda-laden, studies of the time pointed out instead that over 70% of the official Russian newspaper's content originated not from press releases or press conferences from the authorities but from citizens' complaints, enquiries, revelations, and observations (Koch, 1990, p. 17). Consequently, what the USSR exported to the Global South was mostly a model of agitation and mobilization that one might easily assume was propaganda. However, in line with broader discussion, it is better to refer to this as a process of de-professionalization—or, in other words—an attempt to strip journalists from professional autonomy and make them drop traditional normative aspirations often associated with European and US traditions.

Indeed, in her study on the influence of foreign aid on media development and news cultures in Cuba, Sara Garcia-Santamaria (2018) talks about "the Sovietization of Cuban Journalism" and argues that the island's economic dependency on Soviet foreign aid created news cultures and journalistic practices that tried to replicated those in the URSS. For this author, economic and ideological dependency had a lasting impact on the de-professionalization of Cuban journalism in terms of structure, intellectual freedom, and journalistic practice.

> The idealisation of "the Revolution" produced a "Panglossian" media construction of society, presenting an idealised image of the country that hides citizens' daily problems, a senior opinion writer considers. . . . In the face of an external enemy, public self-criticism was interpreted as potentially damaging for national unity, revealing internal weaknesses to "the enemy." Consequently, the journalists were forced to offer a rather simplistic, jingoistic account of society, creating "very repetitive, very transmissive, and very triumphalist" articulations. Therefore, the both closer ties with the COMECOM in the 1970s and the sudden dissolution of the Soviet bloc two decades later had a great ideological impact on Cuban journalism that manifested itself through language, either reproducing Soviet bureaucratic "greyness" or the need to lift people's morals during a "special period" of harsh survival.

Her findings suggest that the Sovietization and de-professionalization of Cuban journalism went hand in hand. However, while the Communist Party stressed journalists' responsibility in the lack of professionalism, the interviews with intellectuals, reporters, and news reporters indicate that Soviet influence on structures and intellectual freedom came with a generalized lack of journalistic agency. This explains, for Garcia-Santamaria, why later official calls to overcome bureaucratic practices and restrictions had limited impact on journalistic practices, since the structure of the media system and a news culture inherited from the Soviet era remains to this day almost untouched.

This lack of professional autonomy and the posterior role that is subservient to the greater aim of supporting the revolution constituted the basis of the de-professionalization in communist countries. According to Silvio Waisbord (2013), professional autonomy is considered as one of the most influential factors that can either prevent or increase journalists' capability to retain their journalistic professionalism. In the case of Cuba, Ethiopia, and North Korea, this meant a model of journalism that did not see itself as an autonomous agent but instead as part of a greater project to bring justice in terms of a socialist utopia. Following this, not only newspapers such as Granma in Cuba copied the style of Pravda of the URSS but also even its news organizations such as Prensa Latina emulated to a great degree the Telegraph Agency of the Soviet Union (TASS).

This includes standardizing the media and eliminating competing forms of journalism for those who complied with AP standards. Therein anti-communism became central in neutralizing other forms of journalism that had developed during the initial stages of the US history. The Red Scares enabled legislation and policies that made large segments of the more advocacy-prone and foreign-language media disappear or become almost invisible. It facilitated a homogenous sea of white commercial press that, even in its more critical episodes such as the Great Depression, stood unequivocally for the market-driven economy, private property, and liberal democracy.

Mainstream journalism practitioners responded to this by emphasizing even further their detachment from ideological structural analysis. Their position was facilitated by the consolidation of Joseph Stalin in power in the URSS, which meant the concretion of National Bolshevism (Brandenberger, 2002) as a political project that shaped the popular imaginary in that country and prioritized explicit propaganda and a sense of national unity. This not only meant the ultimate death or permanent exile of any reminiscence of self-critical and independent journalism in that nation but also signified that the US commercial journalism model could finally claim for itself to be the only paradigm capable of delivering enlightened scientific objective truth.

This exercise of ethical rhetoric that stood in opposition to the Soviet Union model, would be the basis upon which journalism deontology of the 20th century in the West would define itself. One that was deeply grounded in the political economy that sustained the news media—that later became embedded to the Military–Industrial Complex (Der Derian, 2009; McChesney, 2002). As Nancy E. Bernhard (2003) points out, the political economy of the mass media was intimately tied up with the articulation of Cold War policies and objectivity became grounded in fervent anti-communism. In this sense, she adds, the Cold War made propaganda an integral part of American foreign policy and took as its casualty confidence that the United States would triumph in the marketplace of ideas. Many journalists during that period held strongly the belief that in the crusade against Communism, truthfulness should be a distinguishing feature of US propaganda. In a way, one should add, the Unite States did exactly what the Soviets had tried to do before under Lenin and turn the enterprise of truth-seeking into a national enterprise.

Reshaping journalism would become a US nation-building blueprint for the expansion and consolidation of the Market Society—one that extended way beyond the US borders and became part of the ideological project to establish US hegemony across the Global South. Indeed, contrary to the old European empires, the United States set its path to global power mostly by means of ideological hegemony rather than through the use of brutal force—although it did that too. As historian Jason C. Parker has so eloquently described,

> Yet most people in these areas [Global South] experienced the superpower clash neither as the much-feared mushroom cloud nor the abundantly violent way that Vietnam and Korea did. They instead experienced it as what came to be called public diplomacy—as a multifront media war, launched by the superpowers in the pursuit of strategic and psychological gains, to win them over. The not-infrequent episodes of espionage and armed intervention in decolonization and underdeveloped areas held higher stakes for local life and limb. But the public diplomacy was the more sustained presence, one intruding upon and influencing the day-to-day conversations of these lands and peoples in historic flux. (Parker, 2016, p. 3)

POSTWAR AND THE GLOBAL SOUTH

Most countries in the Global South experienced the Cold War not in terms of armed conflict but mostly in terms of propaganda (Parker, 2016). As the end of the war marked the beginning of a frantic race between the two emerging superpowers there was an increasing need to deploy communication strategies that could attract allies under each orbit of ideological stance. The recent decolonized regions in the world suddenly had then to choose between Western capitalism and Soviet socialism as models for development (Lugo-Ocando & Nguyen, 2017). Hence, the battle for ideas—arguably hearts and minds—became as important as, or even more than, those who fought with bullets and tanks (Lucas, 1999).

In this sense, the first US administration after the war, that of President Harry S. Truman (1884–1972), saw itself as a champion of the free world and thought vehemently that if the new decolonized regions were properly informed they would always choose liberal democracy and the market economy over Soviet authoritarian socialism. Indeed, many documents declassified since then provide testimony that Truman himself claimed to have opposed the involvement of the Central Intelligence Agency (CIA) in covert operations to subvert governments in other countries (despite his clear involvement in places such as Greece, Italy, Turkey, and the Philippines).

In these documents, Truman (1963, 1964) made an emphatic plea that the creation of the Central Intelligence Agency under his administration had the unique and sole purpose of centralizing information given to the president and at no point had he agreed for the CIA to undertake such types of "strange" operations. In his own view, he was instead a believer in the gospel of the free market. Indeed, many years after stepping down as president, in a candid conversation at his home with former CIA director Allen Welsh Dulles, Harry S. Truman agreed with him as to how important the organization and setting up of news initiatives such as Radio Free Europe and others had been for the strategic interests of the United States. Dulles (1964) would go on to record, in a memorandum to General Counsel Lawrence R. Huston, to explain how these media operations, set during the Truman administration, helped the United States to avoid having to intervene militarily in places such as Greece and Italy.

Overall, Truman's foreign policy toward the Global South, particularly in places such as Latin America, was defined in every single sense by the prerogatives of the Cold War and the fear of communist subversion (CIA, 1950; Kirkendall, 1989). His closest allies also thought along the same lines. In a memorandum to President Truman, the then senator Hubert H. Humphrey Jr. (1911–1978) would warn of the ability of the Soviets to appeal to the masses and calls for a strategy that guarantees reaching the hearts and minds of the underdeveloped countries, particularly in Asia (1951, p. 1). Hence, policies and action toward information operations in the Global South were defined by the Red Scares.

Despite this, the Truman administration inaugurated a new era, at least normatively, in international relations. One that was not characterized by the exercise of overt colonial power, except in places such as Puerto Rico and Hawaii, but instead by the quest to expand markets for US products and services through a more hegemonic and subtle form of power. The priority was one and one only; the expansion of the markets for US products and services in order to reduce war surplus, reduce unemployment, and avoid a full recession. As the Hansen's memorandum from the Board of Governors of the Federal Reserve System pointed out:

> The [economic] record [of the United States] has amazed us; it has amazed the world. The achievement in production exceeds anything which even the most optimistic had thought possible. It is a striking demonstration of the ingenuity, resourcefulness, technical knowledge, and organizational skill of the American economy. It is a revelation of what American business, labour, and agriculture can do when there are adequate markets for their goods and services and when they all cooperate together to reach a common goal. . . . Free enterprise has been and will remain the backbone of the American economy [and] expansion is a

necessary condition for the success of free enterprise. (Federal Reserve System, 1944)

This was the model that the United States intended to export to the Global South as a way of expanding the markets and securing stability, both considered to be by the administration as a prerequisite to growth of the US economy and securing for the nation its dominant role in the world.

The Truman administration strongly believed in spreading the ideas and values of free market economy and liberal democracy in the Global South. For this administration, the media presented a key instrument to do so and believed that in a free market of ideas, the United States would triumph in the end. They had the experience of having used radio to reach the Japanese people as part of the public diplomacy and war propaganda efforts during the conflict (Davis, 1945). The administration understood all too well the use of free media in underpinning power. However, it was a time of transition and many gaps were left by the tremendous demobilization of the war apparatus that took place. This included the fact that the Office for War Information ceased to exist, which had until then managed all provision around information and propaganda operations abroad. The office was closed in less than ninety days and very few provisions were made for alternative government bodies to take on those responsibilities (Klauber, 1945). Without it, support and resources for media development and overall US influence in the Global South literally disappeared overnight.

Truman's administration response was the creation of the Interagency Foreign Information Organization (IFIO). It placed emphasis on psychological operations and influencing world opinion and received increasing attention and resources after the outbreak of the Korean War (Lilly, 1968, p. 361). Its creation can be counted as the initial step that led to later programs of public diplomacy and supporting media development initiatives abroad. Indeed,

> As the Cold War continued to build, some officials in the Truman Administration argued that the U.S. needed to do more than it was currently doing to influence the world situation. Based on recommendations from an ad hoc committee headed by Paul Nitze, Truman signed NSC 68 on 14 Apr 1950. NSC 68 called for an intense program of both overt and covert economic, political and psychological warfare to influence the political and psychological conditions in both the Free World and Soviet areas, with a particular aim to foster unrest in Soviet satellite countries. NSC 68 was the hallmark of the American containment strategy of the Cold War.... The Soviet role in the origins of the Korean War galvanized the need for better coordination and planning of psychological warfare at the national level. The Soviets increasingly used propaganda and other unorthodox methods to increase their sphere of influence. The United States needed to find

ways to counter Soviet influence that would not trigger nuclear war. Recognition arose that this was as much a battle of ideas, a battle for the hearts and minds of men, as it was a battle of tanks and artillery. Political and psychological warfare became key weapons in the U.S. arsenal. (Gough, 2003, p. 9)

Having said that, Truman's administration never really seem to have an elaborated and systematic media plan to spread ideas of capitalism and liberal democracy beyond some key discourses and interventions.[6] There was, nevertheless, ample awareness of the need to develop media systems in the Third World that evoked those in the United States if the US model ought to be exported effectively to those regions of the world. In fact, members of his cabinet—including some of his closest advisors—were convinced that by promoting a free press in places such as in Latin America, they could have better access to the public in those countries and effectively saw a government-controlled press as an obstacle for US influence in that part of the world (Mann, 1952, p. 35). Nevertheless, this general sentiment never materialized in any type of specific action plan.

However, one initiative during this administration deserves ample attention in relation to the thesis of this book: the establishment of the US Cultural Exchange Program known as the Fulbright Program. Set in 1946 by United States senator J. William Fulbright, the program has seen thousands of exchanges between scholars, students, and journalists from around the world. It became also a central instrument in the spreading of a particular model of journalism in the Global South thanks to this. President Truman himself would point out:

> This program is vitally important in widening the knowledge and technical ability of the peoples of the twelve participating countries. Even more important, it is helping us all to understand each other better than ever before. And it is proving effective in combatting communist lies and distortions about social, economic and political conditions and objectives in our respective countries. (Truman, 1951)

Indeed, the program was seen as a way of countering Soviet advances in Europe and the Global South and to help educate and train in the US hundreds of journalists from around the world who were exposed to US culture and society while also simultaneously allowing US journalists to travel abroad to evangelize about "best practices" in journalism. The most important aspect of this program was its cultural dimension; one that aimed at fostering a "culture of freedom" (Sussman, 1992) by promoting these type of exchanges.

The Fulbright Program is perhaps the largest international educational and cultural program on the planet and has seen the greatest exchange of scholars and professionals in the world since the fall of Constantinople in 1453. It was also the first large-scale effort of the US government in history to reach out toward international education and came at the time of the end of World War II and the start of the Cold War (Jeffrey, 1987, p. 40). The program went ahead despite the fact that Truman himself did very little to support the bill that appropriated war surplus in Europe and used their sale to fund the exchange program;[7] he nevertheless gave it his blessing and authorized Senator Fulbright to lobby the Congress in order to get it passed (Jeffrey, 1987, p. 44). Once in place the program has seen an extraordinary expansion in the countries it reached—going from 12 to over 130 and allowing scholars and young people from all over the world to live in the United States for a period of time.

In no other area was this program as successful as in the education and training of journalists from the Global South. This was achieved by allowing both students to be educated in the United States in media and mass communication as well as promoting US journalism educators to take their knowledge and teaching into every corner of the world (Arndt & Rubin, 1993). Despite important and legitimate assurance that the Fulbright Program's nature was of cultural exchange, some voices have questioned these credentials and have accused it, at least in its initial period of the 1950s, of serving as a propaganda instrument for US foreign policy (Garner & Kirkby, 2013; Reivich, 2007).

The Fulbright Program was not by any means the only effort deployed by the Truman administration to influence the shaping of journalism in the Global South. Another important initiative was the program to train science journalists in Latin America offered by the OAS. An institution created in 1948 to coordinate effort among nations in the Americas but mostly funded by the United States, which was part of the architecture of the United Nations system (Davis, 1959) and the project of a new type of world order dominated by the United States.[8] Indeed, the dissemination of science in the news media was seen as a fundamental instrument to further US prestige abroad (Coffey, 1960a).

However, one of the most influential and perhaps most sinister legacies of this administration in shaping a particular model of journalism in the Global South was the fact that it planted the "seeds" of McCarthyism (Athan, 1971). It was in this period where anti-communism developed as an overreaching framework that would define both the way that news values and approaches such as "objectivity" were understood and applied to the daily practice of journalism and, the model of journalism that would be exported to the Global South using foreign aid.

To be sure, most historians recognize that McCarthyism was not unique or sudden in the US history and that, on the contrary, as a phenomenon, it can not only be linked to the Soviet Revolution of 1917 but also presented throughout the 20th century as a continuous trend (Athan, 1971). In truth, both Red Scares were fueled by the fear of the masses, something that preceded the revolution and the war, the flux of immigration, again something that precedes the 20th century, and the growing power of the legally constituted trade unions.

AN ORCHESTRATED EISENHOWER

However, it would be under Truman's successor's administration that efforts to shape journalism in the Global South by means of media development initiatives would take form. The starting point would be initiatives to educate and train journalists to report science as the new administration grew wary of the scientific advances of the Soviet Union and the tremendous impact that it was having upon public opinion—home and abroad.

Indeed, Truman's successor and wartime hero, Dwight D. Eisenhower, would take a far more proactive approach when it came to orchestrating an information campaign abroad.[9] Indeed, based on a series of reports, there was a growing concern that the United States was suffering from a decline in prestige abroad (Boggs, 1953, p. 8) and there was the belief that this decline might affect the influence of the United States to conduct its foreign policy. However, members of the National Security Council initially dismissed these reports and Eisenhower himself ordered the report to be suppressed and be recalled from all offices where it had been distributed. Moreover, the president himself blamed a great deal of this decline on the fact that, contrary to the previous government, it was no longer committed to giving away resources to third parties while also blaming instead political opponents. In fact, in response to a report from the Operations Coordinating Board (OCB),

> The President said that he almost blew his top when he first read the report. It was obvious to him that many of the individuals overseas who had sent the views out of which the report had been made, had been appointed to their jobs when they thought that the only way to assure the prestige of the United States overseas was to hand out money. Many of them were New Dealers with the result that the report was badly overdrawn and coloured. (Ileason, 1953a, p. 7)

However, after a series of setbacks in the international arena, the administration increasingly came to accept that US reputation abroad (they used the term "prestige") was in fact in "decline." One of the early responses was the creation of the Committee on International Information Activities (also referred to as the Jackson Committee) in 1953, which, after interviewing over 250 expert witnesses, recommended the expansion of activities in developing countries and the consolidation of information efforts under one single agency, the United States Information Agency (USIA). In 1959, Eisenhower would appoint a second committee to review these findings and draw up a conclusion and it would be called the US president's Committee on Information Activities Abroad (the Sprague Committee) to consider changes in the international situation, which affect the validity of the findings and recommendations in the Jackson report. It recommended an expansion of the UNIA's efforts in developing countries in Africa and Latin America where there was a renewed expansion of Soviet presence and influence.[10]

It is from this background, in the middle of the Cold War and having in mind the main aim of stopping the expansion of Soviet communism, that his administration set in motion a series of efforts to improve the image of the US abroad. One of the key drivers for this discussion was the administration's perception that a gap was left by the disappearance of the Office for War Information under Truman. Hence, as proposed by the Sprague Committee, the administration created the USAI in 1953 (Osgood, 2006; Parry-Giles, 1994). The proposal won support from Eisenhower who was far more media savvy than his predecessor. Not only had he been exposed to the war propaganda machinery during his military career but also he was the first presidential candidate to make full use of the media and particularly television during his campaign (C. Allen, 1993; Osgood, 2006; Parry-Giles, 1994).

The agency was born from the start as an instrument to promote the United States as a champion of freedom and democracy but overall to disseminate "evidence." To be sure, after several discussions in the National Security Council, the members agreed that the agency's mission would be defined in these unequivocal terms,

> The purpose of the U.S. Information Agency shall be to submit evidence to peoples of other nations by means of communication techniques that the objectives and policies of the United States are in harmony with and will advance their legitimate aspirations for freedom, progress and peace. (Ileason, 1953c)

This was a very interesting departure from the missions and statements of previous agencies as it emphasized the function of submitting "evidence" rather than dissemination information. In so doing, the administration was clear that it did not intend to be a propaganda arm—although that was what it was to all intents and purposes—but to coordinate instead efforts to present to the publics abroad the facts that will convince them of the message. This in my view is not just a historical technicality but a central aspect of this era, which indicates what would be, conceptually speaking, Eisenhower's administration's greatest contribution to future debates on international political communication: its embracement of the "free flow of information" paradigm—one that would go on to underpin, even today, US international information policy and propaganda efforts. Indeed, his government focused on delivering news and information in the Eastern block and the Soviet Union itself and it poured important resources in trying to bypass the jamming of Radio Free Europe and other media outlets. Several memorandums and official documents highlight discussion in his cabinet about making sure that television broadcasts reached the Soviet Union's people while making sure of bypassing the Soviet's jamming of Radio Free Europe (Ileason, 1953b, p. 10).

In many ways, the notion of "free flow of information" was deeply shaped by the idea of a free market and the assumption that if people were exposed to the values and principles of the free market and liberal democracy (Lemberg, 2019). Documents of the time show repeatedly that there was consensus among the members of the National Security Council and the president himself that if exposed to policies, values, and ideas of the administration, people abroad would be more sympathetic toward the United States.[11] The significance of this contribution cannot be downplayed in the context of that era as the presence of messages disseminated by the USIA was in fact the only contact with the Cold War in much of the Third World (Cull, 2008) and turned out to be the main conceptual framework for the future debates around the international communication and information order within UNESCO. More importantly for this book, it would go on to define the type and nature of the foreign aid that would be allocated to shape journalism in Africa, Asia, and Latin America.

The administration was centrally concerned with credibility and trust. It was perceived that Radio Free Europe and the Voice of America (VOA) were lacking credibility and seen as mere propaganda instruments (Coffey, 1960b). Hence, it was more inclined to use "private" actors to disseminate "evidence" in the Third World. Hence, this was the period in which we can actually observe the first concrete initiatives of media development, particularly in supporting capabilities among journalists. By 1960, one of the first initiatives was to fund television for educational purposes in underdeveloped areas (USIA, 1960, p. 2). This initiative would include financing equipment, training staff and operators, and providing additional media content.

Overall, it is important to recognize that it was no coincidence that some of the most important efforts to define objectivity as a professional journalistic norm were carried out precisely after the Soviet Revolution had established itself as an alternative paradigm for society. These efforts and actions took place both in the United States and abroad as part of larger geopolitical struggles and in this sense looked to project a standardized model of journalism for which objectivity became a "strategic ritual" (Tuchman, 1972) that could obscure and hide unwanted socio-structural phenomena such as poverty under the guise of quantified factual appearances (Harkins & Lugo-Ocando,

2016c; Lugo-Ocando, 2014). Through global diffusion, the principle of journalism objectivity then became a transnational norm that went beyond the United States and Great Britain into colonial and postcolonial territories of the Global South.

This superimposition of this principle to all other functions of journalism in society help journalism to establish the language of "common sense" as the hallmark for political discussion in the public sphere. In so doing, mainstream commercially driven journalism set the parameters for political debate among the public in a way in which the public examination of society by individuals would be considered from then on only "legitimate" when driven by "factual" analysis rather than by opinion or ideological structural deconstruction. This "common sense" (Gramsci, 2003 [1935]) approach toward reporting the outside world has reduced political debate in the news media to intuitive narratives that allows for superficial explanations of society's wrongs while displacing the blame for them to "the other."

Journalists who work in the mainstream news media then enable and reinforce such type of discursive regimes by using "objectivity" as a core normative value that presumes that the social world can also be analyzed throughout the same type of "scientific rationality" as the natural world. In so doing, journalism has become a postcolonial hegemonic institution in modern society that has been able to claim "truthfulness" while helping to set and protect the parameters of political engagement by linking them to the values of the Enlightenment as a political project while underpinning the discourses of power of the ruling elites (Harkins & Lugo-Ocando, 2016b, 2017).

Thanks partially to this, the mainstream paradigm of journalism—predominantly present in the United States and the United Kingdom—was then able to push other forms of journalistic practices to the margins while presenting "structural analysis" as too "ideological" to be incorporated as a legitimate form of expression and therefore restricting it to the margins of the public debate.[12] To be sure, as a particular way of practicing journalism consolidated over the years as a universal paradigm of journalism (Randall, 2000) and became accepted as the only legitimate source to achieve truth in the news, other forms of journalism practices around news production and dissemination became increasingly marginalized from the mainstream debates as they were considered propaganda or just mouthpieces for opinion (Janowitz, 1975; Schudson, 2001). Therefore, labeling these other journalistic formats and practices as "nonscientific" became the way of de-legitimizing other ways of doing journalism while consolidating the commercial-factual model as the only credible source of news. This could hardly have happened without the menace of the Soviet Union, the workers' struggle and all the resistance movements that were in search of justice and a better world. A quest which, ironically, mainstream journalism deontology claims for itself in today's world.

NOTES

1. To be precise, Bolívar himself had previously imported a press in 1810, which he bought in England with his own money. However, this was lost to enemy hands after the fall of the First Republic. The press donated by Haiti had a similar fate being seized by the Spanish at the battle of Ocumare de la Costa in 1816. In view of this, the British then gave Bolívar another printing press, which he brought from Trinidad in 1817 together with a skilful printer, Andrés Roderick. This was precisely the press that was used by Simón Bolívar to establish *El Correo del Orinoco*, today considered the key newspaper for emancipation. Bolívar created this paper in his attempt to counter the propaganda efforts by the Spanish Crown that had created years earlier their own newspaper, *La Gazeta de Caracas*—later renamed La Gaceta de Caracas—in order to support colonial rule.

2. Yet, even before the arrival of the Spanish print and setting up of the pro-colonial Gazeta in 1808, there were several small artisan prints used to publish news that dated back to the 17th century (Forment, 2013; Rubio, 2017). However, Venezuela was by far one of the latest countries to receive a modern printing machine. The fact remains that modern newspaper production only happened thanks to British, Haitian, and Spanish foreign aid toward that country.

3. Sambrook (2012, p. 5) proposes a synonymous deployment of the words, though admitting that "impartiality, the removal of bias, is the more complex of the two, although objectivity—a disciplined approach to isolate evidence and facts—is still far from easy to achieve."

4. This publication had among its staff John Reed, who left for Russia to write the famous book *Ten Days That Shook the World* (2007 [1919]), which would become a landmark in the accounts of the Bolshevik Revolution.

5. The term "muckraker" was used in the Progressive Era to characterize reform-minded American journalists who attacked established institutions and leaders as corrupt. They typically had large audiences in some popular magazines. There were, of course, other journalists who more openly supported the Soviet revolution such as John Silas "Jack" Reed (1887–1920) whose book *Ten Days That Shook the World* (1919) became one of the most influential accounts about those events.

6. See White House Central Files: Official File. Dates: 1945–1953. Box 1648–1285 March–September 1950 [2 of 4]. Harr S. Truman Library and Museum.

7. See Letter to the Chairman, Board of Foreign Scholarships, on the Fulbright Program. May 11, 1951 [Released May 11, 1951 Dated May 10, 1951]. Harry S. Truman Library and Museum.

8. See Thomas C. Mann Oral History Interview—Oral History Interview with Thomas C. Mann. Opened July, 1979. Harry S. Truman Library and Museum.

9. See Brownell, Herbert, Jr.: Papers, 1877–1988. Box 27 S (1)(2) [Martha Schmidt re Radio Free Europe]. Dwight D. Eisenhower Presidential Library & Museum.

10. See People-to-People Program. Mission of the United States Information Agency, 1954 [DDE's Records as President, Official File, Box 748, OF 247 United States Information Agency 1954 (2); NAID #12648972]. Dwight D. Eisenhower Presidential Library & Museum.

11. See US National Security Council Presidential Records: Intelligence Files, 1953–1961. 1. Country Files/INT Subject Files (22) [Radio Free Europe and Radio Liberty: project support; expansion of overseas broadcasting facilities]. Dwight D. Eisenhower Presidential Library & Museum.

12. Let us not forget that these debates around scientific/rational approaches against irrational ideological (ideologies) did not only happen in the West. In the Soviet Union, they were also at the center of many discussions (Ings, 2017; Pollock, 2006). On the other hand, the emergence of magazines such as *McClure's* and *Time* in the United States was partly attempts to go beyond the overt analysis of social issues (Wilson, 2015).

Chapter 4

Journalism and Postcolonial Aid

In his seminal piece regarding media professionalism in the Third world, Professor Peter Golding (1977) made the point that the expansion of Western journalism models into the Global South was as much about reproducing ideology as the transfer of practices and skills. This is systematically and repeatedly the case in Africa, Asia, Latin America, and the Caribbean. In most of these places, news media outlets were not only set up as the mirror image of those in Europe but also—in many cases—they even had cross-ownership and cross-editorial structures between the center and the periphery (Adesoji & Alimi, 2012; Omu, 1968).

This colonial and post-colonial interventions when configuring media ownership and creating outlets had a profound impact in shaping the news media landscape, the news cultures and more generally the journalistic practices in these regions of the world. Some scholars, such as Marie-Soleil Frère (2012, 2015), have pointed out how in places such as the African continent, the great powers of the times shaped deeply and distinctively the media systems and defined the media in their own colonies. Consequently, today the media systems and news cultures in Francophone and Anglophone Africa still reflect in many ways the distinctiveness of the presence of the British and French colonial powers, which has had a direct impact upon reporting practices and news cultures in these countries.

This, of course, is not to say that these aspects that underpin journalistic practices have remained static in relation to colonial power influence. On the contrary, many of these practices and news institution changed in particular ways that created parallel and distinctive media structures that went on to challenge, in some cases, the same power structures that allowed them to be created in the first place. We can explain these distinctive journalistic practices and approach, at least partially, by means of a multiplicity of factors but above all by the fact that inter-societal communication and civil society were present in the colonies. In light of this, it is important to acknowledge the distinctive historical legacies and nature of conceptualizing journalism both as a social practice and as a political institution rather than see it just as "profession"—at least in the terms described by Samuel P. Huntington (1981 [1951]) when referring to what makes a professional solider. This can allow us then to appreciate the fact that journalism was not only shaped by a grammar that was imposed from above but also by the dynamics of resistance that came from below.

COLONIAL MEDIA POWERS

From the start, colonial powers appreciated the importance of setting up media systems that allowed them to establish communicational hegemonies over their colonies. Consequently, they funded directly or indirectly media outlets that helped them to transfer ideology and project power into the conquered territory (Bruce, 2016; Mano, 2008). This is because symbolic power was for the empires as important as the use of force. Indeed, one of the most evocative paintings of Christopher Columbus' landing on Guanahani Island (named by him later as San Salvador) can help illustrate this point. Painted by the Spanish artist Dióscoro Teófilo Puebla Tolín (1831–1901), it shows Columbus surrounded by his men—heavily armored guards—who will later go on to pillage the continent and impose the King's rule through bloody force. In that same paining, at one side of Columbus, there is a priest holding a cross in the air (inspired perhaps by earlier illustrations that showed men erecting a bigger cross on the beach) while looking at the skies. This, although probably not an accurate depiction of the actual events, is nevertheless a stark reminder that colonial domination was as much about the use of brutal force as the dissemination of particular ideologies as a means of domination through the media available at that time.

Let us make no mistake. The process of European colonization was defined mostly by genocide on a scale never seen by humankind until then; one that allowed a relatively small elite of white men in Europe to impose ruthless power over the great majority of people on the planet (Michalopoulos & Papaioannou, 2016; Pakenham, 2015 [1990]). A process that would go directly to feed the hunger for the capital to kick-start the Industrial Revolution while defining both national and international structures of power for the centuries to come (Bryant, 2006; Weaver, 2018).

However, precisely because it was such a small army, the core of the domination consisted in establishing hegemony. For this, it was necessary to impose cultural paradigms and structures that included religion and new notions of authority. Fernando Báez (2008) has called this "the cultural looting of Latin America." Accordingly, what for the native people in the region was a true catastrophe of Biblical proportions for European colonizers was a simple process of cultural and structural convergence where existing systems of commercial exchange and belief were deliberately squandered to make people poor both economically and culturally as to be able to appropriate power from them. At the center of this, continues Báez, were communication wars that literally were designed to commit cultural genocide. This would be a practice that subsequent European empires would replicate all over their colonies across the globe.

Colonial authorities joined local elites to replicate communication structures of power as hegemonic tools from the North while disrupting and destroying local systems of communication. This was part of a general dynamics of domination. In this sense, Phoebe Musandu (2018) points out the importance of newspapers, both to colonial administrators and different elites, within the power structures in Africa,

> Against this backdrop of racial segregation, economic competition, and political discontent, a few elites within each racial group recognized the potential of the press to help them create conditions that would advance their particular political and economic interest. At various points in time, these individuals established newspapers to gain a new stake in the protectorate's political and economic spheres or to consolidate an existing one (Musandu, 2018).

However, after the end of World War II, the remaining European empires crumbled and other subtler forms of power started to be exercised across the Global South. These new forms of power, based on the expansion of the modern capitalist markets and of cultural hegemony rather than just upon military occupation, required to double efforts in the hegemonic front and this meant shaping the media systems so they could underpin and reproduced practices and ideologies from the North.

The European colonial rule in many parts of the world saw the emergence of the United States as a world superpower, one that had a very distinctive way of dominating through hegemony of the market. However, the US postwar power in the Global South was more about spreading the market economy by means of the liberal and market ideology. It did so by promoting the notion of "development" (Escobar, 2004, 2011) rather than using crude force (although it did so in places such as Korea and Vietnam). The rise of the Market Society—described by Karl Polanyi (2001 [1944])— led by the United States, marked a fundamental shift from the old colonial order into something new that was reflected in the development of an international communications and media systems dominated by US media and culture (Boyd-Barrett & Rantanen, 1998; Mattelart, 2002; Thussu, 2005).

This emerging cultural paradigm that allowed the projection of soft power demanded new hegemonic approaches in Africa, Asia, and the Caribbean.

In Harry S. Truman's presidential files, one finds a series of documents stating exactly this approach. Not only did Truman dismantle the US Office of War Information at the end of World War II, but he also adopted a more laissez-faire approach when it came to controlling domestic information.[1] Truman's administration repeatedly argued, as stated in many documents, that by promoting a "free press" abroad, they could win the heart and minds of the people in the Global South against Soviet propaganda. On the other hand, without the formal propaganda structure, US officials were able to circumvent national governments' restrictions on foreign propaganda (Parker, 2016, p. 34).

This is not to say that there was no genuine aspiration among US officials to foster a "free press" in the Global South or that all these were cynical attempts to grasp power. Nevertheless, it was a period marked by tensions between the United States as an emerging superpower and the old colonial European empires, particularly the United Kingdom. A strong sentiment of anti-colonialism dominated in many Washington circles even if it was only to see the end of European empires and to push for Europe's subordination to the new US geopolitical hegemony (Keohane, 1991; Louis, 1984; Reivich, 2007). These sentiments would become abundant clear in the face of the Suez Crisis of 1956, when the United States would turn its back to its European allies, France and the United Kingdom, to support Gamal Abdel Nasser (1918–1970) in Egypt. More importantly, however, was the growing power, influence, and international presence of the Soviet Union under Joseph Stalin in the decolonized territories, which exacerbated the hawkish views of many anti-communists in the White House and that ultimately led to the blunders in the Vietnam war.

US foreign policy toward media development was directed toward fostering a new world communication and information order that had two basic premises in order to allow the new superpower to project hegemonic power and disseminate its ideology (Lemberg, 2019; Sparks, 2007). On the one hand, that the market economy should be the basis of the political economy of the news media as the only way of guaranteeing a "free press." On the other, there was the need to create a global market for such media. It was in this context that the scholar Wilbur Schramm (1964) wrote a very influential book on "Mass Media and National Development." The book was published in conjunction with UNESCO. The book not only kick-started research into the link between the spread of communication technology and socioeconomic development but also set the overall agenda for scholars and policymakers in relation to their agendas (Sparks, 2007; Wasserman, 2017).

In an overreaching manner, the book reflected in its own time the US principles that would guide future aid for media development stated earlier. Schramm's work set the framework for the notion of "free flow of information," which would dominate for decades to become US policy toward media development. Schramm (1964) argued that mass media in developing countries needed to play three roles—those of watchdog, policy maker, and teacher for change and modernization. It was a conception that was followed to the letter by policy-makers in Washington, DC.

However, the postcolonial era of Foreign Aid for Media Development was not only shaped by US foreign policy and geostrategic priorities. Western European efforts to retain its power and influence in its former colonies, Soviet propaganda efforts to stir revolutions in the Global South, and local movements' struggles to reassert national governance (e.g., Lee Kuan Yew in Singapore and Julius Nyerere in Tanzania) were also very influential over the years. In the case of the old dying European empires, they placed emphasis on foreign aid for assistance in Africa, Asia, and Latin America as these three regions have certain degrees of commonalities in relation to how foreign aid influences and postcolonial settings.

EUROPEAN COLONIES

In this context, Foreign Aid for Media Development and media assistance came in different forms and shapes. Within these efforts, governments were always central as donors, and in many cases, as recipients. The colonial experience was one of nation building but as a power exercise to reassert control over vast amounts of people and territory. Hence, this process of colonial institution building needs to be seen not in terms of developing a democratic framework where governments and individuals could deal fairly in the transactions of power and rely on the rule of law—as many claim—but as part of a wider process of hegemonic settlement to consolidate colonial power.

Contrary to claims that empires such as the British left behind the "rule of law" and other institutions that allowed democracy to emerge from colonial legacy (Gilley, 2018; Killingray, 1986), it was instead the contested nature of, and resistance against, that colonial rule that brought about a new institutional framework. Indeed, the push against colonialism was central in helping to articulate future democratic institutions, which were aspirations that derived from the independence and self-determination movements and the responses they generated against hegemonic power. As Shashi Tharoor (2018) points out,

> By the time of Independence, British India, and many British colonies had elections, political parties, a more or less free press, and the rule of law, unlike the Spanish, Portuguese, French, Dutch, and Belgian counterparts. Democratization

may have been slow, grudging and gradual, but it was also more successful in the ex-British colonies than elsewhere. The Indian nationalist struggle and its evolution through various stages—decorous liberals seeking legislative rights, "extremists" clamouring for Swaraj, Gandhi and his followers advocating non-violent struggle, the Congress, the Muslim League and other parties contending for votes even with limited franchise: all these pre-Independence experiences served as a kind of socialization process into democracy and helped to ease the country's transition to independence. (2018, p. 86)

This process of contestation to the colonial rule shaped the process of institution building in the colonies and also helped define the creation of journalism as a political institution. Having said that, journalism fostered within the empires was foremost a colonial institution that emulated on the periphery of the values and practices of the center, even when practiced by the supposed voices of contestation. Something reflected by George Orwell's work in the Indian Section of the BBC's Eastern Service (1941–1943) when broadcasting radio programs to India. At this time of World War II, India came under real threat of invasion from the advancing Japanese, and there was anxiety in London that the loyalty of the Indian subjects of the Raj might not be relied on in these critical months. As an important part of the work of the Eastern Service, which was viewed as propaganda, the anti-imperialist Orwell found himself part of an institution and discourse devoted to encouraging Indian loyalty to the empire. The rhetoric of Orwell's BBC broadcasts, and particularly the weekly news commentaries he wrote, became then a special and especially conflicted case of colonial discourse, in which Orwell's commitment to the anti-fascist cause became to underpin the BBC's commitment to empire (Kerr, 2002).

This is not to say that journalism was a homogenous colonial institution. On the contrary, as I discuss earlier, colonialism and resistance had equally shaping power in defining journalism as a political institution in the Global South. These forces created a nuanced expression of journalism that was as much an expression of imposition as contestation. Indeed, compared to what happened in the French and Dutch colonies, the freedom of the press was far from achievable within the British Empire's domains, allowing it to become also a feature of resistance to colonial power. In fact, it was the widespread aversion of colonial governors and European officials to press criticism, which gave Africans the impression that press liberty was always in danger of being throttled. By a curious paradox, therefore, the African nationalist press was at once practically free but basically controlled. They key to this paradox was an interplay of complex forces brought into action by Africans, the colonial governments, and the British government (Omu, 1968, p. 279).

Consequently, in many of the British former colonies, one of the most striking features was how the African nationalist movements went to great lengths to safeguard the freedom of the press after expelling their colonial masters. As British subjects, many of whom were trained in Britain, educated Africans assumed that they were entitled to enjoy a free press, which was an essential ingredient in the British political tradition (Omu, 1968, p. 297). This process of resistance to colonial rule was in fact far more important in the idealization for the need of a free press and the articulation of normative deontological aspirations than the efforts of the empire to retain hegemonic control.

This, of course, changed radically with the end of World War II and particularly after independence movements seized power. Two key reasons account for the change. Firstly, as discussed in length in this book, the context created by the Cold War and the spread of Communist propaganda spearheaded by the Soviet Union and its satellites, which funded media efforts in the Global South. Secondly, the consolidation in power of many of the African and Asian independence leaders who became the de facto dictators with no appetite for a free press. This increasing trend of autocratic rule and attacks against the free press ran all the way to the 1980s, which was a terrible time for African journalists. If well, it began as a promising decade as Nigeria returned to civilian rule, the Tanzania People's Defence Force had sent Idi Amin packing, and the liberation struggle in Zimbabwe won independence, it soon became clear that the continent was sinking into its "lost decade" (Martin, 1992).

Within this postcolonial context, it is important to notice how the aid-journalism relationship evolved since the end of World War II when foreign aid started to be substantially directed at disseminating a particular model of journalism practice and education that is aligned with the interests of the wealthy, industrialized northern donor nations. At its core, was the aim of "developing" a journalism model that would be constantly judged against a US-benchmark, politically, economically, culturally, and ideologically. However, the benchmark was not just based on emulating the US model itself but also developing the standardized deontological ethics and a professional normative aspiration that fitted as a piece of the larger puzzle in the emerging new global order constructed by the United States and its allies. One which, under the umbrella of modernization, went to underpin the free market, promote industrialization and push for US-style liberal democracy as a universal paradigm (Lugo-Ocando, 2018; Paterson, Gadzekpo, & Wasserman, 2018). In this context, the accepted mission for journalists was one of pushing toward a type of development model that brought about freedom and market as a unified notion.

FOREIGN AID AND CONFLICT

The end of World War II and start of nationhood for many of the newly independent countries was also marked by conflict itself or the collective trauma from the remains of conflict (Cooper, 1994; Nye, 1999). Indeed, for many parts of the Global South, the postcolonial era was marked by fratricidal war and post-conflict trauma. Nevertheless, the role of foreign aid in media assistance can be traced to events that preceded World War II such as the Spanish Civil War (1936–1939), which can be used exemplify the use of foreign aid as an instrument to assist media during conflict. Not only because it was effectively "the first radio war" where foreign aid was used to intervene in the public sphere (Arasa, 2015; Davies, 1999) but also because by 1936, Spain was, to all intents and purpose, part of what we would call today the Third World. As such, it was deeply underdeveloped, poor and very unequal, and overall politically divided (Beevor, 2012).

The Spanish Civil War became rapidly an international conflict in which the European empires locked horns. It was one that would also mark future developments on the world stage (Keene, 2007; Whealey, 2015). The conflict highlighted larger geopolitical and ideological struggles and in many ways was different from past conflicts. One of these aspects was how the foreign powers created and funded radio stations and how this shaped both propaganda and journalism in Spain during the war. As Arasa (2015) suggests, wars might be fought in the trenches, but equally important are the convictions, feelings, and opinions to underpin the morale on the front and at the rear, which have their own battlefields.

Foreign powers put money and resources not only in gun barrels, but also on the airwaves to influence information and propaganda, given the ideological character of the Spanish Civil War. For example, some of the transmissions were carried out using a German transmitter based in western Spain, which gave limited coverage of the Republican-held east coast, and until radio EAJ-101 was commissioned in 1938 the Nationalists depended upon the Italians for coverage there. In February 1937, the Italians had begun to transmit Radio Verdad (Radio Truth) using high-powered domestic transmitters after their normal programs had closed down. The broadcasts were easily heard in eastern Spain and, by giving an address for correspondence in Salamanca, caused people to assume that this was a new Spanish Nationalist station based in Northern Spain (Davies, 1999, p. 484).

In this conflict, radio would become a true weapon of war. One that would be recipient of large amounts of resources from foreign aid to create and foster new media outlets all over the conflicting territory. Radio became a weapon of psychological operations, which would later be used massively in World War II. During this conflict, foreign powers funded broadcasters from each side of the conflict who used radio clandestinely in enemy territory to undermine the moral of the adversary, contradicting official accounts and creating chaos among their ranks. However, these outlets also reported the war and gave accounts of what was happening even if it was with a propaganda-distorted tone. Or as Arasa (2015) also argues, a medium in which some lied less than others.

What these historical accounts highlight is how different media platforms that have emerged over the decades have been quickly used by the different sides in the broader political struggles. They also show how foreign aid toward media development and assistance has played a crucial role in conflicts and political struggles in the Global South over the years, regardless of which platform it is directed toward. Indeed, in more recent times, Western governments and private foundations have been investing huge sums in media projects in different places, such as in the Arab countries (let us not forget that the origins of Al-Jazeera lay on an initial Qatar-BBC collaboration). This to the point that such intervention has become almost an industry. In this regard, not enough research and scholarship exists about the integration of new media and information assistance by development actors (EU countries and the United States) as part of their democracy promotion programs implemented in prospective democracies. This type of analysis is, to a great extent, non-existent particularly concerning the Middle East, despite the added value it would offer to the understanding of the causes that brought it to the turbulent events of 2011 (Brownlee, 2017, p. 2277).

Indeed, media development aid became a tool for the different powers to support or deny regime change in places such as Syria. Indeed, the presidency of Bashar al-Asad and the process of liberalization (infitah) that he inaugurated created the ideal timing for such investment to take place as they allowed foreign aid to be channeled into the development of a sector and a class—the media and journalists, respectively—that played a crucial role in the outbreak of the revolt in 2011 (Brownlee, 2017, p. 2279). Other powers, such as Russia, Turkey, and Iran, would soon follow suit, funding substantially new media outlets in that country to support different factions in the war that broke while sending their own cluster bombs and tanks.

However, these efforts are not restricted to governments. Private donors have effectively funded a variety of initiatives too. Among them, one could mention not only those on the ground in the places where these events are happening but also virtual spaces in the North where different actors can deploy their own voices. One of them is Global Voices, led by former CNN journalist Rebecca MacKinnon and MIT professor and director of the Center for Civic Media, Ethan Zuckerman. They have received substantial support from George Soros's Open Society Foundation to create new spaces for broader expression from bloggers and journalists around the world, including the Arab world. These initiatives provided counter voices to official accounts and also help disseminate alternative narratives and versions that the authorities were providing during the Arab Spring and other events in the region.

LESSONS LEARNED

So, what are the lessons from the history of colonial hegemony, resistance, and postcolonial arrangements? Firstly, that the original colonial settings were fundamental in establishing the groundwork for existing media system and prevalent news cultures. It is bluntly clear that the configuration of the "media systems" (Hallin & Mancini, 2004, 2011) in these countries today have been a direct result of institution building and hegemonic efforts from the part of the European colonial power and the resistance movements that they generated. Secondly, that journalism in the Global South emerged as a "political institution" that absorbed, accommodated, and contested colonialism within its own deontology. Thirdly, that the context of the Cold War—which led to interventions all over the world—and the increasingly autocratic tendency of many of the leaders who came to power after independence thwarted the possibility of these nations to develop media systems and journalistic cultures that reflected better and more effectively the needs and aspirations of their own societies. In relation to this last point, the greatest lesson is that institution building was an incomplete project in relation to journalism in the Global South given the above reasons.

It is because of this that I suggest that the analysis of the role of Foreign Aid for Media Development—and for media assistance too—needs to be carried out by applying an explanatory theoretical framework that uses the so-called new institutionalism (NI) as a reference. This, as it can act in a complementary manner to the field theory that has traditionally served as the basis of journalism studies analysis in these particular cases (Couldry, 2004; Marques de Melo, 2009). The main reason to adopt this particular approach is that NI focuses on aspects of power, politics, culture, and processual shifts within the institution of journalism.[2] Like field theory, NI gains effectiveness on the mezzo level, linking micro and macro structures, individual, and organizational agency with large-scale forces such as capitalism. It assumes,

> [News] organizations are deeply embedded in social and political environments [suggesting] that organizational practices and structures are often either reflections of, or responses to rules, beliefs, and conventions built into the wider environment. (Powell, 2007, p. 1)

From among several streams of NI, Douglass North's "institutions-as-rules" approach appears highly interesting for this work.[3] North (1990, p. 5) considers organizations as "groups of individuals bound by some common purpose to achieve objectives." They are agents embedded in, and shaped by, institutional frameworks. Similar to Bourdieu's principles of action, North compares institutions to "rules of the game in a society" (p. 3). In this context, the work of those operating in news media outlets is defined by routines and practices that are part of that setting (Ryfe, 2006). For North, institutions are humanly devised constraints that people impose on themselves (p. 5) and that

> structure political, economic and social interaction. They consist of both informal constraints (sanctions, taboos, customs, traditions, and codes of conduct), and formal rules (constitutions, laws, property rights). (North, 1991, p. 97)

While formal constraints often materialize as legally defined constructs, informal constraints are rooted in the realm of culture and history. In this context, it is possible to see how colonialism and post-colonialism defined formal and informal rules for journalism as a political institution.

These "rules that have never been consciously designed and that it is in everyone's interest to keep" (Sugden, 1986. p. 54), such as informal common practices, routines, and discursive formations. Informal rules are usually the outcome of historical struggles such as the case of colonial and anti-colonial tensions. With the same formal rules imposed on different societies, different outcomes or paths are produced (path dependency, Cook, 1998).[4] This explains why, for example, the principles of objectivity and detachment are implemented differently across the globe despite its global diffusion.

North's (1994) contribution notes that the nature of human learning and hence, societal change, is rooted not only in rational choice assumptions but that it is fundamentally shaped instead by actors' subjective frames and representations of a problem. For journalists operating within the context of colonial rule, not only the news agenda and daily news coverage but also the approach toward these issues were defined by the independence struggle and afterward by the tensions emerging from identity and ideology in the construction of nationhood. This means culture and beliefs, "ideologies, myths, dogmas, and prejudices matter" as subjective mental models in understanding decision-making in contexts of uncertainty (1994, p. 362).

This is, in my view, a fundamental notion in helping us understand how journalism became to be in the Global South. Indeed, formal and informal rules developed within the context of colonialism and post-colonialism—and their enforcement shaped the character of the game and how it is played—came to define journalism as a political institution. North (1990, p. 6) sees their economical purpose as to "reduce uncertainty by establishing a stable (but not necessarily efficient) structure to human interaction" within complex environments (p. 6).[5] In the context of postcolonial journalism, this meant keeping in place the political economy of the mass media and remaining within the operational structures developed under colonial rule.

Consequently, European former colonies' media systems inherited (in)material journalistic codes of conduct that were anchored in the notions of objectivity and impartiality as core journalistic principles at the turn of the 20th century (Golding, 1977; Lima, Hohlfeldt, Sousa, & Barbosa, 2014; Skjerdal, 2012). As Tuchman (1972) pointed out, this has served to reduce uncertainty in areas such as confronting powerful governments, law and liability, or more general relations with sources and audiences, while simultaneously making journalistic claims legitimate and powerful.

This theoretical framework is key in understanding the establishment of journalistic legitimacy as one of three taken-for-granted assumptions of the "institutional regime of news" in the former colonies (Sparrow, 2006; Spurr, 1993). The framework of normative assumptions developed after journalists in the colony was required to reduce, in part, the inherent uncertainty in the professional field. In the same way that new independent nations and democracies tend to perpetuate (or extend) particular political institutions after the end of the previous regime—most commonly seen in relation to the criminal justice system and the application of law and order—journalistic normative aspirations, news culture settings and reporting practices and norms were also projected to the new system in most former colonies.

Therefore, the most important legacy for journalism in postcolonial times has been the perpetuation of the normative framework for reporters, which was forged both by colonialism and resistance to it and that in the postcolonial era became increasingly distorted in its ability to reflect its own societies' realities, given the prolonged shadows and tensions of the Cold War (Osgood, 2006; Parker, 2016; Saunders, 2000). This framework would continue to shape the way news was gathered, produced and disseminated even afterward and be influentially present in shaping the media systems of these countries and determining their media ecologies and journalistic cultures and practices, particularly in relation to the more recent historical development of journalism as a political institution in the Global South. This is because it facilitated in imposing models to continue defining news reporting in these countries rather than allowing them to develop their own pathways in creating interpretative communities.

CONTEXT AND RESISTANCE

It is perhaps important, at this point, to conceptualize the reasons why in very few cases we can actually see models that have been imported and implemented as originally designed by donors. Most studies have underlined that attempts to import models often face instead hybridization and domestication by recipients. In other words, it is rare that efforts to establish particular journalistic Western models have actually ended up adopting the particular format that was originally intended. In Latin America, for example, Silvio

Waisbord (2000) exemplifies this by shows how particular types of news reporting, such as critical reporting, can be better defined as "watchdog journalism" rather than as investigative reporting as it is often understood in the tradition of Anglo-American journalism. He reminds us that these societies in the Global South have different traditions in terms of news cultures and reporting practices while being challenged by distinctive political factors; that is, that journalists operating in these societies had to work under authoritarian regimes and dictatorships and that there was no muckraking press tradition. For him, this calls for the analysis of new political, media dynamics, and journalistic cultures that reflect unique settings and realities.

In the following chapters of this book, I have tried to identify variables that explain these elements of integration, domestication, adoption, and contestation. However, these factors cannot be amalgamated nor assumed to be universal. In each society in the Global South, there were and are specific and distinctive elements that have fostered and hindered the adoption of particular models of journalism. In some, they have accelerated imitation and replication of the proposed models while in others particular variables have made the model unviable and led to the failure of the project that were originally supported by foreign aid.

Literature on this is scarce and there is an urgent need to develop a more robust and empirically based system of evaluation and assessment of Foreign Aid for Media Development. So far, most of the assessment and evaluation has been carried by donors themselves and this has been done from a perspective of metrics and quantitative approaches that centered upon reach and use rather that evaluating the nature of the impact and final outcome (Requejo-Alemán & Lugo-Ocando, 2014). Again, using Latin America as an example, over the years, a number of nonprofit investigative news organizations in that part of the world have experienced an important growth and have enjoyed to some increasing success. Indeed, they have won several international awards, uncovered some of the most important scandals in the region, and helped set the news agenda across the continent, bringing about accountability to power in ways that journalism in the region has not done for decades. Moreover, research has shown that these organizations practice public service journalism in ways that the old legacy media has not (Ferrucci, 2017). These efforts have been mostly supported by international funding, which has allowed many regions in the Global South to restore capacities around investigative reporting, which had diminished over the previous years (Requejo-Alemán & Lugo-Ocando, 2014; Scott, Wright, & Bunce, 2018).

These organizations have struggled reaching wider audiences beyond specific elites and creating a critical mass within the general public. In the case of Latin America, previous research suggests that these organizations are in fact limited to a small segment of the public (Meléndez-Yúdico, 2014;

Requejo-Alemán & Lugo-Ocando, 2014). Although these digital-native news organizations are not commercially driven, they do need nevertheless to justify their existence and the resources provided to them by funders by demonstrating reach and impact (Olmedo-Salar & Lugo-Ocando, 2018). In these cases, it is clear that the way assessment is carried out by donors reflect the ideal type or projected model that was originally intended but that tends not to considered the variables on the ground that would reshape the nature of the original-intended aid effort into something more hybrid and local.

Historical context, political system, cultural realities, and access to local resources tend determine degrees of hybridity, adaptation, and contestation. However, it is perhaps the way audiences in these places come to define news cultures by means of the way they themselves consume news that is perhaps the most important variable of all. This is why future works on the role of Foreign Aid and Media Development should center in understanding better this central factor.

NOTES

1. See Harry S. Truman Papers Staff Member and Office Files: Philleo Nash Files. Philleo Nash Papers. Dates: 1925–1998. General Correspondence File. Harry S. Truman Library and Museum.

2. NI is partially subsumed under organizational theory, though institutions and organizations need to be differentiated.

   It is seen by scholars like Kaplan (2006) as a remedy for political and cultural deficits in most existing social theories dealing with news.

3. North's work originates in the economic realm and has been referred to in New Economic Institutionalism. For media studies, also relevant are Cook (1998) and Sparrow (2006)—see also Caballero and Soto-Oñate (2015).

4. For example, political news coverage can be considered as result of the interaction between journalists and politicians and the broader fields they are embedded in. This setting limits the role variations journalists can take in a democracy. Blumler and Gurevitch (1995) identified a more "sacerdotal" attitude of British journalists (considering official institutions like the Parliament as "priestly" and hence newsworthy) with more pragmatic approaches.

5. Transaction costs can roughly be understood as costs of transacting (costly) information and (costly) enforcement, consisting in "the costs of measuring the valuable attributes of what is being exchanged and the costs of protecting rights and policing and enforcing agreements," where they act as sources of institutions (North 1990, pp. 27–32).

Chapter 5

Spreading the Ideology of Objectivity

It is clear at this point that the biggest legacy of Foreign Aid for Media Development and assistance in the past century has been the standardization of journalism normative aspirations and practice in the Global South. This normative paradigm was forged by the emergence of the United States as a new superpower and the exacerbation of the postcolonial tensions created by the geopolitical prerogative of the Cold War. At the center of this new setting were the notions of "objectivity" and "impartiality." Nevertheless, as I also discussed previously, these prerogatives and normative impositions did not go unchallenged. In fact, they were widely contested both by local-national decolonization traditions and independence movements and by the efforts of the Soviet Union to project its own soft power.

Nevertheless, the US paradigm of journalism ended up becoming the gold standard and default model to follow and by which to be measured. So, why and how did "objectivity" manage to spread across the Global South—and be embraced as an idea—despite long-term existing distinctive news cultures aboriginal to those nations? Was the notion of journalistic objectivity, defined in terms of US normative professional claims, so powerful and so well grounded that it was able to override any other approach of how news ought to be gathered, produced, and disseminated?

The answer to this, as always, is context as we have widely discussed in this book. This is because the notion of journalistic objectivity is enclaved in the boarder framework of modernity and underpinned by the language of common sense. That is, the idea that there are absolute and universal truths that are rational and fact-based; an idea that is deeply rooted in the very notion of modern science. For both practitioners and scholars, journalism in the West is fundamentally about truth-seeking human activity and as such provides a type of knowledge that reflects the understanding and description of the world outside. As an official from a donor institution points out,

> We fund journalism projects that support democracy and that brings about transparency. Our resources are allocated to help journalism to bring accountability to society and improve people's lives. This fundamentally means shedding light upon issues that those in power want to remain obscure.[1]

Nothing is wrong with that. The problem arises instead as the West has defined what is truth in its own positivist terms, which is why it is so important to explore what "objectivity" means in this historical context. This as "objectivity" and "impartiality" has been the most important and long-lasting cultural export value for foreign aid.

A SHORT HISTORY OF OBJECTIVITY

As it became increasingly difficult to counter the growing popularity of the press in the 19th century as a platform that agitated and mobilized the masses, a mixture of a new political economy for the media based on advertisement and specific efforts toward de-ideologizing its role in society, started to develop a new setting for how journalists and the news media operated. To be sure, by the second half of the 19th century, in places such as the United Kingdom and the United States, these efforts became progressively less coercive and far subtler. The appropriation and co-option of the news media by commercial enterprises proved to be far more effective in depoliticizing that any deliberate effort made by corporations or governments (Briggs & Burke, 2009; Conboy, 2004). This was achieved by converting the press into a commercial enterprise and turning journalism in to a professional trade that embraced a deontological approach that detached itself from the events that it covered and, that proclaimed its neutrality as a pre-condition to make claims of scientific truth.

In the United States, the task of de-politicizing journalism practice was advanced thanks to the standardization imposed by AP on its members, who demanded the type of neutrality and detachment that today is seen as the underlining aspects of objectivity. AP became then the "de facto" cartel that helped refine the character of news as a commercial and exchangeable commodity. Certainly, AP was not alone in the market but other news agencies such as UPI quickly adapted their own codes of practice and styles to the standards set by AP. This process of standardization occurred in the backdrop of the historical monopolization of international news content by the news agencies (Boyd-Barrett, 1980; Boyd-Barrett & Rantanen, 1998; Diaz-Rangel, 1976).

For this to happen, it was also pivotal in advancing new copyright laws that made the exchange of material and news by local newspapers almost impossible (Baird, 1983; Epstein, 1992). Indeed, thanks to the preferential treatment that the postal services in the United States had given to all newspapers since the foundation of the country, news editors and the public in the United Stated had enjoyed, so far, remarkable and unprecedented access to the news (González & Torres, 2011; Machlup, 1962), which they could lift and copy into their own newspapers. These newspapers had then been able to reproduce and share stories from all over the country and the world without intermediaries and at no cost except for the value of the copies they bought from their competitors. However, with the new copyright laws and the increasing adherence to AP style and norms, journalism in the United States was rapidly driven toward a "professional standardized" model, which soon became the dominant ideological paradigm of what journalism ought to be.

Indeed, Kent Cooper (1880–1965), who served for forty-one years as Executive Director of the AP, was instrumental in leading the process of standardization across places such as Latin America as part of the expansion of the news agency into the Global South markets (Allen, 2016). Not only did he oversee the development of AP's style book but he also promoted the idea that newspapers across the United States needed to adapt to the practices and principles that guaranteed certain standards (Cooper, 1959; Silberstein-Loeb, 2014) and make sure that alternative styles and forms to these standards were excluded from the market (Horne, 2017a). To be sure, Rob Tiffen (1976) suggested that the homogenization of the markets in the Third World was key in the development, growth, and consolidation of AP, particularly after the independence of many former colonies. This homogenization meant that local and national media in the former colonies adopted similar aesthetics and principles in the production of news.

It was in this context in which the theory of journalism objectivity was rationalized as such within the professional guild of news reporters. The deontological aspiration of objectivity soon reached the status of professional ideology (Deuze, 2005; D. T. Mindich, 2000) and went on to dominate the 20th century. Today, objectivity continues to form a cornerstone of the cultural authority of journalism, which still projects its lasting shadow into the new millennium. More important, it became the condition "sine qua non" that would come to define the nature of what could be called—or not—journalism and the key cultural export that would also define journalism in the Global South.

THE NATURAL NORM

Objectivity became not only the default standard, both in the United States and in most of the Global South under Western influence, but also it was seen as the "natural" way of doing truthful news reporting. This way of packaging a cultural product so as to control both its production and consumption is standardization, and something that all elites at all times through history have done to control all types of cultural practices (Horkheimer & Adorno, 2001; Sommerville, 1996). In the case of the news media, it would not be different. To do so in a way that the norm was accepted as legitimate, objectivity had to be given the same type of "naturalization" historical narrative that embraces positivist instrumentalization of science and that anchors itself in the Enlightenment as a political project. In this way, it was presented and sold as the way of achieving "truth" as it reflected facts by means of common sense.

It is worth remarking that journalistic objectivity—as we know it today—originated during the 19th century from the "scientific rationalism" that would go on to justify a particular type of journalism paradigm (Lippmann, 2010 [1920]; Wien, 2005). In the United Kingdom, it appeared closely tied to the PSB regulation system in the face of impartiality, which dominates the regulative and professional wording (BBC, 2016; Secretary of State, 2006),[2] being anchored in the Royal Charter and Ofcom regulations (Hampton, 2008; Sambrook, 2012).

In the United States, on the other hand, the concept is still widely used and linked to the private media and its procedures to guarantee fairness and balance. In other places, given their postcolonial settings, such as India, objectivity has become commonly associated with neutrality, balance, and facticity (see Yadav, 2011, S. 6) while it continues to dominate the public imagination and deontological aspirations of many journalists from around the world (Hanitzsch et al., 2011; McNair, 1998). This was something that became evermore present in the 20th century. As Bernhard (2003) sweepingly concludes,

> In the mid-twentieth century . . . the political economy of the mass media was intimately tied up with the articulation of Cold War policies, and objectivity became grounded in fervent anticommunism.

In describing the dwindling belief that in the crusade against Communism truthfulness should be a distinguishing feature of US propaganda, she writes that by 1948, Congress, the Departments of Defense and State, and the three networks agreed that "All information had military implications." Moreover, "the Cold War made propaganda an integral part of American foreign policy and took as its casualty confidence that the United States would triumph in the marketplace of ideas." Something that was epitomized in the supports and resources allocated toward the idea of "free flow of information" that became to dominate UNESCO and the rest of institutions around media development in that era (Chaparro-Escudero, 2012; Lemberg, 2019; Pineda de Alcázar, 2001; Smith, 1980).

THE GEOPOLITICS OF OBJECTIVITY

It was no coincidence that the main efforts to define objectivity as a professional journalistic norm were carried throughout the Cold War as a nation-building exercise (Pressman, 2017). These efforts and actions took place both in the United States and abroad as part of larger geopolitical struggles and in this sense looked to project a standardized model of journalism for which objectivity became a "strategic ritual" (Tuchman, 1972) that could mantle and hide unwanted socio-structural phenomena such as poverty behind quantified factual appearances (Harkins & Lugo-Ocando, 2016c; Lugo-Ocando, 2014). Through global diffusion, the principle of journalism objectivity then became a transnational norm that went beyond the United States and Great Britain into colonial and postcolonial territories of the Global South.

The 20th century saw how journalists reinforced the discursive regime by using "objectivity" as a core normative value that presumes that the social world can also be analyzed throughout the same type of "scientific rationality" as the natural world. In so doing, journalism has become a postcolonial hegemonic institution in modern society that not only has been able to claim "truthfulness" while helping to set and protect the parameters of political engagement by linking them to the values of the Enlightenment as a political project but also underpins the discourses of power of the ruling elites (Harkins & Lugo-Ocando, 2016b, 2017).

Thanks partially to this, the mainstream paradigm of journalism—predominantly present in the United States and the United Kingdom—was then able to push other forms of journalistic practices to the margins while presenting "structural analysis" as too "ideological" to be taken seriously and therefore restricting it to the margins of the public debate.[3] This, despite the fact that structural analysis provides a method by which one can attempt to understand the way the world is ordered. It assumes a series of principles that can be made overt and whose description makes clears elements of the whole. Structurally, one is interested in the form as well as the specific datum (facts) of the story (Koch, 1990, p. 21). This, to the degree that the structure should be both consistent and predictable as to allow journalists to analyze a specific story as an example of broader social class issues.

Any attempt to historicize the adoption of journalistic objectivity as a normative aspiration in the Global South requires us to acknowledge that it is a notion that is profoundly interwoven with the process of securing authorial dominance over what is truth and expanding cultural hegemony as a way of securing ever growing global markets. This is not to say that bringing about objectivity as a deontological norm in the Global South was only a cynical and deliberate attempt to narrow journalism to a commercially neutral fact-checking activity. However, there was an important effort done in bringing storytelling into industrial and modernist aesthetics that fitted better with the model of journalism practiced by the United States and the United Kingdom within their liberal democracies. Let us remember that all of Woodrow Wilson's efforts to use the League of Nations to expand liberal democracies and all of its institutions around the world in order to secure more international stability and confront the menace of communism emanating from the Soviet Union (Ambrosius, 2002; Knock, 1992) where fallowed up in the post–World War II era with the new architecture of the United Nations and NATO. It is part of a longer historical trend to construct "truth" within Western liberalism at the center as its underpinning ideology (Losurdo, 2014; Rosenblatt, 2018).

In doing so, we also need to recognize that by pushing for objectivity in the Global South using foreign aid, donors tried to replicate what had happened in the United States, which meant, as Kaplan (2006) has explained, the transformation from a partisan press to "objective media." Therefore, these foreign aid efforts in the South reflected the process of institutional and nation building that took place in the US. They carry with them the same implicit rules of journalistic practice caused that mirror the two-party political system, with rising progressive ideas of "public service" and professional autonomy.

Hence, the same process of nation and institution building that we saw in the United States was attempted in the Global South with the view of creating friendly political systems that could help expand the markets. What we call today globalization—and that is referred to as "Americanization" by some (Mattelart, 1996; Roach, 1997)—was a process of market expansion by means of institution building and expansion of the consumer-driven culture. Hence, the guiding principles that shaped the development of US liberal democracy and its market-oriented institutions became also the groundwork for what was exported as the journalism model in the Global South.

OBJECTIVITY AS A CURRENCY

However, the forces that shaped journalism were also deeply rooted in the rise of anti-communism in the United States, which was definitive in the development of its deontology. Journalism ethics was therefore shaped by the tensions that oscillating between a free market economy and its liberal democratic paradigm against the socialist utopia that led to the totalitarian Soviet state and its satellites. This was reflected in the standardizations of practices and in the normative aspirations that emerged while hindering—or enhancing at times—the ability of local and national communities to produce their own historical grammar about how news is produced and exchanged in society.

The news media in the Global South then went on to assume impartiality and objectivity as standard norms while covering issues and events (Golding, 1977; Paterson et al., 2018; Slavtcheva-Petkova, 2019). Advocacy for neutrality then was adopted in the South in the most virulent terms by excluding any alternative forms of journalism, some of which were traditionally far more present. Individual journalists then started to operate within a media system that required them to comply with the notions of objectivity and impartiality as conceived by the Western news media establishment so as to be able to claim to be a legitimate and neutral voice, both on the national and international stage.

The efforts to spread the ideology of objectivity and impartiality through foreign aid were often presented under two flags. On the one side, as Craig LaMay (2009) has pointed out, these efforts were linked to the ideal of freedom of expression as an inherent part of the expansion of democracy after World War II. This, in turn, meant supporting the need for the free flow of information (Nordenstreng, 2011; 2013; Lemberg, 2019). Indeed, the theory of free flow of information was central in the development of the ethos of international communication policy pushed by the United States, the United Kingdom, and their allies (Mattelart, 2003; H. I. Schiller, 1975; Sparks, 2007). The idea that media content should be available and accessible all over the world without restrictions was therefore an inherent part of the central message around freedom and democratic values. Journalism and the news media were, in this sense, neutral vessels that disseminated information among the public and contributed to the creation of a robust and well-informed public.

This ideal of free flow was often linked to the need to promote a "free market of ideas" (Mattelart, 1996; Nordenstreng, 2011). It was one which was brought into place within the larger post–World War II debates around reconstruction and development (Schiller, 1975). These were debates that effectively turn into policy in that postwar period as part of the push for expansion of markets for US capitalism by other Western powers. In this sense, international communication had the primary function of promoting democracy, freedom of expression, and market freedom. This is while opposing Soviet Union efforts into the Third World. The ideal of free flow of information reflected the belief that information and cultural markets should not be controlled or censored and that the function of the state in general, and foreign aid in particular, was to create the infrastructure and conditions for this free flow to happen.

The ideology of free flow together with the related notion of the free market of ideas served both economic and political purposes within the propaganda efforts against the Soviet advances (Lemberg, 2019; Schiller, 1975). In terms of journalism practice in the Global South, the "free flow" ideal became the basis for objectivity (Schiller, 1981). Indeed, in order to be able to flow freely, the argument ran, news needed to become a commodity with universal value and deprived of subjective judgments as to be able to be exchanged in neutral terms in the free market of ideas. This meant seeing objectivity as a scientifically neutral and fact-based object that could lead through its own interpretation of the "receiver" as truth. Therefore, bringing about modernity into the developing world by securing a way of making news that was scientific and impartial toward the facts. Only then, was it claimed, journalism could produce news content that could freely flow across channels and nations in non-ideological terms.

The backdrop for this was, of course, the "cybernetics" approach that defined a great deal of the post–World War II scholarly thinking and policy emanating from UNESCO until the late 1970s (Mattelart, 2003; Nordenstreng, 2011; Stevenson, 1988). In this period, scholars and policy-makers undertook a cybernetic understanding of what to do with communication in developing countries. By this, they meant approaching issues related to communication and development in terms of the science of control and communication, specifically seeing the interaction between automatic control and people as fundamental in the attempts to engineering (actually re-engineering) culture, communication, and social relations at large so as to fall into notions of development provided by assumptions around what is modern.

This is in fact an important and fundamental historical link. Mainly because the re-conceptualization of "objectivity" in terms of anti-virulent communism during this period was central in the dissemination of the news values and journalistic practices that followed. Particularly, as these notions translated into actions that underpinned implementing modernization as an ideology; one that was linked to progress and development within attempts of nation building (Escobar, 2011; Latham, 2000). Indeed, as Michael E. Latham (2000) has argued, there is a strong track record of efforts displayed by the US State Department and other government officials in places such as Latin America in order to use the social sciences and activities relating to them to support nation building in the forms of liberal democracy and market-driven economies.

These efforts included developing journalism as a political institution setting up in the Global South within the framework of modernization and nation building. For example, Tietaah, Yeboah-Banin, Akrofi-Quarcoo, and

Sesenu (2018) studied the extent to which capacity-building assistance to journalists in Ghana fostered particular types of journalistic practices. Their findings suggest that underlying the manifest objectives of building the capacities of beneficiaries was the implicit intent of the aid country of origin to use the media as agents of economic and cultural diplomacy. This means, creating a paradigm for journalism that somehow reflects the ideologies and models of the donor countries and replicating approaches and worldviews within news values.

Since then, not only many scholars but certainly most policy-makers and practitioners see—or intrinsically assume—that objectivity and impartiality are emblems for freedom and scientific truth, which confer journalists with the authorial control over narratives and discourses that can underpin liberal democracy.

Today, foreign aid has adopted a new terminology and uses concepts such as "media capture" against "media diversity" when setting their policies and allocating resources. However, they have the same meaning as in the past: to provide resources in order to build capabilities around objective reporting. To be sure, most foreign aid programs are still defined by this conceptual framework and, despite the end of the Cold War, continue to emphasize in allocating resources upon fostering "diversity" and "plurality" in order to support a more robust "free market of ideas" in the countries where they operate.

OBJECTIVE DISCUSSIONS

This historical context is important and relevant because current aid policy continues to be defined by ideologies and issues of the past even after the fall of the Berlin Wall. This is not only because the original setting of these policies, which was to push for a free flow of information that could underpin a free market of ideas, but also because of the reactions and resistance toward these attempts. In fact, as with the rest of the news values that the West tried to implement in the Global South, the notions of objectivity and impartiality did not go uncontested. Consequently, the set of values that journalists in the Global South embrace today are not only a reflection of one or the other but also—in many cases—both. Moreover, the understanding of what impartiality and objectivity means in these places is far from universal.

Journalism in the Global South today stands on the shoulders of contested ideologies, which explains why it presents such visible and notorious contradictions. On the one hand, journalism in developing countries show similar type of normative aspirations while on the other very distinctive practices that rather respond to the contested values in its formation as a political institution. Journalism in the Global South neither is the homogenous body of normative aspirations that we find in the North nor simply an amalgamation of the latter. It does aspire to truth, one which is factual. However, this truth can have many meanings in different societies as factuality, objectivity, and universality also can mean different things from place to place. This is in the same manner in which the ideal of freedom and equality meant one thing for George Washington (1732–1799), himself a slave owner, and a very different thing for the former slave and father of Haiti's independence, François Toussaint L'Ouverture (1743–1803).

All in all, what this chapter shows is that the ideological framework that made possible the dissemination and adoption of today's news values in the developing word was defined by tensions and conflict. In fact, one can say that the history of journalism all across the Global South was not the simple linear process of hegemonic dissemination and subsequent cultural imposition argued by some, but instead a process in which current values were forged by the heat of contradiction, conflict, and resistance. Contestation toward the overwhelming hegemonic efforts spearheaded by the colonial and post–World War II powers to disseminate particular ideologies of truth were in fact as important in this process as the resources and policies allocated from the center to establish dominance. It would be, as we will see in the next chapter, a struggle that would extend to the very spaces where present and future journalists were being formed, trained, and educated.

OBJECTIVE AUDIENCES

The expansion of the Western model of journalism into the Global South has also meant shaping audiences' expectations and taste of what news stories should look like, while determining what type of aesthetics and structure does people expect in a global scale. We know by multiple studies that audiences are active consumers of media and that media uses are purposive, goal-oriented, and driven by specific motivations, within a wide range of gratifications that vary across individuals and communication processes (Colomina, 1968; Lee, 2013). In the case of news content, people look for news stories that match their expectation in terms of interest, relevance, and overall quality. All three terms, of course, are relative in regard to each community and individual. Particularly in relation to what "quality" means for the general public.

This is because quality is a matter of aesthetics and part of the broader socially constructed reality. The emphasis to produce "quality" news argued by some experts (P. J. Anderson, Williams, & Ogola, 2013; Pennycook & Rand, 2019) as well as other efforts seeking to display certain standards when articulating stories—both mainstream legacy media and new digital-native ones across the globe—do not reflect universal realities or tangible measurable characteristics but instead socially constructed assumptions to which we all ascribe ideals of good taste. In some ways, "quality" in news are in reality cultural determinants around high culture and low culture to which Umberto Eco referred to in his seminal work Apocalyptic and Integrated (Eco, 2011 [1964]). In this sense, taste places values on what we consume as particular cultural artifacts. Hence, our taste on news is set by what we learn to appreciate as valuable and truthful. This taste for what journalism ought to bring in its outputs has been shaped partially by a long positivist tradition that is in itself problematic.

The fact remains that aspirations on what quality news is are vaguely defined within journalistic practice and even less clear in relation to the broader spectrum of news cultures. The notion of "quality" in the news remains not only elusive but also contentious (Anderson et. al, 2013; Martisini and Lugo-Ocando, 2020). On the one hand, the notion of "quality news" and "quality news providers" has centered on the normative claims of journalism being a public service to society; something that is in itself questionable both factually and historically. On the other hand, there is ample evidence to suggest that even when news stories meet particular expectations such as accessibility, reliability, accuracy, validity credibility, impartiality, and balance, the news stories are still not considered to be able to achieve "quality" (i.e., particular news stories that appears in the British tabloid press). This is because, as Michael Lithgow (2012) has pointed out, aesthetics in the news manifest itself as a rationally ambiguous category—one that has a meaning that encompasses both relational and representational dimensions of communication. Moreover, claims about truthfulness have ontological consequences bound in the social commitments and obligations generated through expressive choices and interpellated audiences.

This means that aesthetics is always a matter of power either in literature or in journalism. To be sure, and as Walter Benjamin once suggested, "culture" is not an autonomous realm of values nor there are "independent values of aesthetic" (cited Koepnick, 1999). For news audiences, the culture of relevance and truth plays a central role in the constitution of collective knowledge about the world out there in ways that extend beyond rational argumentation and go into the realm of aesthetic experience. Hence, aesthetical experiences around news are inevitably influenced by power relations.

In light of this and given both the colonial and postcolonial relations of power between the center and the periphery, it is possible to argue that tastes among audiences in the Global South have been influenced and determined in a great deal by external relations to power that over the years have managed to define how people appreciate a particular structure and style in the news. It is important, therefore, for scholars and experts alike to explore this in more depth in ways that can trace the history in the development of news audiences and how Foreign Aid has also affected the way those societies see, interpret, and appreciate news in broader terms. Something that nevertheless would require perhaps another book in itself.

NOTES

1. Interview with official from donor organization on September 10, 2019. Identity withheld at request of the interviewee.

2. Sambrook (2012, p. 5) proposes a synonymous deployment of the words, though admitting that "impartiality, the removal of bias, is the more complex of the two, although objectivity—a disciplined approach to isolate evidence and facts—is still far from easy to achieve."

3. Let us not forget that these debates around scientific/rational approaches against irrational ideologies did not only happen in the West. In the Soviet Union, they were also a motive of discussion as we will explore in a later chapter (Ings, 2017; Pollock, 2006).

Chapter 6

Educating and Training Journalists in the South

Overall, it is possible to suggest that the education and training of journalists in the Global South has been one of the most important and enduring channels through which the key normative values of news reporting were disseminated across the planet in the past 100 years (Murphy & Scotton, 1987; Rodny-Gumede, 2018). In the particular context of the Cold War and referring to Western aid, one can also argue that the same educational channels have been at the cornerstone of the dissemination of "common sense" as the language of news. It has not been, however, a monolithic process as we have already discussed in this book. Hence, in order to analyze the role that aid has had upon shaping the content, message, and values transmitted by means of these educational channels and provision, we have to start by broadening the notions of what journalism education and training means in the particular settings, historical context, and journalistic cultures in which foreign aid was provided.

Despite repeated attempts over the years to universalize and standardize journalism education in the Global South, it remains nevertheless a very broad church. Yes, there are wide and very important general traits and overlaps across countries, nevertheless "journalism is not and never should be disconnected from (the idea of) community," which concretely means that any conceptualization of journalism must always be framed in terms of the society in which it operates (Deuze, 2006). Therefore, the role of foreign aid in defining journalism education across the Global South needs to be seen from the perspective of its own historical and societal specificities. This is because it is, and continues to be, assumed differently within different national and cultural contexts. As Frohlich and Holtz-Bacha (1994) pointed out some time ago, national systems of journalism training are the result of an interplay of the role and function of a society to its journalists, the structures in the field of journalism (e.g., legal regulations, unions, and journalism councils) and, the media system in which journalists operate. Although similarities among countries can be found in particular dimensions, differences in others lead to the great inhomogeneity.

The history of journalism in general is far from the universal and linear account that many historians in the West have suggested (Chapman & Nuttall, 2011; Muhlmann, 2008; Schudson & Tifft, 2005). It is even more the case for journalism education where the creation of a diversity of training provisions, and journalism schools in particular, happened in many cases simultaneously and in parallel. While journalism schools officially started in the United States under the patronage of newspaper publisher Joseph Pulitzer on September 8, 1908, at the University of Missouri, we find evidence of several schools of journalism being created all over the world at the same time.

By 1901, to give an example, Argentina had created not one but two J-schools (Nixon, 1982) although they later closed due to the lack of funds and only reopen in 1934 at the University de la Plata. Some years later Mexico would do the same in 1936 with the setting up of the first formal university degree of journalism at the Universidad Femenina de México, a women's-only college (Cleary, 2003; Ferreira, Tillson, & Salwen, 2000). By 1947, Brazilian journalist Cásper Líbero would establish the school of journalism in São Paulo, that today bears his name and that is the oldest—still running—journalism school in Latin America, known as the Faculdade Cásper Líbero (FCL).

The setting up of journalism schools was part of a broader effort not only to achieve professionalization but also standardization of journalism practices. The many schools that followed Missouri in the United States copied curriculums and syllabuses that placed particular emphasis upon liberal arts but at the same time strengthened skills such as writing and news reporting in a certain manner. One that would follow AP "guide" and "style." This would be a model that would then be extended to the Global South, where not only syllabuses but also core values of the curriculum would be adopted in Africa, Asia, and Latin America (Deuze, 2006; Murphy & Scotton, 1987). By the early1950s, at the time that many places in the Global South had already inaugurated formally their first degrees in journalism, the AP publication was formalized into the stylebook. This, together with other similar efforts from Western international news agencies and broadcasters such as the BBC and Reuters became the standard reference for most member and non-member news bureaus throughout the world. More importantly, these efforts would go on to set the framework for normative professional aspirations for many newspapers and J-schools from around the globe (Golding, 1977; Horne, 2017b; Silberstein-Loeb, 2014). Let us not forget that many of the first professors and instructors in these schools were journalists themselves who had come right of the industry, one that had its own hierarchy where correspondents of the international news agencies such as AP were consider to be at the top.

One also needs to highlight that education and training of journalists are nevertheless distinctive yet related ambits. Consequently, it would be simplistic to study the history of journalism education only from the optic of the formal provisions such as J-schools and universities. It is a history that also needs to recognize the role of professional guilds of journalists in the formation of subsequent generations of news reporters. Brazil, to give an example, had already created its first guild of journalists and professional writers in the mid-19th century (Lima et al., 2014) and there is ample evidence that these associations of "professional" reporters and writers provided mentoring and support to its members.

Education and training nevertheless meant different scopes and approaches. On the one hand, journalism education has been linked to providing a liberal arts background with a sufficient understanding and grasp for the skills to produce news stories. On the other, training was often set by journalists themselves or within the news organizations for which they worked. In the United Kingdom, for example, where journalism schools came very late into being university journalism education, they did not become a significant endeavor until the 1970s. Before that, most of the training was run by the industry-based National Council for the Training of Journalists (NCTJ) and later on by the also industry-based Broadcast Journalism Training Council (BJTC) and Periodical Training Council (PTC), depending on which media platform journalists used (Delano, 2000).

All in all, education and training offered by the US and European governments and organizations have historically focused on setting particular reporting standards by replicating professional deontological practices and values among practitioners in the Global South (McCurdy & Power, 2007). The normative framework is one that reflects the aspiration of fostering a type of news reporting that serves as a watchdog to power, that is committed to liberal democracies and that is professionally autonomous from government and private interests. The education efforts, therefore, have made emphasis over the years upon incorporating topics into to the curriculum that reflect the values that donor countries are keen to set as golden standards.

These efforts also include pushing for agendas that touch upon topics such as corruption, how resources and budgets are allocated and used, and overall that promotes transparency and political freedom. The particular angle of these educational and training efforts justified their existence over the years by arguing that they can help to improve the overall "quality" of journalism practice in these countries and have a lasting impact upon society in more general terms. Journalism, in this context—it is argued—can play a pivotal role in modernizing nations and bringing about liberal reforms and more openness.

REAL INTENTIONS

So far, so good, one would expect. However, there is a baffling paradox that needs to be addressed. One that emerges from this account and that sets in motion the problematization of this area of study. How is it that these efforts and resources have often been exported to places that by no measure exhibited any "democratic" conditions for journalism to be practiced (Josephi, 2010)? That is unless we accept that in many of those cases, it was more about exporting a particular system of values—to push for regime change—than actually addressing "quality," as problematic as that last notion can be in the context of journalism theory and practice.

To be sure, foreign aid for media assistance and media development cannot be disassociated from the ideological and geopolitical struggles that marked the 20th century as we have widely discussed throughout this book. The great powers showed systematic concern with the type of media that operated outside their borders, something that can be traced to at least modern colonial times. However, it was after World War II that the United States and its allies, in the face of Soviet advancement on the world stage, started to invest heavily in the training of journalists and other forms of media assistance and control in the countries they occupied.

Furthermore, even after the collapse of the Berlin Wall, Western governments, nongovernmental organizations, foundations, and others doubled their concerted efforts to assist Eastern European countries that had left the Soviet Block in order to develop capabilities in this field. By some estimations, the US government spent at least $600 million through media foundations alone during the decade after the fall of the Berlin Wall (Becker & Vlad, 2005).

It was not only governments that would act as donors. All over the South, multiple private and Third Sector organizations also intervened by both allocating resources and organizing themselves to provide education and training. One of the earliest examples of this was the Association of Catholic Bishops "Aktion Adveniat," which was one of the first NGOs to organize journalism courses (Nixon, 1982). These consisted of nine months of short courses delivered each year for some twenty-five journalists during the 1970s based on a syllabus that included writing, ethics, and particular case studies around science journalism, something that we will return to later to comment on.

More recently, to give another example, we can also look at the SembraMedia, which is a nonprofit organization that supports digital media entrepreneurs and journalists by providing technical training, market intelligence, networking opportunities, consulting, and, perhaps more important, financial resources. This organization launched in 2019 under the "Velocidad" initiative that allocated more than $1.5 million in grants and professional consulting supporting independent news organizations in Latin America. This fund operates under the direction of SembraMedia and the International Center for Journalists (ICFJ), with financial support from Luminate. Particularly important in this fund is how much of the resources are allocated to training and education and, key to this, how much of these resources are destined to guarantee "diversity" of voices (Warner & Iastrebner, 2018).

Other NGOs that have provided in the past and continue to allocate today resources toward journalism include George Soros's Open Society Foundation (United States), the Konrad Adenauer (Germany), Fundación Carolina (Spain), and Toda Peace Institute (Japan), among hundreds of large and small institutions that have provided training, education, and curriculum development in this field. One important caveat refers to the fact that most are independent from governments in terms of funding, although not all. In fact, many "private" organizations that provide support to journalism education and training programs are heavily dependent upon state resources, which have led to accusations in some cases of been a façade for foreign governments to meddle in the internal affairs of other nations (Fijałkowska, 2011; Golinger, 2005).

In light of all this, one can see how the central focus of foreign aid has been—and continues to be—that of supporting a particular model of journalism. One that is fact-based, objective and overall defined by its commitment to "common sense" as a discursive framework. Moreover, the general conclusion is that foreign aid destined to support journalism education and training has been an exercise that seeks the promotion of the democratic ethos by means of its support for diversity and freedom of the press.

AMOUNT AND NATURE OF "HELP"

In this context, Foreign Aid for Media Development has delivered support to both areas: education and training. However, the extent of investment in media assistance from donor countries remains largely unknown and most figures for spending on journalism education and training are often not available. In fact, few studies have looked specifically at the financial aspects and amounts of resources allocated toward media assistance and media development, let alone how much money has been destined to educate and train journalists or the nature of that spending.

Nonetheless, proxy studies and anecdotical evidence suggest that these amounts have been of important significance over the years and that they responded largely to ideological and public diplomacy prerogatives (Becker & Vlad, 2005; Ogundimu, Oyewo, & Adegoke, 2007; Schiffrin, 2010). On the one hand, there was an estimated $1 billion spent on media assistance each year by non-US organizations until the mid-2000s. On the other, initiatives such as the Fulbright Program in the United States and Chevening in the United Kingdom have consistently had journalism and media studies among their top priorities when allocating scholarships for potential students from developing countries.

Moreover, organizations such as the British Council and many other similar ones have consistently funded a great number of events and support mechanisms around the world in order to support short-term courses and master classes in journalism as well as exchanges and visits for groups of journalists. These short courses include many organized by the United States Agency for International Development (USAID), which is an independent agency of the US federal government that is primarily responsible for administering civilian foreign aid and development assistance (Nixon, 1982, p. 19). These budgets have also included publishing monographs, translating others, and donating books and teaching materials to libraries of universities and schools of journalism. More recently, these efforts have tended to focus more upon developing online support websites and online resources to foster particular types of approaches and practices toward reporting.

All in all, journalism education and training have been a long-standing interest for donor countries and has been particularly central to public diplomacy efforts, particularly since the Cold War. From the end of World War II, financial foreign assistance to journalism education and training has expanded to incorporate universities, teaching and training organizations, NGOs, and local provisions destined to develop not only news reporting but also new areas such as public relations, social media skills and a wide set of subjects that today relate to the increasingly broader spectrum of elements that can support and influence the news media. However, despite this growth and the expansion into new areas, foreign aid for media assistance and development destined to educate and train present and new professionals in the Global South remains largely focused on disseminating and reproducing a particular set of values and practices.

Important however to notice is the fact that from the evidence and studies available, we can single out some general patterns. Firstly, it is important to note that both formal education and the training of journalists have received over the years their fair share of foreign aid resources. However, the aid provided is distinctive in terms of its nature in periods of time among specific programs, in relation to curriculum development and also in regard to quantity of the resources allocated. One can also observe that donor governments have historically allocated resources and engaged with universities and other higher education institutions. They have done this via support for libraries, particular programs that fund exchange and visits by scholars, offering scholarships for postgraduate and undergraduate studies abroad and, providing general support for curriculum development.

Secondly, we can see that NGOs are far more engaged directly with news media outlets and journalists themselves. They tend to support and develop shorter courses that are far more centered on improving skills and supporting better practices. In many of these cases, such as the Fundación Ángel Ramos in Puerto Rico in the 1970s, journalism courses were short and lasted at the most a few months (Subervi-Vélez et al., 2020). Over the years, the time span of these provisions has become shorter and we find increasingly more that they take the form of very short workshops and online provision (Nixon, 1982).

Another very important area of journalism education and training has been the support that foreign assistance has provided in the area of radio. Initial efforts to expand particular formats and approaches to producing radio news can be traced back to the 1930s during the Spanish Civil War and the training of Arab journalists in Morocco to support Franco's war efforts in Spain (Arasa, 2015). The BBC, on the other hand, made extensive inroads in radio journalism training during the postwar with its efforts to develop a broadcasting system in British Colonial Africa between 1946 and 1956, which colonial officials argue was an instrument for national development (Armour, 1984, p. 359). In reality, however, radio was used as a medium to project imperial soft power across the different colonies (Kuitenbrouwer, 2016).

More recent efforts included the training of journalists in Africa, Asia, and Latin America by European public service broadcasters such as the BBC, Radio Netherlands,' Radio France Internationale (RFI), and the German Deutsche Welle, among others. These efforts have included workshops in a variety of countries and flying over to Europe hundreds of journalists from the Global South in order to work in these organizations for a short period of time while providing free international content to fill the airwaves in these countries (Osung, 2018; Segura, 2018). Perhaps one of the most significant initiatives was the Radio Nertherlands Training Centre América Latina, established in San José, Costa Rica in 1968 that operated until 2008 (Prieto Castillo, 2008; Uranga & Pasquini, 1988) and which followed similar efforts in other parts of the region (Mrázek, 1997). This center provided education and training to journalists from all over Latin American and the Caribbean in a diversity of areas that covered technical skills as well as international law. These training sessions and provision included elements of ethics and normative deontology as well as areas of specialism such as science and technology. As Pablo Hernández, former correspondent in Latin America of this station, points out:

> The network not only provided training for journalists but also produced a series of materials to help us do our jobs. A lot of these books, guides and materials gave very practical advice about how to produce good quality radio but mostly

about news and procedures to follow. This was not only for us working for Radio Netherlands but also for all journalists working with affiliated stations. I mean the local ones, the ones that broadcast our news bulletins and programmes.[1]

Today, a great deal of foreign aid that goes into journalism training and education continues to be channeled through universities and NGOs. This is increasingly the case as less aid destined to education and training is provided by traditional mainstream media outlets and more is delivered instead either by central governments, multilateral organizations, or NGOs. Indeed, most international aid for training programs performed by European public service radio networks have by now all but shut down (Prieto Castillo, 2008), while international television organizations offer nowadays little or no provision for the training and education of reporters in the Global South.

One of the reasons for the decline of foreign aid support to the traditional channels of education and training for journalists is the fact that it was used in the past to support anti-democratic forces and military coups (Alvear & Lugo-Ocando, 2016; Segura, 2018). Hence, not many governments—particularly the United States—are keen to associate themselves directly with foreign aid toward media development in general. Even more as many journalists and reporters who have participated in educational and training programs supported by these funds have been accused of spying for foreign governments or being agents for political destabilization in the service of these governments or individuals. For example, Hugo Chávez in Venezuela—as Vladimir Putin also did in Russia—constantly refers to foreign aid used to pay journalists who were critical toward his regimes. His accusations were based on the work of US-Venezuelan lawyer Eva Golinger (2005), who paradoxically went later to work for Russian Television, which is now considered a "foreign agent" by the US government.

The accusations against journalists in Venezuela just for the simple reason of attending a training session or having been a recipient of a scholarship (Golinger & Landau, 2006) led to persecutions and in some cases to imprisonment of reporters. Many of these programs are increasingly the subject of criticism by those who see the danger of particular agendas being advanced through charitable work (Barker, 2008; Browne, 2010). In Russia, under Vladimir Putin, a foreign agent law was issued, which was developed after large anti-Putin protests in 2012 and that has largely targeted NGOs. That same year, a new law was issued that incorporate the possibility of declaring journalists and bloggers as "foreign agents" (Roth, 2019). Needless to say, many of these attacks have been directed toward international organizations providing the education and training of journalists such as the Central European University, funded by George Soros, which was "forced out" of Hungary by the government (Walker, 2018).

These types of attacks are by no means new. During almost the whole of the Cold War, each side accused the media on the opposite ideological spectrum of being funded to subvert and spy against each other. Organizations such as the Latin American Faculty of Social Sciences (known in Spanish as Facultad Latinoamericana de Ciencias Sociales or FLACSO), which sponsored many forums and programs around journalism and communication came under suspicion regarding funding. Similarly, there were numerous cases of journalists who went to study abroad only to return and find no jobs as they were seen to have sold out to foreign powers. Hence, since the 1970s, there was increasing awareness about the need to avoid direct and explicit showing of this aid. Many funders then started making concerted efforts to elude direct funding, redirecting through a third-party NGO, or just focusing on "non-political" areas such as health and science.

SCIENCE JOURNALISM AS A TROJAN HORSE?

One of the areas to which foreign aid toward journalism education and training was directed so as to avoid explicit "politicalization" was science and technology. In fact, science journalism became a true beachhead to advance Western journalism values and practices across the globe, even within nations and societies that were very antagonistic to the idea of liberal democracy. Nevertheless, initial efforts to push for science journalism training were far from an attempt to promote covert operations or slip through hidden agendas. Instead, the initial resources allocated were part of a larger effort within the Cold War to win the propaganda war.

This is not only because the Truman administration was convinced at the time of the superiority of Western science technology[2] but also because the administration was advised that these efforts would pay off by bringing the type of rationality and objectivity that Soviet propagandists could not match. Indeed, far from cynical assumptions, politicization was not a consideration in these initial efforts. On the contrary, science reporting was seen as a special form of rhetoric (Anderson, 1970). One that was built upon the most objective and factual understanding of reality and that could advance truth in ways that no other news beat could due to the nature of the subject area itself. During this period, support for science journalism was given directly and indirectly such as the UNESCO and Kalinga Foundation Trust in India, joint efforts since 1952 to support and recognize the work of science journalists.

This push for science journalism happened in the context of the Cold War where science and technology were the key factors underpinning the notions of exporting Western "development" and "modernity" and, until the late 1950s, a stark reminder of Western superiority (Lugo-Ocando & Nguyen,

2017), which, of course, would crumble in the public imagination under the weight of the political metaphors produced by the launched in 1957 of the Sputnik 1 and Laika and finally quashed by the return of Cosmonaut Yuri Alekseyevich Gagarin after his capsule Vostok 1 completed one orbit of Earth on April 12, 1961. No wonder the juggernaut of science and technology was the primary weapon of propaganda during the Cold War (Edwards, 1997, p. ix) as initially it supported the narrative that portrayed technology and cultural freedom as the great saviors of the West. The space race in particular but also advances in medicine, engineering, and other areas of society played toward this narrative (Oreskes, 2014). To be sure, the race toward scientific and technological progress became at the forefront the Cold War and a key part of the propaganda rhetoric that dominated the overall narratives of the time.

The more into the Cold War and the greater the Soviet advances were, the less secure the West became of itself. Indeed, under the Eisenhower administration (1953–1961), the United States suffered some of its greatest propaganda defeats including the stalemate in Korea in 1953, the triumph of Castro in Cuba and the Soviet initial supremacy in space. Some authors have called this "Eisenhower's Sputnik moment" (Mieczkowski, 2013), when the space race for world prestige seem to be all but lost for the United States.

Qualitative assessment of the news coverage given to the Soviet Union launch of the Sputnik satellite in October 1957 using the *New York Times*, *St. Louis Post-Dispatch*, and *Los Angeles Times* as samples indicate depictions of dramas of defeat, of national mortification, and of doom and dread toward the Soviet menace (Lule, 1991). To be sure, US public reaction to the launch of the Sputnik satellite was one of monumental shock and fear. This as the Soviets' space supremacy sent shockwaves across the West influencing nearly every aspect of US life: from an immediate shift toward science in the classroom to the arms race that defined the Cold War, the competition to reach the moon, and later the birth of the Internet (Dickson, 2019; Ichikawa, 2018). The US news media both promoted, and at the same time downplayed, the space race during those years (Marlin, 1987), which seems to correlate with the lukewarm attitudes and support toward science journalism education in the Global South during that same period. Subsequently, and contrary to the Truman administration, Dwight D. Eisenhower gave far less emphasis upon supporting the expansion of a free media and independent journalism in the Global South and instead allocated more resources toward overt and covert propaganda efforts. This went along also to increasing US interventionism in places such as Guatemala, Iran, and the initial US involvement in Vietnam, among others.

A new impulse to support science journalism education and training in the Global South took place under the John F. Kennedy (1961–1963) and

Lyndon B. Johnston (1963–1969) administrations, which re-engaged with Truman's initial attempt to support journalism in the Global South. Renewed confidence in the ideological and technological superiority of the West underpinned these efforts despite important setbacks such as the consolidation of the Cuban Revolution in power and the start of the Vietnam war. In Latin America, the OAS programs on this front deserve particular attention. For example, several workshops organized in Colombia and Venezuela plus scholarships to study abroad were channeled through organizations such as the Inter-American Institute for Cooperation on Agriculture, which placed great emphasis on education and training (Samper, 1964, p. 7).

More explicit efforts to educate and train journalists can also be found within OAS initiatives over these years. This is because the OAS has a mandate regarding the creation and dissemination of scientific knowledge to promote development stemming from its Charter that proclaims that the historic mission of the Americas is to offer human beings a land of liberty and a favorable environment for the development of their personality and the realization of their just aspirations. This reaffirms its commitment to give primary importance within their development plans to the encouragement of education, science, technology, and culture, oriented toward the overall improvement of the individual, and as a foundation for democracy, social justice, and progress (OAS, 1948). Over the years, the OAS developed and implemented a series of initiatives to support the education and training of science journalists.

In more recent times, in adopting the Declaration of Santo Domingo in 2010, the OAS launched the Inter-American Scientific Journalism Project. The main purpose of this project is to strengthen the capacities for dissemination and popularization of science. It includes subregional seminars to train journalists, policy-makers, and other professionals in the private sector; the creation of an Inter-American Portal of Scientific Journalism as a mechanism for dissemination of information on science and technology information for the general public; promoting communication between journalists, scientists, media representatives, and public officials as well as other initiatives across the region.

One important characteristic today is that science journalism education and training tend to be delivered through Third Sector and multilateral organizations rather than universities or formal higher education institutions. Not one of the fourteen top-ranking universities in Latin America have among their syllabus science journalism or science communication among their core subjects. That is also the case for many programs in Africa, Asia, and Latin America where science journalism has for a long time disappeared from the curriculum. So, the question is: Why have these resources declined? Well, the answer seems to be far broader, as the decline is across the whole of the contributions that historically were made to universities as they became more critical of foreign aid and less willing to accept it openly.

COMMON TRENDS

In education and the training of journalists, we find important overlaps and convergence between the different programs and among donor countries' efforts deployed in the Global South, which tend to foster particular skills and be Western-centered (Howard, 2003). In addition, foreign aid is directed in great measure toward sustaining programs of study abroad that are based on scholarships for local journalists from the Global South. To the United Kingdom's Chevening scholarship program that has brought over 50,000 exceptional professionals to study in British Universities since 1983, many of whom are journalists, we have to add other initiatives, such as the Commonwealth Scholarships and private or semi-private ones such as the Journalist Fellowship Programme at the Reuters Institute, which is based at the University of Oxford, the program sponsors mid-career journalists who are fully funded and receive a stipend to cover living and travel costs. Similar initiatives are found in the United States with the Fulbright Program that aims at improving "intercultural relations, cultural diplomacy, and intercultural competence between the people of the United States and other countries through the exchange of persons, knowledge, and skills" and the University of Harvard-based/Nieman Foundation-sponsored fellowship programs for journalists.

Although a global map of these programs is still needed and should be part of a future research agenda, we can count many similar programs in the Netherlands such as Nuffic, which is the Dutch organization for internationalization in education (an independent, nonprofit organization based in The Hague, the Netherlands but related to the Ministry of Education, Culture & Science and the Dutch Ministry of Foreign Affairs). Others include, the Australia Awards, which aim to "promote knowledge, education links, and enduring ties between Australia and its neighbours," and which incorporate and coordinate resources from the Department of Foreign Affairs (DFAT), the Department of Education, and the Australian Centre for International Agricultural Research (ACIAR).

However, not all donors that support the education and training of journalists and media professionals are located in the North. As a reminiscent of the broader efforts to export its model during the Cold War, Cuba remains committed to provide scholarships for journalists from the Global South to undertake graduate programs on the island. Particular attention deserves to be paid to the International Institute for Journalism José Martí—that takes its name from the famous journalist and Cuba's independence national hero. The institute's program of short courses is actually relatively independent from ideological constraints and focuses instead on technical skills or broader issues, such as population, social exclusion, and science and technology, to name but a few. Many of these provisions have been developed in conjunction with the United Nations and other international organizations (IIPJM, 2018). Having said that, individuals who study in Cuba are often selected or self-selected based on their ideological affinities.

In these cases, individuals are brought to the donor countries to study journalism in a host university that delivers a curriculum that reflects all the values and common practices that we have discussed in this book. In addition, these students often live under privileged conditions with a stipend during their studies with access to services and goods that normally are not available to the citizens of that country while keeping little contact with the latter. This often translates in an experience that is broadly positive and that ends up reinforcing their worldviews toward the host country and their status of buyers in the market for loyalties.

Not all education and training programs are delivered in the host countries. Foreign Aid is also widely allocated to fund courses, symposiums, events, and a variety of master classes across the globe in the countries of origin of the journalists. These resources have funded over the years a variety of events. In her extraordinary account on the CIA involvement in the cultural propaganda efforts during the Cold War, British journalist and historian, Frances Hélène Jeanne Stonor Saunders (2000), exposed how the United States deployed systematic efforts to infiltrate and co-opt cultural movements in order to combat political influence from the Soviet Union and expand American political influence. Armand Mattelart (2003) has made similar points when highlighting how the CIA and the US State Department funded a series of events and conferences that helped underpin key concepts in media and communication studies. It is therefore not surprising that during the Cold War, many other of these conferences, events, symposiums, and workshops were also funded in order to help shape journalism as a political institution in the Global South.

RESISTANCE AND RELUCTANCE

It is possible to argue that the journalism curricula in many countries in the Global South was originally copied from journalism degrees in the Global North and thereafter transferred to media systems and political frameworks in very different contexts. This led to accusations that journalism curricula in the Global South reflects values and practices grounded in Western normative ideas of the role and function of journalism (Rodny-Gumede, 2018). Consequently, goes the argument, they ignore the particular realities and contexts in the countries where they are implemented. This is far more than just a relativist critique as it also highlights important postmodern issues.

However, and despite this criticism, attempts to universalize syllabus have continued. In 2007, the UNESCO published a proposed journalism curricula (UNESCO, 2017). This generic model, it argued, could be adapted according to each country's specific needs. The effort aimed at incorporating "full cognizance of the social, economic, political and cultural contexts of developing countries and emerging democracies, highlighting the connection between democracy and journalism and arguing for a more cross-disciplinary approach within journalism training centres."

UNESCO-commissioned experts for the initial development of the journalism education curricula initiative, who then solicited a response to their first draft from twenty senior journalism educators "who were deemed to have considerable experience working in developing countries and emerging democracies." The revised draft design thus featured a list of courses for both undergraduate and postgraduate levels, a brief description of each course and an outline of fundamental journalism competencies. Journalism instructors with experience working in developing countries or emerging democracies were then "carefully selected from Africa, Asia, Europe, the Middle East, and North and South America" to write the syllabuses for seventeen core courses. The draft curriculum was then reviewed by other "experts" in Paris.

Needless to say that as laudable as the intentions of this effort might be—and UNESCO has become a different institution today—it still reflects the traditional top-bottom approach that dominated the Cold War and seeks to "standardize" journalism education. One of the things that the groups pushing forward this initiative failed to see, which perhaps explained the lack of progress in implementing such a curriculum model, is that the Global South way left behind the quest for standardization.

First, because for years there has been a great awareness of the agency in the attempts to implement universal curriculums in journalism studies. Scholars in those parts of the world are well aware of the consequent prospect of compromising the journalistic autonomy of beneficiaries of training aid and that this brings into question their capacity to contribute to sustainable development in their countries (Tietaah et al., 2018). Second, because J-schools are no longer the training grounds that once were imagined but critical spaces that were positively tainted by radical and critical trends such as decolonization and Marxism. Indeed, during the 1960s and 1970s, journalism schools in places such as Latin America and India shifted from a modernization approach to a critical neo-Marxism approach and even though Latin American journalism and mass communication education has recently shifted away from its neo-Marxist past (Ferreira et al., 2000) they nevertheless retain their overall critical framework. One that rejected not only attempts to standardize a journalism curriculum but that got away with journalism training as a dominant format to form future generations.

Indeed, all across the Global South, the history of curriculum development in journalism education has been both one of adaptation and rejection. There is a historical narrative for which early attempts of globalization—which was a "euphemism" for standardization as the term carries a residue of postwar US hegemony (Simonson, Morooka, Xiong, & Bedsole, 2019)—were characterized by both power and resistance. In this sense, authors from all over the Global South have argued for the need to "decolonize" journalism curricula and practices from the prevailing Western models. These efforts have to go both ways. Hence, the need to also de-Westernize media studies of higher education in the North. The dominance of particular paradigms in terms of journalism curricula and practices and how certain narratives dominate the discussions around what journalism curricula in non-Western and developing countries requires is a material reality. How many scholars from the Global South were able to see or provide feedback to a "universal" curriculum model as that proposed by UNESCO? How many can afford to travel and participate in meetings in Geneva, New York, Washington or Paris? Yes, there is a need for a different approach to content and delivery, which places more emphasis on the value of local research and knowledge as a pedagogical and epistemological tool (Papoutsaki, 2007). But in the face of the material realities of how the Foreign Aid for Media Development—and we must recognize UNESCO's proposal as this—is designed and implemented—it is regrettable and expected that little will change.

Poutsaki has suggested that many developing countries have experienced colonization and therefore the imposition of Western educational systems, where local ways of acquiring knowledge were systematically neglected and undermined (Papoutsaki, 2007, p. 80). So, if this is the case, she argues, the challenge is for journalism to move away from the dominant principles contained in normative media theory, ethics, and practice. The question is that journalism education normative aspirations continue to be dictated by power and resources. This continues to be the case, where priorities and hierarchies of learning continue to be set from the top. For example, denial by international agencies and Western governments that they support media assistance programs does not hold water in Syria, or in the rest of the region. The high number of activists and journalists trained by international organizations is a clear indication of this multifaceted strategy (Brownlee, 2017, p. 2289).

In this sense, it is worth highlighting particular cases such as that of the BBC Media Action, which is an important player in the field of media development in Syria. Despite its high level of competence and successful history of international media assistance, Syria has not been an easy ground to work on, given the regime's tight supervision and the suspicion overlooking any foreign activity. BBC Media Action was among the pioneer organizations implementing media assistance programs in Syria. Juliette Harkin, BBC journalist and specialist in Syrian media, affirmed in our first interview that Syria was selected, among seven other Middle Eastern countries, for a £1.5 million project between 2004 and 2007. The project, the Arab Media Dialogue Programme, consisted of building partnerships with Arab media organizations and training the management and staff of media agencies. Harkin, project manager of the program and based in Damascus at the time, said that the program in Syria consisted in the organization of training in journalism skills, business, and management for selected journalists, editors, and managers, working in partnership with both state and private media outlets (Brownlee, 2017, p. 2283).

We can say that that educational and training programs for journalists in the Global South present a mixed picture. On the one hand, they have been about capacity building but on the other, they have hindered the potential of a homegrown understanding of what journalism should be about in that specific society. In Ghana, for example, the assistance to journalists has fostered and inhibited at the same time independent and indigenous journalistic practices and normative frameworks. Some research in that country has suggested that underlying the manifest objectives of building the capacities of beneficiaries was the implicit intent of the aid delivered to the country of origin to use the media as agents of economic and cultural diplomacy. This with the consequent prospect of compromising the journalistic autonomy of beneficiaries of training aid and brings into question their capacity to contribute to sustainable development in Ghana (Tietaah et al., 2018).

Equally important is to highlight the degree of contestation and agency provided by the individuals themselves who over decades participated in these educational programs. As Merlyn Lossada, professor of digital journalism at the Universidad del Zulia explains:

> Originally, we were called the School of Journalism as it was named given in its creation in 1958. In that time, there was not a lot of books or materials in Spanish and overall research was scarce. So, a lot of the materials we used were translations from the English. The US Embassy donated many of the books we used and several professors went to study there. Over the years, however, the scholars became increasingly critical and started to produce their own research and books. Finally, even the name of the school change to "Social Communication" as by then it became clear that we needed an alternative model to communicate things, one that responded to our own needs.[3]

This historiography of the transition that occurred in many journalism schools is confirm by the research in the evolution of the teaching of journalism in Latin America, which has recorded the same path in several places of the continent (Cuenca, 1998; Martín-Barbero & Rey, 1997; Nixon, 1982).

Scholarships and resources from the United States, Europe, and the Soviet bloc allowed individuals to study abroad and also provided financial assistance to train in situ reporters, allowing transfer knowledge, skills, and normative values. In this sense, agency from the part of participating journalists and academics who taught in journalism schools in the Global South is crucial in understanding why there is such degree of assimilation, adaptation, and contestation across the spectrum. It helps us also explain why and how Foreign Aid end up producing many innovations and interesting projects and ideas that were not originally intended, or even desired, by the donors.

Nevertheless, despite important levels of contestation, aid remained crucial in setting and spreading a particular paradigm of journalism because graduates still had to work in media organizations. Their professional ideologies then were subject to further influence by the need to integrate into larger professional communities that already worked around well-established news cultures, normative aspirations, and professional practices. These organizations continue to push for a language of common sense set around the notions of objectivity—although less explicit than in the past—impartiality and balance. The interpretative communities working within these organizations assumed that "facts" are the basis of truth and often obviate for context, history, and structural analysis. It is a paradigm that continues in the very present to privilege a particular type of news reporting while excluding others as legitimate forms of communicating news and that, in many cases, bows to the powerful while claiming to expose truth.

NOTES

1. Interview with Pablo Hernández on November 12, 2019.
2. Harry S. Truman Papers Staff Member and Office Files: Psychological Strategy Board Files (1951–1953).
3. Interview with Professor Merlyn Lossada on October 2, 2019.

Chapter 7

Foreign Aid for Media Development in the Digital Age

What started as early as the 19th century with resources from the new Republic of Haiti to support the emancipation of slaves in South America by providing Simón Bolívar with a printing press and money to set up a pro-independence and pro-abolition newspaper in Venezuela, has over the years developed into multiple efforts from around the world to project soft power and promote ideologies and geopolitics across the globe. This remains at the core of the relationship between the allocation of resources on the part of foreign governments and their efforts to project influence and power.

Monroe Price (2019) has placed media development efforts within the frame of actions coming from strategic communicators, such as the state, transnational corporations, and religions, which seek to foster support for their general positions around the world. He has suggested that these actions need to be understood within a framework that he refers to as "a market for loyalties" (Price, 2002b, 2019), which suggest that there are "sellers" who use history, dreams, and myths, which then they convert into power and wealth by using them to mobilize the "buyers" or citizens into embracing values and norms. In the case of the influence of foreign aid upon shaping journalism practice in the Global South, this framework can help explain why these resources are so important in fostering particular models and values around news gathering and news production.

However, as we have discussed in this book, even accounting for such a frame, we find a gradient of intentions and actions that present to us a rather more complex and, at times, hectic picture of what happens on the ground. We have seen examples of foreign aid toward media assistance being used to promote military coups as well as resources being allocated to foster investigative reporting capabilities that allow journalists to denounce tax evasion and political injustices from the very same donors who provided the aid in the first place. This is not to say that donor money is not central in defining the news agenda, as it has been robustly argued by some scholars, who have not only underpinned the importance of journalistic agency and contextual variables in the journalist-donor relationship but also have tried to explain the workings of donor power (Scott, Bunce, & Wright, 2017; Wright, Scott, & Bunce, 2019). Nevertheless, as these same authors have also acknowledged, we need to highlight too "the potential significance of contradictory dynamics" as well as to account for the fact that is a subject about which we still know very little; particularly when the donor resources are allocated to journalists and media outlets from the Global South. Hence, as useful as it is in many aspects, the notion of market for loyalties does not address completely some crucial aspects of the function of fostering particular models of journalism in the Global South.

Indeed, contrary to their counterparts in the North, media outlet recipients of foreign aid are often assigned particular functions, which justifies, to a great degree, the support. On the one hand, efforts toward media development almost always are linked to particular conceptions around nation-state building and more often than not tend to be linked to fostering diversity (Jones & Waisbord, 2010). To be sure, the combination of these two objectives is crucial to the efforts of exporting liberal democracy and the market-driven economy.

Let me be clear in this, the framework of market for loyalties is helpful in explaining a lot of how Western aid operates regarding media development and media assistance and, it is particularly useful in understanding agency and intentionality when there is a linear cultural and ideological relationship between donor and recipient. Nevertheless, it falls short from providing an equally sound explanatory framework for aid coming from other centers of power, which seen today are far less concerned with exporting models, values, or principles and instead are more interested on extending economic influence under the narrative of multilateralism.

The prime example of this—albeit not the only one—is the aid coming from China at an age where "socialism" is no longer an exportable ideal. China has nevertheless increased its donations at a geometrical rate over the past few years (Kitano & Harada, 2016; Vieira, 2019). China's practice of sending resources to neighboring countries goes back to the early 1950s, although some of this assistance does not fit neatly within a modern conception of overseas development assistance. This is because it was a response to the pressures of perceived US containment efforts and US foreign aid programs in Asia during the Cold War. In light of this, China launched its own self-described external assistance programs, which included military and food assistance to North Korea and Vietnam to support their struggles against US and French military forces, respectively, in the early 1950s (Cheng,

2019). More recently in 2018, China decided to restructure its foreign aid management system by establishing the China International Development Cooperation Agency (CIDCA), a bilateral aid agency that places particular focus on financially sustainable projects but that still prioritizes the advancement of China's diplomatic interests (Liao, Cheng, Harris, & Xu, 2018). The transformation of the Department of Foreign Aid of the Ministry of Commerce into the CIDCA had two purposes. On the one hand, it allowed it to provide aid based on commercial criteria rather than just political and diplomatic aims. On the other, it gave it more freedom and flexibility to operate as it effectively became a quasi-autonomous NGO (or quango).

Without a proper ideological model to export, foreign aid from China in the past two decades has been all about expanding markets and commercial interests rather than exporting values (Liao et al., 2018). This explains why so little investment has been made in media development compared to the United States, despite the fact that the overall ratios of assistance are similar between both countries. Here, we should highlight that the notion of "a market for loyalty" might be useful only to a certain degree as on the ground China is not really looking for a market to which to export its values or a particular political model nor even gain long-term loyalties from Third World countries. Instead, its efforts are directed to grasp new markets and gain a degree of political influence seem far more pragmatic than the ideological and cultural actions for hegemony that the United States sought in the post–World War II era. China might claim openly that it continues to fight imperialism, colonialism, and hegemonism but in practice its foreign aid efforts present a remarkable degree of pragmatism that merges political and economic interests in a project that responds to both domestic and international constraints, where the economy retains predominance over diplomacy (Vieira, 2019).

DIFFERENT STROKES

Despite the United States' historical uniqueness in the post–World War II era as a donor who exported a particular model of journalism that would go on to underpin liberal democracy and market economy, it had nevertheless very important overlaps and convergent elements with many European donors. Indeed, beyond the very distinctive characteristics and nature of Foreign Aid for Media Development between the United States, which has tended to fund more traditional journalism practices, and the Europeans that pivoted toward investing rather in a variety of creative projects and cultural formats, one cannot but observe the remarkable convergence between their programs in relation to their focus and approaches toward developing journalism as a political institution in the Global South.

There are some important overlaps and commonalities in relation to the United States and some European countries—particularly France, the Netherlands, Spain, and the United Kingdom. They present, for example, an important convergence in the way they have been directed over the years to create, develop, and assist media outlets. They all have also delivered an important amount of resources to support the education and training of journalists by means of scholarships, the organization of workshops and conferences, and providing resources and access to materials.

Over the years, countries such as Japan and Germany have played catch-up—although not in terms of the amounts spent by the United States—in relation to some of these approaches (Dreher, Nunnenkamp, & Schmaljohann, 2015; Manning & Malbrough, 2012). For example, since the 1980s, Japan has funded a series of media initiatives in Asia such as the Philippines, which is the third-highest Asian recipient of Japan's official development assistance (Pollard, 1996). There is also the case of Germany, which saw an important expansion of foreign aid toward media development and assistance since the same decade, particularly in places such as the North of Africa and the Middle East through direct government assistance and private organizations in order to promote democratization in those regions (Carapico, 2002).

Beyond important common trends, one must also mark some of the key features that seem to characterize these aid programs and which show distinctiveness between US and European approaches. If well, transatlantic comparisons provide important spaces of overlap, as we mentioned, no less certain is that they are different in a variety of ways. US aid has tended historically to place emphasis on supporting education rather than training with scholarships programs such as the Fulbright although there is an ample history of also funding directly and indirectly workshops, conferences, and a variety of events. In other cases, levels of transparency also show important divergent approaches. For example, foreign aid from certain donors is given to particular projects that go to tender while others do not, such as setting up a new newspaper in El Salvador (Salar & Lugo-Ocando, 2018).

US SUPREMACY

Beyond these emerging players in the world scene, the United States continues to lead by far Foreign Aid for Media Development and media assistance. This is not only in relation to the amounts given—where the United States is still by far the greatest donor—but also because it continues to dominate the scaffolding of international aid as it was its chief architect after the war. Since the 1970s, US foreign aid has tended to have a greater presence in Africa and Latin America, while the types of journalistic projects that are increasingly funded are mostly native digital ones. This is a departure from early Cold War assistance programs and covert support for legacy (traditional) news media outlets.

However, to imagine that the United States somehow provides organic support to Third World media that is quantifiably as robust and discernible to detail would be a mistake. Instead, US-sponsored media development programs are often fragmented and poorly funded overall, making up a tiny fraction of overall development spending. The amounts are fragmented and there is literally little coordination even within the donor countries. In the United States, there is an estimated $625 million spent on media development each year that comes from a variety of sources, which includes governments and private institutions (CIMA, 2019). Very few donor countries actually disclose how much money they allocate toward media development. This is without mentioning the fact that private funders only disclose occasionally what they provide toward media development. For example, we know that since 2003, Soros's Foundation has spent over $48 Million funding media organizations all over the world. Soros resources also go to fund other foundations in turn such as the Tides Foundation, which then make their own donations. All this based a very complex accounting system, which makes it almost impossible to account for what actually is given and who are all the recipients (Gainor, 2014). Other private donors are literally black boxes when it comes to disclosing how much money they provide to media projects in the Global South as it is not stated in any of their reports.

Hence, more research in this area is urgently needed considering the fact that the OECD recent reports showed that countries such as the United Kingdom aid spending in 2015 totaled 0.7 percent of gross national income, which was exceeded by only five countries: Denmark (0.85%), the Netherlands (0.75%), Norway (1.05%), Luxembourg (0.95%), and Sweden (1.4%). The OECD figures also showed that the largest development assistance donors by volume were the United States, the United Kingdom, Germany, Japan, and France. Aid flows from the thirty major international donors who make up the OECD's Development Assistance Committee totaled $131.4 billion (£107 billion) in 2015 (Quinn, 2017).

Having said this, the amount of money spent on media development is just a fraction of the overall development assistance resources that are allocated worldwide. The way the resources are allocated varies not only from donor to donor but also from recipient to recipient. However, and despite this variety in aims, intentions, and outcomes, we can point out to important common trends within the way most of this aid has been allocated.

The US foreign aid funding model toward media development projects and media assistance initiatives tends to undertake a top-down approach. This happens even when it is allocated to support grassroots projects. This is not to say that there is no consultation with those on the field. On the contrary, over the years, donors have gotten better at placing their ear to the ground and seeking advice and feedback from the end users. In so doing, the US-based Centre for International Media Assistance (CIMA), an initiative of the National Endowment for Democracy (B. Anderson)— which itself receives an allocation of resources from the US Congress in the form of a grant awarded through the US Information Agency—has set several criteria to understand how their own work can be assessed and evaluated.

One dimension is "effectiveness," which looks at how media development programs are designed and implemented. It examines what should be the tools used for diagnostics and evaluation and asks about the impact of media development interventions. The other dimension is "sustainability," which assesses the legal and political enabling environment for media and explores how can the media organizations they support achieve financial independence while fulfilling normative aspirations around standards of professionalism. However, studies around this point suggest that sustainability needs to be understood in a broader sense and indicate that perhaps too much focus has been placed on a particular interpretation of what it means (Requejo-Alemán & Lugo-Ocando, 2014). The other issue, as we have sufficiently discussed in this book, relates to the type of standards that have been disseminated and pushed. Finally, there is the dimension of "innovation" that assesses what are the contributions made by the donation in terms of new practices and helping the media landscape to change, while introducing new trends.

This analysis highlights the fact that there is a complex and very divergent structure of media aid architecture across the globe despite US dominance. It also suggests that media development and assistance efforts from the United States are mostly set up to promote democracy through alternative and non-collateral, bottom-up support (Brownlee, 2017). This underlines that the system of aid reflects different interests and degrees of engagement in order to gain political influence in particular regions or support specific objectives in particular conjunctures.

NATION BUILDING

By now it should be clear that the Foreign Aid for Media Development and assistance is a global phenomenon that has historically demonstrated its link with what today we call public diplomacy as well as having roots in colonialism and market expansion. We have also seen that it is not homogenous or even organic in its aims or outcomes. We can find public and privately funded efforts from governments and NGOs. Some have been deployed to support traditional forms of journalism while others work within specific remits.

In a very broad sense, we can argue that there are nation-building efforts and diversity efforts. Within the first, we find peace-building approaches in different parts of the world. Among them, for example, we find Lola Mora funded by the Dutch-based WorldCom Foundation, a nonprofit organization involved in the development of communication systems in Africa and Latin America. Lola Mora has managed to support and fund a series of projects around gender and social justice, which are produced in a variety of languages. In the Democratic Republic of the Congo, it has worked in the field of denunciation, information, and political pressure using telecommunications as exceptional tools to shorten distances and to be a speaker to alert local populations on the levels of danger and insecurity where they live. There is a whole universe of efforts that support peace-building journalism and which include, among many others, organizations such as the initiative for Media for Peace and Human Dignity developed by the Fondation Hirondelle, a Swiss nonprofit organization founded in 1995 that provides support for the defense of "rigorous and responsible journalism in contexts of conflict, post-conflict, humanitarian crisis or democratic transition."

Nation building has always been a central function of the media (B. Anderson, 2006 [1983]; Chasi & Rodny-Gumede, 2016; Price, 2002b) and as such journalism as a political institution was pivotal in helping to develop the foundations of the type of democratic ethos that cemented the United States. In the Global South, journalism has been seen as a potential source for accountability and social cohesion, which in a particular form has the possibility of supporting nation building. For example, Ahmed (2016) has argued that the notion of development journalism continues to have enduring relevance in Asia and Africa, particularly in post-conflict societies that are promoting nation building, this despite the fact that for some, the concept is outdated. Instead, he argues, that development journalism is relevant today in current political dilemmas such as those in places like Somalia where conflict has made literacy rates and overall capabilities recede.

There is a long history of foreign aid toward media development and media assistance in supporting nation building. It became particularly acute during the Cold War as new independent countries emerged in the international scenario while the big super powers were competing to secure their adherence to one or the other's orbit. This meant that a great deal of these resources allocated are so in order to make sure that journalism supported, in the case of the US and European government-led efforts, liberal democracy and market economy as the basic foundations for the newly created states. However, these ideological pressures do not come only from official donors but also from private ones such as foundations. In this last case, some research shows that digital-native news organizations sometimes pursue foundation funding even when the journalists within those organizations do not agree with those foundation's beliefs about journalistic practice:

> In other words, journalists working in newsrooms that are recipients of foundation funding may find themselves folding engaged journalism techniques into their news routines—whether they want to or not. The result is a situation where these foundations have arguably more control over news production processes than advertising [had in the past towards the old traditional legacy media]. (Ferrucci & Nelson, 2019, p. 53)

This view is shared by other experts who have argued that if well funding quality journalism and giving reporters the resources to carry out important work is critical, not less important is to remind ourselves that new financial model for news production is also changing approaches and practices toward coverage. Hence, argue these scholars, we need to follow best practices to ensure that direct funding of news content remains a source of strength for independent media of equal partnership and not a marriage of convenience exercising undue pressures upon journalists and their news agenda (Schiffrin, 2010, 2017).

Equally, the Soviet Union deployed during the Cold War similar systematic and orchestrated actions toward supporting a particular type of news media in places such as Cuba and Vietnam in ways it could cement the ideal of a socialist nation under one flag (Garcia-Santamaria, 2018; Parry, 1967). These other cases are also illustrations of the use of journalism for nation building, regardless of the reservations one can have with regard to the ideological stance or practices that they deployed. They were not really alternatives, as neither they were set to recognize and foster local-national forms of journalistic practices and news values. They were just other efforts to "modernize" these societies in the ideological terms of the socialist donors and bring them into their own ideological and market orbit within the context of the Cold War.

Although nation building is no longer the global priority it once was for media development and assistance, it remains nevertheless at the core of justifying foreign aid in certain parts of the Global South. Looking at a range of cases of intervention of USAID-sponsored fieldwork, Krishna Kumar (2006) has reminded us of the continued US efforts in places such as Afghanistan, Bosnia-Herzegovina, Central America, Indonesia, Russia, Serbia, and Sierra Leone and how international media assistance programs in these post-conflict areas remains important. Indeed, Foreign Aid for Media Development and assistance, particularly in relation to building up capabilities around journalism, remains particularly relevant in post-conflict areas.

However, it no longer tends to be directly managed by government agencies—although they are still the main players—but instead increasingly outsourced to third parties—most of them NGOs or Foundations—despite the continuous flow of government resources. In this sense, in a world where there is no longer any real ideological threat to the market economy—although still plenty against liberal democracy—the Western foreign aid supports the development of journalism as a political institution should be now conceived, within our analysis, more as part of the broader efforts to foster both capabilities and institutions that underpin democracy and by default promoting the free market economy.

It is important, perhaps, at this point to underline the fact that the nation-building function of foreign aid is, above all, a normative objective. In claiming so, donors claim that they are helping to build a stronger democracy (in the case of Western aid) or a fairer and socialist society (as in the case of the Soviet help in the past). These are by all means normative claims that were linked to the ideological stance of those who allocated resources toward media assistance and development. On the ground, one can observe that there is a persisting dichotomy between the stated objectives of promoting the creation of democratic states and the covert propaganda intentions to foster regime change (or support in some cases) that favors the donor country in terms of political influence and access to the market.

The dichotomy between normative claims and Realpolitik continues to be today—way after the end of the Cold War—at the very core of the tensions between government/private foundations claims around efforts to fund journalism and what they try to achieve in practice. It is as if there were a law of motion still steaming from the Cold War dynamics that continues to prevail in the world map even when no longer seems to make sense in the traditional terms in which it was originally designed and implemented. Nevertheless, they continue to be important as donations toward media aid and assistance from the West are have both a normative function—to improve journalism practice—and practical—as to help strengthen and spread the ideologies of liberal democracy and free market.

The function of journalism toward nation building can be argued explicitly and implicitly. In the first case, debates around journalism for development centered upon the role that news reporting should have in the Global South. For example, they key political leaders in countries, such as Indonesia, Malaysia, and Singapore argued that there were particular "Asian values" in the practice of journalism in their own countries, which demanded specific normative approaches. In these countries, they argued, the press should promote order to maintain social, cultural, and political values that a society upholds. They highlighted the importance of cultural values in determining what the press should be and do in society. Hence, the press should promote Asian values and underpin nation building, given the postcolonial setting and needs for development.

These explicit claims are today seen cynically by those who claim that there were nothing nut attempts to justify censorship and state control (Romano, 1998; Sparks, 2007) and broadly speaking, they are right to pinpoint so. However, they also need to be contextualized in the ideological propaganda struggle during the Cold War in the process of postcolonial efforts to bring about modernization in terms of market economy reforms. Hence, it is also possible to argue that the support to spread a Western model of journalism was also a nation-building effort that needs to be analyzed within the same context.

PROMOTING DIVERSITY

The second normative function of Foreign Aid for Media Development and for assistance efforts is to promote and foster diversity. One of the key arguments around this function is that a plurality of voices is a vital sign of a healthy democracy. Western-supported media initiatives are often guided by the need to address information scarcity. Stanislav Budnitskiy (2016) points out that this paradigm derives from the assumption that audiences have limited or no access to alternative sources of news and related information. This was the raison d'être during the Cold War for the establishment of BBC and Radio Free Europe shortwave Russian-language broadcasts, which provided some of the very few sources of information behind the Iron Curtain not censored by the Communist authorities. Although the media environment today is very different from the one we had in the 1970s, the rationale for recent media diplomacy initiatives remains similar, which is to fill the void created by domestic censorship and provide information that is arguably "otherwise unattainable."

Effort after effort from governments, multilateral institutions, and Third Sector organizations are almost entirely focused and justified by the push to promote "diversity." Promotion of media diversity is part of the so-called media democracy promotion and is a form of international development aid that is not always recognized (Ganter, 2018). Nevertheless, one can argue that efforts around Foreign Aid for Media Development and assistance are in most cases efforts to support liberal democracy in the way it is conceptualized in Western countries.

Some problems stem from this approach; one that sees the function of aid as promoting diversity. The very fact that in today's world, information is not only abundant but in fact overwhelming is a distinctive feature of the present. Contrary to the Cold War thesis, access to information is no longer the problem that it once was. Moroever as besides the most totalitarian regimes such as North Korea, absolute censorship is no longer possible as it once was. The problem of today seems rather to get audiences to pay attention to a particular source or piece of information instead of simply providing information as the main goal (Budnitskiy, 2016). State-sponsored censorship in the 21st century face obstacles that past censors and propagandists could never have imaged. The advent of the internet has given rise to the rapid and easy dissemination of information and has created the type of porosity that makes it impossible to close communication with the outside world. The way pre-digital dictatorial states operated in relation to censorship and propaganda is over. With very few exceptions, no dictator can today completely seal a society from the outside news or control to the point where little is allowed beyond direct or indirect influence of the propagandist is no longer possible.

Attempts from the government to control the flow of information through methods such as firewalls and deletion of posts as happens in countries such as China, and to a lesser degree in Russia, are now less likely to succeed. People have found ways to bypass censorship in a variety of ways. China's "Great Firewall" is bypassed and censored materials accessed on a routine basis. Hence, as some scholars have argued,

> In the age of instant information, marketing a regime or ideology demands a whole different set of policies and summons a new set of audience responses. When information borders no longer coincide with state borders, it becomes increasingly difficult for propagandists to make falsehoods believable and truths evadable. While citizens of illiberal governments are now able to be more aware of what is out there and what they can want, the growing wave of self-censorship becomes increasingly apparent. Simultaneously, nations attempt to champion their narrative against other ones in an increasingly globalized world. (Ma, 2016)

We live now in the age of "cultural chaos" (McNair, 2006) where information is widely available for those savvy enough to know how and where to find it and, how to use it. But the concept of "cultural chaos" also implies that this overload of information and widespread access to it has unintended consequences, including the dissemination of rumours, Fake News and all osrt of conspiracy theories that have come to distort public opinion. Indeed, the advent of the internet initially appeared to be a liberating force for good that assigned quasi-axiomatically a pro-democratic function for journalism as a political institution. By enhancing its ability to be a critical scrutineer, Fourth Estate and source of common knowledge for the public sphere would be strengthened. As Professor Brian McNair (2018) himself has suggested, today these same digital platforms are being utilized with great effect by the opponents of liberal democracy as tools that fuel and drive authoritarianism, surveillance, and the darkest ideological conflicts rather than just cultural democratization.

The other key element that we also need to bear in mind is that in the marketplace of foreign aid donors, there are many players. Hence, we should acknowledge that while foreign aid has been used in the past to support media diversity, which overall has been a positive outcome that brings about pluralism and healthy democratic debate not least through that we have also witnessed an age where the rise of pluralism has also meant an increase in populist rhetoric, post-truths, and hate speech to pre–World War II levels. In some countries, hate speech is deployed by grassroot and civic organizations (Lazaridis & Veikou, 2017) and has been funded from abroad. It is worth noticing that funding for media projects comes in all shapes and forms.

The hedge fund billionaire Robert Mercer, for example, has funded a string of media projects that are set to underpin nationalism (Swenson, 2018) including $3 million to support the US-based Media Research Center, a media watchdog group run by conservative activist Brent Bozell (Levine, 2017). In this sense, this rainbow of objectives and ideological aims can make diversity also be a true Pandora's Box, with no guarantee that liberal freedom would come out at the end.

Equally, we find a world network of media outlets, particularly broadcasters, that have been created by religious organizations. They extend from radio and television networks funded by the Evangelical and Catholic churches (Lugo-Ocando et al., 2010; Schultze & Woods, 2009) to faith-based organizations buying existing news provisions, such as the case of the News World Communications, an international news media company founded in 1976 by Unification Church leader Sun Myung Moon, which bought in the year 2000 the United Press International news agency. These religious have extended their operations to the Global South and funded media outlets and operation in Africa, Asia and Latin America. These projects have their own faith-based ethos while providing news provisions in their programs.

The second issue relates to the market forces that themselves were once argued to guarantee freedom as that associated with the market. Indeed, as I have argued in other parts of the book, there is a long-standing philosophical tradition that argues that freedom of the media is grounded firmly upon private property and the market. This tradition underpins the optimism and self-assuredness of Western liberalism that assume that media freedom would gradually give room to pluralism and media democracy and that a healthy and robust market for ideas is the best way to achieve this. However, over the years, it has become harder to sustain confidence in traditional pillars of media independence as media systems in the Global North became dominated by runaway commercialism, clientelism, and partisanship (Waisbord, 2019,

p. 55) all marked by ownership concentration and corporate interests defining the news agenda.

The assumption that one can promote diversity by means of strengthening the market does not hold water in many cases. Mostly as competition often results in converging news agenda and over-focuses on particular beats and issues. Although it might seem to some counterintuitive, diversity and competition are in many cases mutually exclusive. Pierre Bourdieu (1997) pointed out some years ago when referring to television journalism that competition, far from automatically generating originality and diversity, it often tends to favor instead the uniformity of supply. By this, one could argue that because the mainstream news media traditionally has had to compete for the same markets—so as to be able to turn audiences into exchangeable commodities—then it has also had to follow similar agendas and produce similar content. Hence, competition might improve the quality of the news content as presumably people will consume the "best" ones but in no way does this mean that this content will be different across the front pages or screens that reach the public.

One of the distinctive features of news media in the past decades was their investigative practices and they scoops that they were able to produce thanks to them. However, they were among the first casualties of shrinking newsrooms, particularly in light of decreasing resources, smaller and fragmented audiences, and the redirection and increased concentration of ad revenues toward social media and search engines. The market in this case did not foster great journalism but instead in stream most of the media into a spread of cost-saving/cost-cutting madness that wiped entire segments of the press and reduced the capability of the media landscape to cover effectively society (Chyi & Tenenboim, 2019; Nielsen, 2015; Picard, 2008). This phenomenon has been taking place across the globe at different scales.

In the Global South, investigative reporting has also had to deal with similar challenges. However, their situation is aggravated by the fact that news media outlets operate within smaller and less robust markets, face greater political pressures and censorships, and lack a sufficiently strong institutional framework to protect them, given the legacy of past dictatorships and colonial rule. It is because of this, that Foreign Aid for Media Development and assistance toward the South tends to allocate resources to fund enterprises where not only politics but also market failure makes these initiatives unviable in many places in the Global South.

One example of this is the Latin American radio network Fe y Alegría, run by the Jesuit order of the Catholic Church. Latin America at large lacks the resources and, in most cases, the political will to develop and sustain PSB in the way it has developed in Europe. However, Fe y Alegría has been able to deliver an alternative model of PSB by means of the Instituto Radiofnico Fe y Alegra (IRFA), which provides what by all standards can be described as PSB (Lugo-Ocando et al., 2010). This organization, as with many others, are dependent upon donation from abroad and they fill a gap that is left by the market failure to provide similar media services. Mónica Marchesi, former news producer, points out:

> Over the years, our organization was devoted to produce news from the ground about what we called "the popular." That is, news about those excluded and left behind. In fact, our motto was, "we start where the roads end" signaling that we cover the places and areas that had no roads or services. Where the poorest lived. As you can assume, that is not a news beat that attracts many adverts. We used to get resources from the central and local government but also through the Jesuits donations from abroad. This allowed us to do the type of journalism that no one else was doing.[1]

Subsidizing media initiative is the nature of foreign aid, hence by default one must assume that these resources support media initiatives that are not necessarily viable as commercial enterprises or that at least need seed funding to kickstart. However, it also creates the dilemma of supporting what in many cases are media projects that are not sustainable in time. To be sure, sustainability has been a central focus in current research around Foreign Aid for Media Development and assistance (Requejo-Alemán & Lugo-Ocando, 2014; Tietaah et al., 2018).

This focus has brought into question the ability of these media initiatives to survive beyond the end of the funding from the donors, which in some cases is limited. In her own research on this topic, Clare Cook (2016) points out that the media in restrictive environments—mostly operating in politically closed regimes—often rely on media development funding to survive. Yet, they are increasingly expected to diversify revenue as they wean themselves off grant dependency. This demand to generate revenues while continuing journalism in some of the most challenging environments globally is an uphill task for some of them. Her empirical data points to important tensions that call for pragmatic approaches by those leading these outlets. This brings, in turn, present important ethical dilemmas to the values and norms that motivated the creations of these outlets in the first place, which are left with choices that oscillate between entrenched dependence on grant funding, commercial reluctance, and commercial reconciliation with the market.

This is a common problem of many other areas of funding for foreign aid where development projects are unable to subsist without the resources (or in some cases without the leadership) of the donors (Cooke & Kothari, 2001). Nevertheless, in terms of assessment and evaluation of these projects, the mindset continues to be one that prioritizes the market logics in order to support financial sustainability in the medium and longer term (Abbott, 2019; Foster, 2019). This is despite the fact that many of these same voices recognize the need for a wide supportive framework that allows the foreign aid-funded news organizations to be sustainable in the long run. Nevertheless, the fulfillment of organizational and financial sustainability of local media organizations needs to be part of any donor exit strategy (Foster, 2019; Howard, 2003).

On the ground, there seems to be a different perspective. In this sense, Craig LaMay has pointed out that journalists in developing countries have come to understand that neither political efforts in the face of assistance nor the market left to its own devices are able to support good journalism,

> The irony of this, as both development theory and free expression theory recognize, is that neither markets or governments work very well in the absence of reasonable complete, accurate and timely information. So, though the "public interest" may not be susceptible to definition in economic terms, for journalists the thrust of the thing is straightforward: It is all about serving the information needs of the listeners and viewers so that the actions they take as citizens have real meaning. How to sustain this mission is the problem. (LaMay, 2009, p. 273)

Research in the field shows that there is increasing preoccupation from the donor organizations with measuring success of the funded media projects due to additional requirements from their own constituency regarding accountability, transparency, and effectiveness. The problem is how to measure success with such intangible aims such as democratizing, diversifying, and enhancing freedom of speech? This is a riddle that is commonly faced by Third Sector organizations operating in the field without a possible resolution in sight (Easterly, 2002; Requejo-Alemán & Lugo-Ocando, 2014). First, because the aims and objectives of the donor's constituencies are not always as clear as they could be, leading to unmanaged expectations. Second, because the nature and development itself of each project once it takes off might distance itself from what it was originally supposed to be. Third, because cutting off aid for any of the above reasons could be seen as interference from the donors or meddling with the project itself—something that donors nowadays try by all means to avoid. So, for the accountability of how the money was used and some very basic quantitative indicators that can be provided, there is very little that realistically one could expect to be "measured." In addition, the idea itself that "success" of one of these projects can be determined by its ability to financially sustain itself beyond donors' resources is problematic as these projects were funded in the first place given because of the market's failure to make these projects viable (Salar & Lugo-Ocando, 2018).

SUPPORTING INVESTIGATIVE REPORTING

Foreign aid has been allocated in recent times to support journalism initiatives that carry out investigative reporting. This is particularly the case as the entire news media landscape across the globe has been supporting less and less this type of news reporting over the past decades (Houston, 2010; Starkman, 2014; Tong & Sparks, 2009). The main rational for such focus lays down to several factors but two are perhaps the most influential. First, the actual market gap and potential impact that this genre of journalism practice can have upon the wider society. Second, the cost-benefit and efficiency that investment in these types of projects present to the already-present and potential donors in terms of supporting journalism.

Indeed, it is here where donor countries and organizations see they can make a greater contribution toward building up journalism capabilities in the Global South. In Latin America, for example, this funding has supported investigative nonprofit journalism initiatives directed toward at exposing corruption and abuses of power. In so doing, the resources allocated by donors have allowed the creation and expansion of digital-native news organizations that foster investigative journalistic practice that no longer are possible to undertake in the traditional newsrooms based on the legacy-traditional media, given the lack of resources, and in many cases, of political will.

The gathering and dissemination of news based on investigative reporting among these initiatives is often conducted by nonprofit small organizations, which compromise a few veteran and experienced reporters with more junior and not that experience young recently graduated or even students. These small organizations of journalists who have come to work together, creating research-based centers for investigative journalism, tend to operate mostly in the capitals of these countries and be funded by international donors. Such sites are part of a growing phenomenon in Latin American journalism, which was estimated to include by 2018 some 668 non-corporate, digital-native news projects from Latin America (Warner & Iastrebner, 2018). Some hope that the fact that these emerging forms of news media are slowly but inexorably establishing more and more loyal audiences would allow them to be self-sustainable in the future. SembraMedia, a nonprofit organization that is mapping these initiatives across the region, has built a directory that includes for-profit corporations as well as nonprofit organizations, which encompasses 45 percent of the directory (Warner & Iastrebner, 2018). César Batiz, one of Venezuela's leading investigative journalists and currently the director of Poderopedia and El Pitazo, two of the best-known sites in that country for investigative reporting, points out that funding comes in multiple forms.

> We do a lot of our budget from crowdfunding. Some of that comes from abroad and you can say it is part of the support we receive. Without this support it would be impossible to do investigative reporting. We are a nonprofit organization and we do not operate on an advertisement or subscription basis. We strictly depend on donations that come from home and abroad from individuals and organisations.[2]

This is one of the key characteristics of foreign aid toward media, which today come in all shapes and forms. In this book, however, I have deliberately placed emphasis on government foreign aid but I have also made it clear that today this is highly fragmented and distributed through third parties. In this sense, the US-based CIMA is one of the leading funders; however there are a variety of other funders.

One example is the Konrad-Adenauer-Stiftung (KAS), a German political party foundation associated with, but independent of, the center-right Christian Democratic Union (CDU). The foundation has seventy-eight offices and runs programs in over 100 countries, many of which are in Latin America and are directed toward supporting investigative reporting. The KAS is largely financed by German federal and land government funds and some consider it to be a think tank rather than a foundation (Weilemann, 2017). In Latin America, KAS has funded a variety of projects around news media that not only include investigative reporting but also academic research around the news media itself reporting issues such as poverty (Kitzberger & Pérez, 2008). As one of the grant administrators points out:

> We are constantly seeking projects that strengthen democracy. We know this can be problematic to many as it might be seen this as interfering with domestic issues. However, we in this office are all nationals of this country and our job is to support initiatives that will bring more and better information to the public. We do not tell them what to do but only review applications and then fund projects that can help to promote this objective.[3]

These days funding for media development and assistance is a wide and very diverse landscape. Funders are spread and funding itself comes in a variety of ways from direct resources allocated for day-to-day operations through contributions toward particular investigative projects. In all, the landscape is far more complex and distinctive these days than it ever has been. In a way, that is an important and positive aspect as there is far more diversity in the field—and projects that in the past would not get funding are more likely to get it today. The downturn is that the field has become increasingly opaque and confusing. Transparency about funding and lack of accountability to the wider society with regard to who is paying for what continues to be a big challenge.

Beyond this, a very important question remains unanswered so far. Why are these resources allocated to these news organizations rather than to the traditional legacy media outlets, such as national and local newspapers and broadcasters, which not only have better infrastructure but are currently craving for additional resources for their newsrooms? To answer this question, it is important to look at the problematic history of Foreign Aid for Media Development in the Global South and the tainted reputation that it brings with it. Few news editors or producers working in the traditional legacy news media in the Global South would be likely to accept these contributions openly, moreover as it can mean additional censorship or even prosecution from their own governments as they could be labeled as "foreign agents," a practice that is increasingly more common among many governments across the globe (Roth, 2019; Sonne & Fassihi, 2012).

This situation, nevertheless, seems to be changing to some degree as more and more traditional newspapers in the Global North are accepting support from international donors. *The Guardian* newspaper in London, for example, today carries out content on its online platform that is sponsored by organizations such as the Bill and Melinda Gates Foundation. Such support has made more visible, for example, particular news beats that in the past did not receive as much attention from the newsrooms in the legacy media outlets (Lugo-Ocando & Nguyen, 2017; Scott, 2014; Scott et al., 2017). One can expect that if this trend continues, it will be caught up, at some point, by the legacy media in the Global South but perhaps only in some particular news beats (those that are less problematic such as science or general social issues such as poverty).

However, this is not the only reason as to why Foreign Aid for Media Development and assistance is channeled to these new digital-native organizations. Donors also want to improve diversity and plurality and to do so, they have to densify the composition of the media ecology. As one official from a donor organization operating in Latin America told me:

> Our mission is not only to help improve journalism in this country but to help the development of capabilities that are just not there for one reason or the other. The traditional news media, and I say this openly, has had it chance to produce these types of news reporting over the years. In some cases, they have done a tremendous job in doing so but in most cases they didn't. The organization we support here is far more proactive in setting the news agenda and has far less constraints in determining what subjects they investigate. Yes, they are subject to political pressures but they can move faster to cover issues and subjects that the old newspapers cannot or won't cover.[4]

There are also issues around competition. Indeed, the same interviewee explains that as these digital-native projects are set with donor assistance resources in the first place, there is no issue when it comes to other players seen this as giving privilege to one over the other.

> I mean, it is unlikely that a major newspaper would approach us to request funding to do investigative reporting. They are commercial enterprises after all . . . they, I assume, would be reluctant to do this. However, if one did so, let's say. I mean hypothetically, let's say. And the word got out, it might be the case the other would criticise this and see us as supporting unfair competition. I mean, another newspaper would perhaps say why are you subsidizing that other newspaper? You see. I mean, it would be a difficult scenario for us having to justify one or the other. With the news organization we currently support here there is no problem as they are not perceived to be a commercial competition, at least not in the traditional sense.[5]

This strategy of supporting digital-native initiatives rather than the legacy news media outlets has had a degree of success and in countries such as Mexico and Peru, digital-natives have been at the forefront of setting the news agenda and exposing wrongdoings in those societies (Harlow & Salaverría, 2016; Requejo-Alemán & Lugo-Ocando, 2014). However, this lack of engagement with the wider media landscape has also limited in some cases the reach and potential of the works that have been carried out. This has led to some suggesting changes to the way the foreign aid is allocated toward supporting investigative reporting. For example, the US-based "Fund for Investigative Journalism" provides competitive grants and fellowships for investigative projects that can go to up to $10,000 to cover out-of-pocket expenses, such as travel, document collection, equipment rental, and small stipends, as part of the general budget. The resources are provided by the Scripps Howard Foundation, which so far has allocated over $4.5 million worldwide. This scheme suggests a process of tender and far more accountability and transparency but is not perfect, according to others:

> Yes, we could perhaps go to a grant scheme in which both legacy media and digital native compete for funding to carry out investigative reporting. However, this will defeat two of our donor objectives. Firstly, it would not necessarily contribute to greater pluralism and diversity in the media landscape and secondly, if the money goes to the legacy media then it does not really contribute with supporting new capacities or training new generations of journalists because simply that is not the way that the traditional media works.[6]

This last answer also suggests a wider issue with foreign aid donors; the fact that they see themselves as agents of change. Indeed, on most donors' websites one can find phrases such as that they are there to help "transform" the lives of people or contribute to "changing society." This change, of course, more often than not translates into inducing particular values that replicate and underpin forms and practices of journalism as they are conceived in the Global North.

NOTES

1. Interview with Mónica Marchesi on July 21, 2019.
2. Interview with César Batiz on May 10, 2019.
3. Interview with officer of an NGOs. Identity withheld at request from the interviewee.
4. Interview with an official from a donor organization. Identity withheld at the request of the interviewee on March 12, 2019.
5. Interview with an official from a donor organization. Identity withheld at the request of the interviewee on March 12, 2019.
6. Interview with an official from a donor organization. Identity withheld at the request of the interviewee on March 12, 2019.

Chapter 8

Shaping Values and Practices

The greatest historical contribution toward media development made by the allocation of foreign aid has been to establish a framework of values and news cultures that have helped standardize journalism practice in the Global South in ways that are ideologically and culturally convergent with those set in the Global North. The prevalence of a "common sense language" that has come to define news narratives and discourses together with axiomatic assumptions about what truth are, without doubt, a fundamental contribution of decades of funding toward individual journalists and collective news organizations in former colonial parts of the world.

Having said that, despite the fact that the process of standardization became one of homogenization in relation to practices and aesthetics of journalism, the exporting of a particular model of news production was somehow contested both by existing native forms of communicating news and by external ideological competitors to the ideal of liberal democracy and the market. However, the collapse of the Soviet Union with its propaganda machinery meant the end of global ideological competitors to the ideal of a liberal type of journalism that today prevails as the fundamental paradigm across the globe.

In normative terms, recent surveys among journalists suggest that they aspire to follow a particular way of doing journalism (Hanitzsch, 2016; Hanitzsch et al., 2011; Mellado et al., 2012). One that is often defined by the notion that journalism should be objective, impartial, and factual to be able to tell the truth. However, these same studies also suggest that not even these set of broad normative aspirations are monolithic nor homogenous. There is a range of complexity in the aspirational professional values across the globe and a set of distinctive grammars (Das, 2012; Edeani, 1993; Gloria, 2000; Wasserman, 2017). This is partly because the particular journalism model that was disseminated and at times imposed had always to face a great degree of amalgamation, challenge, and contestation from both local and international forces that shaped the specific way in which journalism as a political institution and journalism as a social practice came to be in each particular place.

Consequently, the self-assigned watchdog role of journalists, which has traveled far beyond well-established liberal democracies, presents important gaps between professional ideals and actual reporting on the ground, which is particularly wide in transitional countries (Mellado & Van Dalen, 2017). This gap between normative aspirations and practice also suggests, as it has also been discussed here, important caveats within the recipients of foreign aid. It also underlines the existence of issues and circumstances that make journalistic practice distinctive in these places as reporters respond in unique ways to their own challenges. To analyze these responses and acknowledge that there are different ways of bringing news to the people is crucial in a moment in which the profession is undergoing tremendous challenges and experimenting structural changes. As James Wahutu from New York University's Media, Culture, and Communication points out when referring to Africa,

> This is not to suggest that media organizations in these countries have cracked the code. Instead, it's about recognizing that there is useful knowledge about how to work under hostile regimes in African media markets. It's about moving away from the "we are the best" bubble of journalism that has existed in American and British media for a long time. It's about having the humility to learn from others in the pursuit of being good stewards of this thing we call democracy. (Wahutu, 2019)

Normative aspiration versus practice is not the only gap that we find when it comes to the function of foreign aid in fostering a particular model of journalism. The other important gap to be explored is between intentions from donors and outcomes from recipients of aid, which provides a different vector of analysis.

For example, a lot of the efforts have been placed to avoid "media capture," which is the ability of certain governments to consolidate power by expanding their control over the media system. In response to this, several donors have made funding available to strengthen the ability of the news media on the ground to carry on reporting beyond the need to depend on official advertisement and in the face of government pressures. Nevertheless, the result of this has not always been necessarily a greater diversity of outlets but perhaps the creation of specific niche ones.

This other gap can shape—or contribute to shape—mainstream journalism practice in the Global South. This is because this other gap between initial intentions and final outcomes has been historically determined by social and political contexts in each case and not by a particular deontology or professional aesthetics.

Overall, the outcomes have been mixed and the initial aims of donors have not always landed on their feet or met the initial expectations. Rather, the outcomes of these efforts have produced a variety of cases, which in some circumstances have even gone against the donors' set of interests or presented scenarios and outcomes completely unexpected.

In this sense, research suggests that there are important distinctions between what happens with the resources allocated in the Global North and those provided to develop and assist media organizations and journalists in the Global South. While there seems to be indication of undue influence upon recipients in the West itself (Scott et al., 2017; Wright et al., 2019) other evidence in the South is not that conclusive (Requejo-Alemán & Lugo-Ocando, 2014). This is not to say that donors do not exercise influence as they always do in one way or the other, even if this is by means of changing values and approaches within the news cultures of the recipient societies. Instead, we are reminded of the complexity and diversity in the field once we take a closer look at expectations versus outcomes.

The other question that remains to be addressed is about the ability of these aid efforts not only to shape journalism in the Global South but actually to hinder the potential to development of alternative ways of understanding and doing news in these same societies. This is, paradoxically, something that runs against the normative aim of foreign aid to promote diversity. If the current focus of aid is to foster diversity, then one could expect that resources allocated should go into promoting a variety of media outlets and practices. The fundamental issue is to define what is understood by each side as "diversity." The North and South have had, historically speaking, very different ideas of what media diversity means on the ground. The notion of diversity in the West is one strongly linked to the ideal of free market of ideas and competition among privately owned mainstream media organizations—although at times with the participation of public service broadcasters to correct market failures.

In the South, on the other hand, mainstream media outlets have for decades exercised oligopolies for news and information, given the constraints of the market and the limitations of the institutional and political framework to support a free press hence diversity means instead the possibility of inclusion of voices from below. In this sense, the Global South perspective of diversity, to cite Gayatri Spivak (2010 [1988]), relates to the ability of the "subaltern classes" to speak and represent themselves—not in terms of their ability to speak in itself but rather regarding the possibility of being heard by those in power. This would mean widening the spaces and strengthening the capabilities for the multiple voices that exist in a given society to be heard. That can only happen by providing not only additional channels—as foreign aid has done by multiplying media outlets through the allocation of resources—but also making these channels really alternative in terms of their aesthetics and formats.

In most cases, aid has often been allocated under a very traditional liberal approach, one that still focuses on voices and agendas that are already present in the public sphere. It has contributed to adding channels but not in making them really alternative and distinctive in terms of forms and aesthetics. Community-based journalism cannot happen if the formats are imposed in terms that replicate the ones in the North rather than allowing its own grammar to be deployed. One can argue that it is not so much the nature of the resources that have been allocated but both agency and intentionality within particular ideological contexts that have come to determine the outcome and nature of the aid provided.

CARRY-ON VALUES

Having said that, we also need to acknowledge that if well foreign aid can be pursued for altruistic reasons, neither government nor donor can sustain these types of investment in the long term without evidence that it somehow benefits its own society and interests (Price, 2019, p. 20). Hence, Foreign Aid for Media Development and assistance is ultimately a hegemonic exercise for power. One for which the promotion and dissemination of values and normative aspirations was always intended to foster a particular model of making news that, in turn, reflected the wider ideological commercially driven Western construct.

Consequently, aid allocation in this field has been part of consistent effort to bring about universality to key journalism values, such as objectivity, impartiality, and fairness. In this book, I have argued that at the end, journalistic objectivity—as other elements of the professional ideology in news reporting—was not just an occurrence that floated from above and then was embraced bellow. Instead, it was a norm that developed by assimilation and contestations as a quest for credibility and authorial control over "truth" and in contraposition to external forces. It was one forged against the backdrop of the advances made by the proletariat, other subaltern classes and groups during the struggles that dominated the 20th century, which at times used the news media to agitate and organize the masses.

The efforts of "domestication"—or co-option—of journalism as a political institution in the Global South were carried out by promoting a particular deontology and aesthetics of journalism, which pushed forward the market ideology. To be sure, this was a model that was defined by a professional ideology that reflected the principles of free market principles, private property, and that are nowadays associated with liberal democracy (Steel, 2013). This model, as we have seen, was exported across the globe—at least partially—thanks to foreign aid. It met, nevertheless, resistance and competition from existing local practices and other international centers of power and ideology.

Today, citizen journalists in Africa—to give an example—show at times a clear antiauthoritarian edge, marked antipathy toward government regulation and most see themselves as subject to the same ethics that guide traditional journalism from the West; a deontology marked by neutrality and impartiality to tell the truth (Mutsvairo, Columbus, & Leijendekker, 2012). Nevertheless, the same journalists who appear convergent in many regards have very distinctive understanding of what truth is and a distinctive deontology on the ground when it comes to facing day-to-day realities in their own societies.

The type of journalism that we practice in the Global South is therefore a chimeric creature that is product of geopolitical forces, class struggles, and national-individual tensions and undertones that shaped how we make news today in that part of the world. The fact that our journalists have to write taking cover because of the daily bullets of the gangs around where they live or having to produce stories in countries where there are effectively no institutional frameworks to protect them—having, therefore, to negotiate every single story with the subjects they interview and in many cases compromise—does not make them less of a journalist.

Under these circumstances, the norm of "objectivity" and its signaling of detachment from opinion and value judgment has for too long stood as a measuring rule to set apart professional news reporters in the North from those in the South. This artificial distinction is a legacy of the counter-revolutionary efforts to confront the propaganda efforts from the Soviet Union and should be recognized for what it has been: a rhetorical strategy of hierarchical power to dominate truth in a world that has been for over a century deeply divided in ideological, political, and economic terms.

Yes, journalism in the Global South is a hybrid outcome of the age of Enlightenment, a historical period that itself provided for enormous contradictions and elements for contestations. Moreover, as those living in the Global South at the time experienced this period in Dickensian terms. While for many white male elites in Europe, they were best of times, as it brought an age of wisdom, reason, light, and as spring of hope, for most in the South, it was the winter of despair that brought colonial destruction, slavery, and death.

Indeed, journalism in the South grew up in the orphanage of a schizophrenic political liberalism that claimed universal rights for white European men while enslaving the entire African continent and killing millions of its citizens in colonizing wars. As news reporting in the Global South grew up, it was later adopted by the abusive foster father of the Cold War. However, and despite all these abuses, our own neglect and manipulated daughter has grown up to gain her own place in history. It is a history that has to be yet told. So far, our daughter has written hard news stories using the 5WH and Invert Pyramid techniques for powerful newspapers, international news agencies, and global media conglomerates that have served over the years, good causes but also the most murderous dictators (Alvear & Lugo-Ocando, 2016; McChesney, 2010). Nonetheless, journalism in the South has also raised its voice against injustices committed against the Bolivian miners by means of the radio waves in a local radio station (Edeani, 1993).[1] The fact that scholars or practitioners in the North decide, or not, to call one journalism and not the other, is irrelevant, as both are part of our own very own grammar and history of news.

In a story that recognizes that even in those cases in which projects like those mentioned earlier had at some point support from abroad, they nevertheless developed in most cases their own standards for autonomy and deontology and managed to provide their communities with an alternative agenda. This is because the history of Foreign Aid toward Media Development and assistance is not linear nor its impact has been one sided, given all the counterflows and contestations across history.

WRITING ITS OWN STORY

To write its own story, journalism in the Global South needs to come to terms with the fact that the normative aspirations it upholds do not belong to her. They belong instead to an age and place where white man went to conquer, steal, rape, and enslave in the name of civilization while waging great wars that killed millions and threatening with nuclear annihilation. A civilization that claimed to be objective and scientific in the way it understood the world product of the Enlightenment while, at the same time and paradoxically, using that same scientific rationale to justify and perpetrate the most atrocious and unspeakable crimes to the people of the South (Losurdo, 2014).

Enrique Dussel in his critique of the Cartesian philosophy, upon which modern scientific thinking was built and journalism is still inspired, has argued that the ideals of objectivity, neutrality, and distancing of the object of the study are deeply flawed. He rejects the supposed neutrality that characterizes the "quantitative indeterminacy of any quality" since—he argues—that it is in reality nothing more than the point of view of the white, European male for whom things are white and black (Moraña, Dussel, & Jáuregui, 2008). Santiago Castro-Gómez (2007, p. 83) goes further to define Cartesian ideals as the "zero-point hybris" to refer to an epistemic model in which the observer observes the world from an unobserved observation platform, in order to generate a true and out of all observation doubt. For him, modern science is built on the myth of the zero point of observation with which it pretends to resemble God. It is a hybris in which insolent mortals want to be like the gods but without having the capacity to be them, he adds.

The influence of Cartesian philosophy has been central to the normative claims of journalism in the West (Davis, 2010; Hearns-Branaman, 2016). It was a philosophy erected as an epistemic model and canon of hegemonic thinking from the 18th century onward and one that would come to also define newsgathering and dissemination, not because of the power of the ideas, but because of the gun power of the cannons and bayonets of the successive empires. Indeed, as the European thought was imposed, knowledge and epistemologies of the colonized peoples were inferiorized and displaced (Appadurai, 2006; Dabashi, 2015). This was a systematic and orchestrated strategy of conquest that must be understood from the triangulation of all the elements that enabled colonial power to be fully exercised. Castro-Gómez (2007) calls it the strategy of conquest through epistemological violence. One that sought to impose the privilege of the white, male, European, and Christian in all aspects of life. Let us not forget that time after time the conqueror justified his conquest by arguing "objective" conditions of underdevelopment and lack of civility (Fitzgerald, 2007; Tharoor, 2018) that was "needed" to be resolved with the civilizing mission of the occupying empire (or in more modern times, thanks the "natural" modernizing forces of the market).

Journalism's professionalism is deeply embedded to this Cartesian philosophy. Hence, it has become an activity in which the observer pretends to observe from a point zero; one of assumed detachment and neutrality. The hegemonic positioning of Western journalism implied subsequently the minorization of the knowledge produced by other interpretative communities in the South and the disappearance and exclusion of the knowledge they created. News became what the new model said it ought to be and discourses and narratives started to gravitate around what the frames of the new model imposed. Agendas, news beats, and foremost issues were co-opted by a new professional dynamic that constantly tries to standardize approaches and practices under the umbrella of professionalization. Ramón Grosfoguel (2011), perhaps hyperbolically, refers to this as the process of "the recurrent genocide of native and local epistemologies by the West." Despite this hyperbole, we all should acknowledge that there is a lot of truth in this.

Journalists are an "interpretative community"—as Barbie Zelizer reminds us (1993, 2009)—and, it is one that constantly creates and circulates knowledge (Bødker, 2015; Donsbach, 2014). This is true for those working in the Global North as well as their counterparts in the South. However, not all knowledge is recognized or circulated equally. Normative aspirations and practices deployed by journalists in the North have become standard to which the "others" have to adhere (very similar to what also happens in the global academia). While experiences and contributions from the North have historically been used to shape the standards of professional practice, not enough is done to feedback from the Global South. As James Wahutu (2019) has pointed out:

> It's time for media organizations [in the West] to realize that the terrain has shifted, and they are no longer at the pinnacle of journalism holding political elites to account. I hope they realize the necessity of borrowing a leaf from journalists in regions such as Africa. What media organizations and journalists are going through now has been the reality for African organizations since Nnamdi Azikiwe's West African Pilot and Thomas Mboya and Kwame Nkrumah's elucidations of what it meant to be a postcolonial journalist.

Journalism in the Global South operates today under a preset but contested moral order that inherited from the emergence of Europe and later the United States as rulers of the world. This was an age in which cultural hegemony as we understand it today became to be. It was during this period that the standards of journalism as a political institution were set and as such it defined the model of professional practices that would be later exported to the South, partly, thanks to foreign aid. Nevertheless, the disseminating and imposition of this model was to be a contested enterprise; what would be born from these tensions was something distinctive and unique.

HYBRID PRESENTS AND FUTURES

If well, some will still find the burden of evidence around the thesis of multiple points of emergence for journalism grammars somehow unpersuasive, I think that there is enough indication to create the necessary burden of doubt as to question the notion that the United States "created" journalism's grammar as we know it today in the South. What most likely happened, in my view, was an attempt to impose a particular grammar by means of orchestrated cultural expansion and nation-building efforts to promote market-driven postcolonial settings. All this, while pre-existing forms of news reporting in the Global South where either offset or became hybrid manifestations of the tensions created by clash between assimilation and contestations to these very same efforts of imposition.

Consequently, journalism in the Global South presents formats, styles, and approaches, which are unique and distinctive, regardless of repeated attempts to standardize it in the frame of a commonsense language that saw no truth beyond "objective facts" and that rarely recognized existing structure, culture or history in the way that it narrated news stories. In the face of this, the South has constantly invented and reinvented news and storytelling, by incorporating its own interpretation of how to carry out the quest for justice on its own terms. Yes, journalism in the South continues to aspire to an elusive ideal of professionalism marked by objectivity, impartiality, and independence, but down on the ground, it practices and embraces very distinctive aesthetics and deontology to those in the West.

At times, it is a journalism of accommodation, survival, and resistance—as during the military juntas—at others it is the only voice of the excluded as reflected in the news songs in Creole of Radio Enriquillo in Haiti, the Bolivian miners' radio or the prose of Palagummi Sainath in India. These distinctive voices have provided evidence that journalism has particular and distinctive grammars. In the Global South, there are indeed nationals and local, which developed in parallel from tensions and clashes between the external impositions for standardization and the resistance to them from below. Indeed, as José Marques de Melo has argued when referring to journalism in Brazil as a modern enterprise, "journalism is a universal phenomenon, but it is anchored in national territories" (Marques de Melo, 2009).

For all the globalization that modernity brought about into journalism's history, these grammars are, at the end of the day, our very own national grammars. They have been invented and reinvented in many places while being developed simultaneously across the globe. The grammars of journalism in the Global South are, needless to say, diverse and distinctive. They incorporate rich cultures and traditions that reflect historical convergence, overlaps, tensions, and struggles. This is in fact the main common character in the Global South that there is not one but an infinite number of grammars. In this sense, in places such as India, truth does not mean facts but justice while in my own home country, Venezuela, recognizing that there are many truthful versions and interpretations that describe the same events and people that we all observe, is part of our trade. No, this does not mean we accept the idea that there are "alternative facts" but that we acknowledge that things can have different meaning for different people and that no event in the news ever happens in a vacuum.

Therefore, if we really want to understand news reporting as a global phenomenon, then we need to accept that national and local grammars were also invented in each country and by a diversity of communities. Yes, it is true that anyone reading the same story in a popular mainstream newspaper in London and then doing the same in Mexico City will recognize overlaps and commonalities, but it is also certain that the same reader will encounter also very divergent manners of telling a story and distinctive truths in them. In places such as Haiti, for example, the long tradition of journalism that diverges greatly from what the North calls news reporting and which dates back to the era of slavery—which allowed them to come together against their oppressors—was essential in creating the sense of nation (Anderson, 2006 [1983]), one that allowed blacks from all over Africa, who did not have in some cases the same language or belong to the same ethnic group, to come together and unleash their struggle for freedom and create the very first modern Black Republic that gave the world the first truly sense that the universal human rights were for all people in this planet (James, 2001 [1938]; Nesbitt, 2008; 2009).

Indeed, the Global South journalism grammars meant—among many, many other things—Haitian blacks donating European white aristocrats in South America a print to publish a pro-independence newspaper and asking in return to do a type of journalism that was not only going to report about the tragedy of slavery but denounce it as a crime. This is something that journalism practitioners, today's donor agencies, and scholars of all sort need to bear in mind for current and future enterprises that aim at creating capabilities in the Global South.

The agenda among donors is that if there is the true intention to foster capabilities, then they need initiatives that work with existing expressions of journalism that already have their own local grammars, which reflect the reality on the ground. These projects, let us not forget, have found ways to bypass total blackout, strict censorship, and repression in their own societies, as we saw following the overthrow of democratically elected President Jean-Bertand Aristide on September 30, 1991. In those darkest moments, Radio Enriquillo, a local radio station operating from the Dominican Republican border, managed to evade censorship and kept the Haitians informed of what was happening in the country by singing the news (Ruquoy, 2017). This was by no means the type of journalism that foreign aid tends to support or fund, nor the ideal type of grammar to which many of our textbooks define as objective and factual news reporting, but it was a stark reminder that journalism in the Global South adopts its own forms.

Let us also keep in mind that despite having distinctive grammars, journalists in the South share common ground with their counterparts in the North in their common pursue of truth. This in the same way that individuals share common normative aspirations for social justice either if they work as mainstream reporters of the *New York Times* or as part of the wave of Hip-Hop performers who deliver the news to the poorest areas of the Bronx, New York (McLeod, 2002). They share different traits and even newsgathering practices, such as interviewing, observing, and structuring news stories in particular accessible formats. They, nevertheless, diverge perhaps in the way truth is constructed. This is because, for the rapper or Creole singer, truth is about networking around social justice, not only presenting facts. An ideal that just now mainstream journalism in the West is starting to grasp due to the decline in the traditional business models that had co-opted the voices of so many and the emergence of new technologies that have revolutionized gathering and dissemination of news—by starting to see itself rather "as cultures of circulation" (Bødker, 2015).

Today, despite convergent normative aspirations, journalism has many grammars, which reflects different aesthetics, deontology, and forms of understanding truth. For Indian journalist, Palagummi Sainath, there are three kinds of objectivity. The first, he says, is the "the objectivity of the pure sciences, were something that can be verified, checked, and examined," is "very desirable and ... admirable but ... not replicable beyond a certain degree in the social sciences and in journalism." The second, the "North American" doctrine of journalism objectivity, which he calls "a fraud." This is because it defends the powerful by weakening the arguments against power. It "really ends up giving the last word to authority and the powerful." The third kind of objectivity, says Sainath, that has "strived for" is "personal objectivity," which is "the honesty with which you deal with a subject."

> The first thing about being honest is to accept that our value systems have an impact on us. Now, the day that we accept that journalism is a very subjective art is the day we begin striving for objectivity. Now, if I start with the myth that I am objective then you will be actually committing a serious disservice to your readers, or viewers, or listeners. If you start from the point of view that we all have our deep subjectivities, we all are affected by our sensitivities and our socialization then you know what to look out for. You know the biases and the prejudices to watch out for when you write. (Kale, 2015)

For over 100 years, foreign aid from the West has tried to shape, at times intentionally and at times not, the way we understand and practice journalism in the Global South. In this regard, Diana Lemberg has documented in detail the US efforts to promote a particular model of expanding news audiences and markets. She has shown that in the decades following World War II, American free-flow policies reshaped the world's information landscape, though not always as intended. Through burgeoning information diplomacy and development aid, Washington diffused new media ranging from television and satellite broadcasting to global English. But these actions also spurred overseas actors to articulate alternative understandings of information freedom and of how information flows might be regulated (Lemberg, 2019).

In doing so, these efforts fostered a particular model of news reporting that reflects liberal democracy and market economy values. They also forged a set of normative aspirational values that have come to define both aesthetics and deontology of journalism while determining the format and aesthetics of news reporting and the nature of journalism as a political institution within democratic societies. In all these respects, it has succeeded beyond its initial expectations but not necessarily in the ways initially thought. Instead, its success is mixed and complex as it struggles between resistance and contestations within the particular histories and societies.

In this sense, the allocation of Foreign Aid into Media Development has challenged and successfully produced alternative news cultures and journalistic identities in the very same places where it aimed to standardize journalism practice. Recipients of aid all over the world have constantly found ways of using foreign aid to develop their own news agendas and fostering localized styles and practices all this regardless of the original intention of the donors. Therefore, the challenge now for all of us is to start reconciling the ethical impositions of standardization from the West with the deontological needs and realities on the ground in each and every one of the very own distinctive constituencies of the Global South, which today more than ever crave for being able to share truthful news while also fulfilling their quest for justice.

NOTE

1. Scholars from the Global South have more or less written this story that includes media outlets, such as the radio stations, operated by the Bolivian mining workers union, which are considered one of the first examples of grassroot media providing alternative content (Aguirre, 2017) and the Colombia-based Radio Sutatenza, which broadcast cultural and educational programs between 1947 and 1994 and is considered as one of the paramount examples of educational and community-oriented radio (Bernal-Alarcón, 2012; Hurtado, 2012).

References

Abbott, S. (2016). *Rethinking public service broadcasting's place in international media development.* Retrieved from Washington, DC: https://www.cima.ned.org/wp-content/uploads/2016/02/CIMA_2016_Public_Service_Broadcasting.pdf.

Abbott, S. (2019). Evaluating success: What should we be measuring? In N. Benequista, S. Abbott, P. Rothman, & W. Mano (Eds.), *International media development: Historical perspectives and new frontiers.* Oxford: Peter Lang Publishing Inc.

Adesoji, A. O., & Alimi, S. (2012). The Nigerian press and the challenge of private newspaper ownership: A study of the Nigerian Tribune, 1949–2009. *Journal of African Media Studies, 4*(3), 357–376.

Adorno, T. W., & Horkheimer, M. (1997 [1944]). *Dialectic of enlightenment* (Vol. 15). London: Verso.

Aguirre, J. (2017). Una breve historia de la palabra con sentido el camino de la radio boliviana hacia su fin educativo. *Punto Cero, 22*(34), 31–37.

Ahmed, I. (2016). Development journalism and its potential contribution to the state building: The case of Somalia. *Malaysian Journal of Communication, 32*(1), 437–454.

Aizpurua, R. (2011). Revolution and politics in Venezuela and Curaçao, 1795–1800. In K. Wim & G. Oostindie (Eds.), *Dutch Atlantic connections* (pp. 97–122). Leiden: KITLV Press.

Aldroubi, M. (2017). Bahrain says Qatar's media is making diplomatic crisis worse. Retrieved from https://www.thenational.ae/world/gcc/bahrain-says-qatar-s-media-is-making-diplomatic-crisis-worse-1.620047.

Allen, C. (1993). *Eisenhower and the mass media: Peace, prosperity, & prime-time TV.* Chapel Hill, North Carolina: University of North Carolina Press.

Allen, G. (2016). Catching up with the Competition: The international expansion of Associated Press, 1920–1945. *Journalism Studies, 17*(6), 747–762.

Alonso, P. (2004). *Construcciones impresas: panfletos, diarios y revistas en la formación de los estados nacionales en América Latina, 1820–1920.* Mexico, DF: Fondo De Cultura Economica.

Álvares, P. (2017). El periodista de la Revolución: John Reed y los días que conmovieron al mundo. Retrieved from https://mundo.sputniknews.com/cultura/201710311073623786-periodista-john-reed/.

Álvarez, F. (2010 [1978]). *La información contemporanea*. Caracas: Agencia Venezolana e Noticias.

Alvear, F. J., & Lugo-Ocando, J. (2018). When geopolitics becomes moral panic: El Mercurio and the use of international news as propaganda against Salvador Allende's Chile (1970–1973). *Media History, 24*(3–4), 528–546.

Ambrosius, L. (2002). *Wilsonianism: Woodrow Wilson and his legacy in American foreign relations*. New York: Springer.

Anderson, B. (2006 [1983]). *Imagined communities: Reflections on the origin and spread of nationalism*. London: Verso Books.

Anderson, C. (2018). *Apostles of certainty: Data journalism and the politics of doubt*. Oxford: Oxford University Press.

Anderson, C. W. (2018). *Apostles of certainty: Data journalism and the politics of doubt*. Oxford: Oxford University Press.

Anderson, C. W., Downie, L., & Schudson, M. (2016). *The news media: What everyone needs to know*. Oxford: Oxford University Press.

Anderson, P. J., Williams, M., & Ogola, G. (2013). *The future of quality news journalism: A cross-continental analysis* (Vol. 7). Routledge.

Anderson, R. L. (1970). Rhetoric and science journalism. *Quarterly Journal of Speech, 56*(4), 358–368.

Appadurai, A. (2006). *Fear of small numbers: An essay on the geography of anger*. Durham, North Carolina: Duke University Press.

Appy, C. (2000). *Cold War constructions: The political culture of United States imperialism, 1945–66*. Amherst, Massachusetts: University Massachusetts Press.

Arasa, D. (2015). *La Batalla de las Ondas en la Guerra Civil Española*. Maçanet de la Selva, Girona: Editorial Gregal.

Armour, C. (1984). The BBC and the development of broadcasting in British Colonial Africa 1946–1956. *African Affairs, 83*(332), 359–402.

Arndt, R. T., & Rubin, D. L. (1993). *The fulbright difference: 1948–1992*. Piscataway, New Jersey: Transaction Publishers.

Athan, T. (1971). *Seeds of repression. Harry S. Truman and the origins of mccarthyism*. New York: Quadrangle Books.

Atkinson, R., & Durden, P. (1990). Housing policy in the Thatcher years. In *Public policy under thatcher* (pp. 117–130). Springer.

Atton, C., & Hamilton, J. F. (2008). *Alternative journalism*. London: Sage.

Báez, F. (2008). *El saqueo cultural de América Latina. De la conquista a la globalización*. México, D.F: Debates.

Bailey, O. G., & Harindranath, R. (2005). Racialised 'othering'. In S. Allan (Ed.), *Journalism: Critical issues* (pp. 274–286). Maidenhead, Berkshire: Open University Press/McGraw-Hill Education.

Bailey, R. (1990). The slave (ry) trade and the development of capitalism in the United States: The textile industry in New England. *Social Science History, 14*(3), 373–414.

Baird, D. G. (1983). Common law intellectual property and the legacy of international news service v. associated press. *The University of Chicago Law Review, 50*(2), 411–429.

Baldwin, D. A. (1969). Foreign aid, intervention, and influence. *World Politics, 21*(3), 425–447.

Bamba, A. B. (2013). Transnationalising decolonisation: The print media, American public spheres and France's imperial exit in West Africa. *Journal of Transatlantic Studies, 11*(4), 327–349.

Banning, S. A. (1998). The professionalization of journalism: A nineteenth-century beginning. *Journalism History, 24*(4), 157.

Banning, S. A. (1999). The professionalization of journalism: A nineteenth-century beginning. *Journalism History, 24*(4), 157–160.

Barbero, J. M. (1981). Retos a la investigación de comunicación en América Latina. *La Revista ININCO, 1*(2), 35–45.

Barbero, M. (2010). *Comunicación y desarrollo en la era digital*. Paper presented at the Asociación Española de Investigación de la Comunicación, Malaga. http://www.portalcomunicacion.com/monograficos_det.asp?id=155.

Barea, M. E. R. (2016). *Imperiofobia y leyenda negra: Roma, Rusia, Estados Unidos y el Imperio español*. Madrid: Siruela.

Barghoorn, F. C. (2015). *Soviet foreign propaganda*. Princeton, New Jersey: Princeton University Press.

Barker, M. (2008). The Soros media 'empire': The power of philanthropy to engineer consent. *Swans Commentary*, July, 14.

Barnes, T. (1981). The secret Cold War: The CIA and American foreign policy in Europe, 1946–1956. Part I. *The Historical Journal, 24*(2), 399–415.

Barrera, C. (2004). *Historia del periodismo universal*. Madrid: Grupo Planeta (GBS).

Bavier, R. (2014). Recent trends in US income and expenditure poverty. *Journal of Policy Analysis and Management, 33*(3), 700–718.

BBC. (2016). *Editorial guidelines*. Retrieved from London: http://www.bbc.co.uk/editorialguidelines/.

Beard, R. L., & Zoerner, C. E. (1969). Associated Negro Press: Its founding, ascendency and demise. *Journalism Quarterly, 46*(1), 47–52.

Becker, L. B., & Vlad, T. (2005). *Non-US funders of media assistance projects*. Retrieved from Athens, GA: https://www.grady.uga.edu/coxcenter/Activities/Act_2005_to_2006/Materials05-06/Knight_International_Report_December_2005_v16.pdf.

Beevor, A. (2012). *The battle for Spain: The Spanish Civil War 1936–1939*. New York: Hachette.

Beltrán, L. R., Herrera, K., Pinto, E., & Torrico, E. (2008). *La Comunicación antes de Colón. Aportes a la comunicación indígena*. La Paz: Centro Interdisciplinario Boliviano de Estudios de la Comunicación (IBEC).

Bernal-Alarcón, H. (2012). Radio Sutatenza: un modelo colombiano de industria cultural y educativa. *Bolitin Cultural y Bibliografico, 46*(82), 5–15.

Bernhard, N. (2003). *US television news and Cold War propaganda, 1947–1960*. Cambridge: Cambridge University Press.

Bernstein, C. (1977). *The CIA and the media*. Retrieved from http://lust-for-life.org/Lust-For-Life/_Textual/CarlBernstein_TheCIAAndTheMedia_20oct1977_35pp/CarlBernstein_TheCIAAndTheMedia_20oct1977_35pp.pdf.

Betsill, M., Corell, E., Burgiel, S., & Andresen, S. (2008). *NGO diplomacy: The influence of nongovernmental organizations in international environmental negotiations*. Cambridge, Massachusetts: MIT Press.

Bird, S. E., & Dardenne, R. W. (2009). Rethinking news and myth as storytelling. In K. Wahl-Jorgensen & T. Hanitzsch (Eds.), *The handbook of journalism studies* (pp. 205–217). Abingdon, Oxon: Routledge.

Black, J. (2001). *The English press 1621–1861*. Stroud, Gloucestershire: Sutton.

Blackburn, R. (2006). Haiti, slavery, and the age of the democratic revolution. *The William and Mary Quarterly, 63*(4), 643–674.

Blanchard, P. (2008). *Under the flags of freedom: Slave soldiers and the wars of independence in Spanish South America*. Pittsburgh, Pennsylvania: University of Pittsburgh Press.

Blomley, N. (2007). Making private property: Enclosure, common right and the work of hedges. *Rural History, 18*(1), 1–21.

Blumler, J. G., & Gurevitch, M. (1995). *The crisis of public communication*. London: Routledge.

Bødker, H. (2015). Journalism as cultures of circulation. *Digital Journalism, 3*(1), 101–115.

Boggs, M. (1953). *Memorandum to the president of the United States: Discussion at the 157th Meeting of the National Security Council, Thursday, July 30, 1953*. Retrieved from Washington DC.

Borges-Rey, E. (2016). Unravelling data journalism: A study of data journalism practice in British newsrooms. *Journalism Practice, 10*(7), 833–843.

Bourdieu, P. (1997). *Sobre la televisión*. Barcelona: Anagrama.

Boyd-Barrett, O. (1980). *The international news agencies* (Vol. 13). London: Constable Limited.

Boyd-Barrett, O., & Rantanen, T. (1998). *The globalization of news*. London: Sage.

Brandenberger, D. (2002). *National Bolshevism: Stalinist mass culture and the formation of modern Russian national identity, 1931–1956* (Vol. 93). Cambridge, Massachusetts: Harvard University Press.

Brandenberger, D. (2014). *Propaganda state in crisis: Soviet ideology, indoctrination, and terror under Stalin, 1927–1941*. New Haven, Connecticut: Yale University Press.

Bräutigam, D. A., & Knack, S. (2004). Foreign aid, institutions, and governance in sub-Saharan Africa. *Economic development and cultural change, 52*(2), 255–285.

Braveboy-Wagner, J. A. (2009). *Institutions of the Global South*. Abingdon, Oxfordshire: Routledge.

Brendon, P. (1983). *The life and death of the press barons*. New York: Atheneum Books.

Brennan, J. (2015). The Cold War battle over global news in East Africa: Decolonization, the free flow of information, and the media business, 1960–1980. *Journal of Global History, 10*(2), 333–356.

Brewer, J., & Staves, S. (2014). *Early modern conceptions of property.* Abingdon, Oxfordshire: Routledge.

Briggs, A., & Burke, P. (2002). *A social history of the media: From Gutenberg to the Internet.* Cambridge: Polity.

Briggs, A., & Burke, P. (2009). *A social history of the media: From Gutenberg to the Internet.* Cambridge: Polity.

Broersma, M. (2004). Transnational journalism history. *Contemporary European History, 13*, 211–222.

Broersma, M. (2019). Americanization, or: The rhetoric of modernity: How European journalism adapted US norms, practices and conventions. In K. Arnold, P. Preston and S. Kinnebrock (Eds.), *The handbook of European communication history* (pp. 403–419). Hoboken, New Jersey: John Wiley & Sons, Inc.

Bromley, M. & Slavtcheva-Petkova, V. (2019). *Global journalism. An introduction.* London: Macmillan International, Higher Education; Red Globe Press.

Brovkin, V. N. (1998). *Russia after Lenin: Politics, culture and society, 1921–1929.* London: Psychology Press.

Browne, H. (2010). Foundation-funded journalism: Reasons to be wary of charitable support. *Journalism Studies, 11*(6), 889–903.

Brownlee, B. J. (2017). Media development in Syria: The Janus-faced nature of foreign aid assistance. *Third World Quarterly, 38*(10), 2276–2294.

Bryant, C. (1985). *Positivism in social theory and research.* London: Macmillan International Higher Education.

Bryant, J. M. (2006). The West and the rest revisited: Debating capitalist origins, European colonialism, and the advent of modernity. *The Canadian Journal of Sociology, 31*(4), 403–444.

Budnitskiy, S. (2016). Cold War no more: The west's obsolete media diplomacy towards Russia. Retrieved from https://global.asc.upenn.edu/cold-war-no-more-the-wests-obsolete-media-diplomacy-towards-russia/.

Burns, T. (2016 [1977]). *The BBC: Public institution and private world.* London: Springer.

Burtt, E. A. (2014). *The metaphysical foundations of modern physical science: A historical and critical essay.* Abingdon, Oxfordshire: Routledge.

Bushnell, D. (1950). The development of the press in Great Colombia. *The Hispanic American Historical Review, 30*(4), 432–452.

Bushnell, D. (2003). *Simón Bolívar: Liberation and disappointment.* London: Longman Publishing Group.

Business-Report. (2019). Google news initiative innovation challenge to launch in Africa. Retrieved from https://www.iol.co.za/business-report/technology/google-news-initiative-innovation-challenge-to-launch-in-africa-21423595.

Bustamante, E., Bisbal, M., Honpehayn, M., Getino, O., Canclini, N. G., Barbero, J. M., Trejo, R. (2008). *La cooperación cultura comunicación en Iberoamérica.* Agencia Española de Cooperación Internacional.

Caballero, G., & Soto-Oñate, D. (2015). The diversity and rapprochement of theories of institutional change: Original institutionalism and new institutional economics. *Journal of Economic Issues, 49*(4), 947–977. doi:10.1080/00213624.2015.1105021.

Calabrese, A., & Burgelman, J.-C. (1999). *Communication, citizenship, and social policy: Rethinking the limits of the welfare state.* Lanham, Maryland: Rowman & Littlefield.

Carapico, S. (2002). Foreign aid for promoting democracy in the Arab world. *The Middle East Journal, 56*(3), 379–395.

Carey, J. W. (2000). Some personal notes on US journalism education. *Journalism, 1*(1), 12–23.

Carey, J. W. (2007). A short history of journalism for journalists: A proposal and essay. *Harvard International Journal of Press/Politics, 12*(1), 3–16.

Carlson, M. (2017). *Journalistic authority: Legitimating news in the digital era.* New York: Columbia University Press.

Carroll, T. F. (1919). Freedom of speech and of the press in war time: The espionage act. *Michigan Law Review, 17*(8), 621–665.

Castells, M. (2011). *The power of identity: The information age: Economy, society, and culture* (Vol. 2). John Wiley & Sons.

Castro-Gómez, S. (2007). Decolonizar la universidad. La hybris del punto cero y el diálogo de saberes. In S. Castro-Gómez & R. Grosfoguel (Eds.), *El giro decolonial. Reflexiones para una diversidad epistémica más allá del capitalismo global* (pp. 79–91). Bogota: Siglo del Hombre Editores.

Chakravartty, P. (2009). Modernization redux? Cultural studies & development communication. *Television & New Media, 10*(1), 37–39.

Chambers, S. (2015). *No god but gain: The untold story of Cuban slavery, the monroe doctrine, and the making of the United States.* London: Verso Books.

Chapman, J. L., & Nuttall, N. (2011). *Journalism today: A themed history.* New Jersey, New York: John Wiley & Sons.

Chaparro-Escudero, M. (2012). Medios de comunicación y democracia. Lecciones desde América Latina. *Commons: revista de comunicación y ciudadanía digital, 1*(1), 15–34.

Chasi, C., & Rodny-Gumede, Y. (2016). Ubuntu journalism and nation-building magic. *Critical Arts, 30*(5), 728–744.

Chatterjee, P. (1993). *The nation and its fragments: Colonial and postcolonial histories* (Vol. 11). Princeton, NJ: Princeton University Press.

Chehonadskih, M. (2017). The comrades of the past: The soviet enlightenment between negation and affirmation. *Crisis Critique, 4*(2), 87–105.

Cheng, C. (2019). The logic behind China's foreign aid agency. Retrieved from https://carnegieendowment.org/2019/05/21/logic-behind-china-s-foreign-aid-agency-pub-79154.

Chyi, H. I., & Tenenboim, O. (2019). Charging more and wondering why readership declined? A longitudinal study of US Newspapers' price hikes, 2008–2016. *Journalism Studies, 20*(14), 2113–2129.

CIA. (1949). *Standardization of arms program in the Western Hemisphere.* Retrieved from Washington DC.

CIA. (1950). *Soviet capabilities and intentions in Latin America.* Retrieved from Washington DC.

CIMA. (2019). Media development funding. Retrieved from https://www.cima.ned.org/what-is-media-development/funding/.

Claeys, G. (2018). *Marx and marxism*. London: Pelican.
Cleary, J. (2003). Shaping Mexican journalists: The role of university and on-the-job training. *Journalism & Mass Communication Educator, 58*(2), 163–174.
Coffey, J. (1960a). *Memorandum for: Mr Charles Saunders. Office of teh secretary health, education and walfare*. Retrieved from Washington DC.
Coffey, J. (1960b). *Notes, staff meeting 25 April 1960, 2 to 6 pm. Subject: RL/RFE - PCIAA 3*. Retrieved from Washington DC.
Colomina, M. (1968). *El huésped alienante un estudio sobre audiencia y efectos de las radio-telenovelas en Venezuela*. Maracaibo, Venezuela: Universidad del Zulia. Escuela de Periodismo, Centro Audiovisual, Colección Ensayos.
Conaghan, C. M. (2002). Cashing in on authoritarianism: Media collusion in Fujimori's Peru. *Harvard International Journal of Press/Politics, 7*(1), 115–125.
Conboy, M. (2004). *Journalism: A critical history*. London: Sage.
Conboy, M. (2006). *Tabloid Britain: Constructing a community through language*. Abingdon, Oxfordshire: Taylor & Francis.
Connerton, P. (1980). *The tragedy of enlightenment: An essay on the Frankfurt School*. Cambridge: Cambridge University Press.
Cook, C. (2016). Money under fire: The ethics of revenue generation for oppositional news outlets. *Ethhical Space: The International Journal of Communication Ethics, 2*(3), 66–80.
Cook, T. E. (1998). *Governing with the news. The news media as a political institution*. Chicago: University of Chicago Press.
Cooke, B., & Kothari, U. (2001). *The new tyranny?* London: Zed Books.
Cooper, F. (1994). Conflict and connection: Rethinking colonial African history. *The American Historical Review, 99*(5), 1516–1545.
Cooper, K. (1959). *Kent Cooper and the Associated Press: An autobiography*. New York: Random House.
Corvalán, L. (2003). *El gobierno de Salvador Allende*. Santiago de Chile: LOM ediciones.
Couldry, N. (2004). Media meta-capital: Extending the range of Bourdieu's field theory. In D. Swartz & V. Zolberg (Eds.), *After bourdieu. Influence, critique, elaboration* (pp. 165–189). Amsterdam: Springer; Kluwer Academic Publishers.
Cuenca, G. (1998). *La enseñanza de la comunicación y el periodismo en Venezuela*. Caracas: Prensa de la Universidad Central de Venezuela.
Cull, N. (2008). *The decline and fall of the United States Information Agency: American public diplomacy, 1989–2001*. New York: Palgrave Macmillan.
Cull, N. J. (2008). Public diplomacy: Taxonomies and histories. *The Annals of the American Academy of Political and Social Science, 616*(1), 31–54.
Curran, J. (1978). The press as an agency of social control: An historical perspective. In *Newspaper history: From the 17th century to the present day*. London: Constable, 51–75.
Curran, J., & Seaton, J. (2002 [1981]). *Power without responsibility: Press, broadcasting and the internet in Britain*. Routledge.
Curran, J., & Seaton, J. (2009). *Power without responsibility: Press, broadcasting and the internet in Britain*. Abingdon, Oxfordshire: Routledge.
Dabashi, H. (2015). *Can non-Europeans think?* London: Zed Books Ltd.

Daly, G., Mooney, G., Poole, L., & Davis, H. (2005). Housing stock transfer in Birmingham and Glasgow: The contrasting experiences of two UK cities. *European Journal of Housing Policy, 5*(3), 327–341.

Das, J. (2012). Environmental journalism in Bangladesh: Active social agency. *Journalism Studies, 13*(2), 226–242.

Davies, A. (1999). The first radio war: Broadcasting in the Spanish Civil War, 1936–1939. *Historical Journal of Film, Radio and Television, 19*(4), 473–513.

Davis, D. (1971). *The fear of conspiracy: Images of un-American subversion from the revolution to the present*. Ithaca, New York: Cornell University Press.

Davis, E. (1945, 04–26–1945). [Letter to the President of the US Harry S. Truman].

Davis, H. (1959). A new look at Latin American relations. *World Affairs, 122*(2), 48–52.

Davis, M. (2010). Why journalism is a profession. In C. Meyers (Ed.), *Journalism ethics: A philosophical approach* (pp. 91–102). Oxford: Oxford University Press.

De Balzac, H. (2009 [1843]). *Monografía de la prensa parisina [Los periodistas]*. Sevilla: Comunicación Social.

Defty, A. (2004). *Britain, America and anti-communist propaganda 1945–53: The information research department*. Abingdon, Oxfordshire: Routledge.

Delano, A. (2000). No sign of a better job: 100 years of British journalism. *Journalism Studies, 1*(2), 261–272.

Dellamea, A. B. (1996). La formación de divulgadores y periodistas científicos en la Argentina. Retrieved from https://www.oei.es/historico/salactsi/dellamea3.htm.

Der Derian, J. (2009). *Virtuous war: Mapping the military-industrial-media-entertainment-network*. London: Routledge.

Deuze, M. (2005). What is journalism? Professional identity and ideology of journalists reconsidered. *Journalism, 6*(4), 442–464.

Deuze, M. (2006). Global journalism education: A conceptual approach. *Journalism Studies, 7*(1), 19–34.

Dewey, J. (1991 [1927]). *Public & its problems*. Athenes, Ohio: Ohio University Press.

Diaz-Rangel, E. (1976). *Pueblos sub-informados*. Caracas: Monte Avila Editores.

Dickson, P. (2019). *Sputnik: The shock of the century*. Lincoln, Nebraska: University of Nebraska Press.

DiNicola, R. (1994). Teaching journalistic style with the AP stylebook: Beyond fussy rules and dogma of 'correctness'. *The Journalism Educator, 49*(2), 64–70.

Donsbach, W. (2014). Journalism as the new knowledge profession and consequences for journalism education. *Journalism, 15*(6), 661–677.

Dreher, A., Nunnenkamp, P., & Schmaljohann, M. (2015). The allocation of German aid: Self-interest and government ideology. *Economics & Politics, 27*(1), 160–184.

Dulles, A. W. (1964). *Memorandum fo Mr Lawrence R. Houston* (Box No. 24). Independence, MO: Harry S. Truman Presidential Library.

Duniway, C. A. (1906). *The development of freedom of the press in Massachusetts*. London: Longmans, Green, and Company.

Dunn, J. (1982). *The political thought of John Locke: An historical account of the argument of the 'two treatises of government'*. Cambridge: Cambridge University Press.

Durham, M. G. (1998). On the relevance of standpoint epistemology to the practice of journalism: The case for "strong objectivity". *Communication Theory, 8*(2), 117–140.

Earle, R. (1997). Information and disinformation in late colonial New Granada. *The Americas, 54*(2), 167–184.

Easterly, W. (2002). The cartel of good intentions: The problem of bureaucracy in foreign aid. *The Journal of Policy Reform, 5*(4), 223–250.

Easthope, A. (1990). Trade unions in British Television news. *The Yearbook of English Studies, 20,* 102–120.

Eco, U. (2011 [1964]). *Apocalípticos e integrados.* Sevilla: Debolsillo.

Edeani, D. O. (1993). Role of development journalism in Nigeria's development. *Gazette (Leiden, Netherlands), 52*(2), 123–143.

Edwards, P. N. (1997). *The closed world: Computers and the politics of discourse in Cold War America.* Cambridge, MA: MIT Press.

Ehrenberg, J. (2017). *Civil society: The critical history of an idea.* New York: New York University Press.

Eisenstein, E. L. (1980). *The printing press as an agent of change* (Vol. 1). Cambridge: Cambridge University Press.

Eley, G. (2002). *Forging democracy: The history of the left in Europe, 1850–2000.* Oxford: Oxford University Press.

Elliott, P., & Golding, P. (1974). Mass communication and social change: The imagery of development and the development of imagery. In E. De Kadt & G. Williams (Eds.), *Sociology and development* (pp. 229–254). London: Tavistock Publications.

Eltis, D., & Engerman, S. L. (2000). The importance of slavery and the slave trade to industrializing Britain. *The Journal of Economic History, 60*(1), 123–144.

Emmenegger, P., H'Ausermann, S., Häusermann, S., Palier, B., & Seeleib-Kaiser, M. (2012). *The age of dualization: The changing face of inequality in deindustrializing societies.* Oxford: Oxord Press University.

Epstein, R. A. (1992). International news service v. Associated Press: Custom and law as sources of property rights in news. *Virginia Law Review,* 85–128.

Epstein, R. A. (2003). The necessary history of property and liberty. *Chapman Law Review, 6*(1), 1–30.

Escobar, A. (2004). Development, violence and the new imperial order. *Development, 47*(1), 15–21.

Escobar, A. (2011). *Encountering development: The making and unmaking of the Third World.* Princeton University Press.

Federal-Reserve-System. (1944). *Postwar employment program.* Retrieved from Washington, DC.

Feldman, L. (2011). Partisan differences in opinionated news perceptions: A test of the hostile media effect. *Political Behavior, 33*(3), 407–432.

Ferreira, L., Tillson, D. J., & Salwen, M. B. (2000). Sixty-five years of journalism education in Latin America. *Florida Communication Journal, 27*(1/2), 61–79.

Ferrucci, P., & Nelson, J. L. (2019). The new advertisers: How foundation funding impacts journalism. *Media and Communication, 7*(4), 45–55.

Feuer, L. (1962). American travelers to the Soviet Union 1917–32: The formation of a component of new deal ideology. *American Quarterly, 14*(2), 119–149.

Fijałkowska, A. (2011). Hugo Chávez y la guerra mediática en Venezuela. *Itinerarios: revista de estudios lingüisticos, literarios, históricos y antropológicos, 1*(13), 191–206.
Filler, L. (1993). *The muckrakers*. Palo Alto, California: Stanford University Press.
Fischer, S. (2013). Bolívar in Haiti: Republicanism in the revolutionary Atlantic. In C. Carla, D. Raphael, D-G. Luis, & H. Clevis (Eds.), *Haiti and the Americas* (pp. 25–53). Jackson, Mississippi: University Press of Mississippi.
Fitzgerald, T. (2007). *Discourse on civility and barbarity*. New York: Open University Press.
Fitzpatrick, S. (2002). *The commissariat of enlightenment: Soviet organization of education and the arts under Lunacharsky, October 1917–1921*. Cambridge: Cambridge University Press.
Folkerts, J. (2014). History of journalism education. *Journalism & Communication Monographs, 16*(4), 227–299.
Forment, C. A. (2013). *Democracy in Latin America, 1760–1900: Volume 1, civic selfhood and public life in Mexico and Peru* (Vol. 1). Chicago, Illinois: University of Chicago Press.
Forrest, R., & Murie, A. (2014). *Selling the welfare state: The privatisation of public housing*. Abingdon, Oxfordshire: Routledge.
Foster, M. (2019). The revenue paradox of digital news media. In N. Benequista, S. Abbott, P. Rothman, & W. Mano (Eds.), *International media development: Historical perspectives and new frontiers*. Oxford: Peter Lang Publishing Inc.
Frère, M.-S. (2012). Perspectives on the media in 'another Africa'. *Ecquid Novi: African Journalism Studies, 33*(3), 1–12.
Frère, M.-S. (2015). Francophone Africa: The rise of 'pluralist authoritarian' media systems? *African Journalism Studies, 36*(1), 103–112.
Freyssinet, J. (2010). 1974–1984: une décennie de désindustrialisation? *Le mouvement social, 232*(1), 113–114.
Frohlich, R., & Holtz-Bacha, C. (1994). Structures of inhomogeneity – Dilemmas of journalism training in Europe. Retrieved from https://files.eric.ed.gov/fulltext/ED377537.pdf
Fuentes-Navarro, R. (1992). El estudio de la comunicación desde una perspectiva sociocultural en América Latina. *Diá-logos de la Comunicación*, Retrieved from https://core.ac.uk/download/pdf/47248344.pdf.
Fuenzalida, V. (2000). *La televisión pública en América Latina: reforma o privatización*. Santiago: Fondo de Cultura Económica.
Fuller, B. F., & Elmore, R. (1996). *Who chooses? Who loses? Culture, institutions and the unequal effects of school choice*. ERIC.
Gainor, D. (2014). Soros spends over $48 million funding media organizations. Retrieved from https://www.mrc.org/commentary/soros-spends-over-48-million-funding-media-organizations
Gallagher, W. (2016). *How the post office created America: A history*. New York: Penguin.
Ganter, S. A. (2018). International development aid beyond money: The push and pull of media democracy promotion in three Mercosur countries. *Journal of Latin American Communication Research, 6*(1–2), 1–19.
Garcia-Santamaria, S. (2018). The sovietization of Cuban journalism. The impact of foreign economy dependency on media structures in a post-soviet era. *Journal of Latin American Communication Research, 6*(1–2), 135–151.

Garner, A., & Kirkby, D. (2013). 'Never a machine for propaganda'? The Australian-American fulbright program and Australia's Cold War. *Australian Historical Studies, 44*(1), 117–133.

Gauthier, G. (1993). In defence of a supposedly outdated notion: The range of application of journalistic objectivity. *Canadian Journal of Communication, 18*(4), 497.

Gilley, B. (2018). The case for colonialism. *Academic Questions, 31*(2), 167–185.

Gilmartin, D. (2015). The historiography of India's partition: Between civilization and modernity. *The Journal of Asian Studies, 74*(1), 23–41.

Gloria, G. M. (2000). Media and democracy in the Philippines. *Media Asia, 27*(4), 191–196.

Glück, A. (2016). What makes a good journalist? Empathy as a central resource in journalistic work practice. *Journalism Studies, 17*(7), 893–903.

Go, J. (2008). *American empire and the politics of meaning: Elite political cultures in the Philippines and Puerto Rico during US colonialism*. North Carolina: Duke University Press.

Golding, P. (1977). Media professionalism in the Third World: The transfer of an ideology. In C. James, M. Gurevitch, & J. Woollacott (Eds.), *Mass Communication and Society* (pp. 291–308). London: Edward Arnold.

Golinger, E. (2005). *El código Chávez: descifrando la intervención de los EE. UU. en Venezuela*. Caracas: Fondo Editorial Question.

Golinger, E., & Landau, S. (2006). *The Chavez code: Cracking US intervention in Venezuela*. Northampton, MA: Olive Branch Press.

González, J., & Torres, J. (2011). *News for all the people: The epic story of race and the American media*. London: Verso Books.

Gorman, L., & McLean, D. (2003). *Media and society in the twentieth century: A historical introduction*. Hoboken, New Jersey: Wiley-Blackwell.

Gough, S. (2003). *The evolution of strategic influence* (Strategy Research Project). U.S. Army War College, Carlisle Barracks, Pennsylvania 17013.

Gramsci, A. (2003 [1935]). *Selection from the prison notebooks*. London: Lawrence & Wishart.

Greer, A. (2018). *Property and dispossession: Natives, empires and land in early modern North America*. Cambridge: Cambridge University Press.

Gregory, A., & Halff, G. (2013). Divided we stand: Defying hegemony in global public relations theory and practice? *Public Relations Review, 39*(5), 417–425.

Grey, G. (1952a). *Memorandum to Frank Gardiner Wisner, Deputy Director of Plans CIA*. Retrieved from Chapel Hill, North Carolina.

Grey, G. (1952b). *Report to the president of the United State of America*. Retrieved from Chapel Hill, North Carolina.

Grosfoguel, R. (2011). Decolonizing post-colonial studies and paradigms of political-economy: Transmodernity, decolonial thinking, and global coloniality. *Transmodernity: Journal of Peripheral Cultural Production of the Luso-Hispanic World, 1*(1). Retrieved from https://escholarship.org/uc/item/21k6t3fq

Gross, M. (2017). The dangers of a post-truth world. *Current Biology, 27*(1), R1–R4.

Habermas, J., & Habermas, J. (1991). *The structural transformation of the public sphere: An inquiry into a category of bourgeois society*. Cambridge, Massachusetts: MIT Press.

Hagedorn, A. (2007). *Savage peace: Hope and fear in America, 1919*. New York: Simon and Schuster.

Haithcox, J. P. (2015). *Communism and nationalism in India: MN Roy and comintern policy, 1920–1939*. Princeton, New Jersey: Princeton University Press.

Hajkowski, T. (2013). *The BBC and national identity in Britain, 1922–53*. Retrieved from https://www.manchesterhive.com/view/9781847793010/9781847793010.xml

Hall, C., & Rose, S. O. (2006). *At home with the empire: Metropolitan culture and the imperial world*. Cambridge: Cambridge University Press.

Hallin, D. C., & Mancini, P. (2004). *Comparing media systems: Three models of media and politics*. Cambridge: Cambridge University Press.

Hallin, D. C., & Mancini, P. (2011). *Comparing media systems beyond the Western world*. Cambridge: Cambridge University Press.

Hampton, M. (2008). The "objectivity" ideal and its limitations in 20th-century British journalism. *Journalism Studies, 9*(4), 477–493. doi:10.1080/14616700802113060.

Hampton, M. (2010). The fourth estate ideal in journalism history. In A. Stuart (Ed.), *The Routledge Companion to News and Journalism* (pp. 3–12). Abingdon, Oxfordshire: Routledge.

Handlin, O., & Handlin, L. (1989). Who read John Locke? Words and acts in the American revolution. *The American Scholar, 58*(4), 545–556.

Hanitzsch, T. (2016). The WJS 2012–2016 study. Retrieved from http://www.worldsofjournalism.org/.

Hanitzsch, T., Anikina, M., Berganza, R., Cangoz, I., Coman, M., Hamada, B., . . . Moreira, S. V. (2010). Modeling perceived influences on journalism: Evidence from a cross-national survey of journalists. *Journalism & Mass Communication Quarterly, 87*(1), 5–22.

Hanitzsch, T., Hanusch, F., Mellado, C., Anikina, M., Berganza, R., Cangoz, I., . . . Karadjov, C. D. (2011). Mapping journalism cultures across nations: A comparative study of 18 countries. *Journalism Studies, 12*(3), 273–293.

Hanusch, F., & Hanitzsch, T. (2017). Comparing journalistic cultures across nations: What we can learn from the worlds of journalism study. *Journalism Studies, 5*(18), 525–535.

Harcup, T. (2011). Alternative journalism as active citizenship. *Journalism, 12*(1), 15–31.

Harkins, S., & Lugo-Ocando, J. (2016a). All people are equal, but some people are more equal than others. In J. Servaes & T. Oyedemi (Eds.), *The praxis of social inequality in media: A global perspective* (pp. 3–20). Lanham, Maryland: Rowman & Littlefield.

Harkins, S., & Lugo-Ocando, J. (2016b). How Malthusian ideology crept into the newsroom: British tabloids and the coverage of the 'underclass'. *Critical Discourse Studies, 13*(1), 78–93.

Harkins, S., & Lugo-Ocando, J. (2016c). Victorian discourses of poverty and race in modern journalism. In L. Matthews-Jones & A. O'Neal (Eds.), *Re-visioning the victorians*. London: Palgrave MacMillan.

Harkins, S., & Lugo-Ocando, J. (2017). *Poor news: Media discourses of poverty in times of austerity*. London: Rowman & Littlefield International.

Harkins, S., & Lugo-Ocando, J. (2019). *Poor news: Media discourses of poverty in times of austerity*. London: Rowman & Littlefield International.

Harlow, S., & Salaverría, R. (2016). Regenerating journalism: Exploring the "alternativeness" and "digital-ness" of online-native media in Latin America. *Digital Journalism, 4*(8), 1001–1019.

Harrison, D. (2003). *The sociology of modernization and development*. Abingdon, Oxfordshire: Routledge.

Hart, F. B. (1919). Power of government over speech and press. *The Yale Law Journal, 29*, 410.

Hart, J. (2013). *Empire of ideas: The origins of public diplomacy and the transformation of US foreign policy*. Oxford: Oxford University Press.

Harvey, D. (2007). *A brief history of neoliberalism*. USA: Oxford University Press.

Haynes, J. E. (2000). The Cold War debate continues: A traditionalist view of historical writing on domestic communism and anti-communism. *Journal of Cold War Studies, 2*(1), 76–115.

Hearns-Branaman, J. O. (2016). *Journalism and the philosophy of truth: Beyond objectivity and balance*. Abingdon, Oxfordshire: Routledge.

Hochschild, A. (2017a). When dissent became treason. Retrieved from http://www.nybooks.com/articles/2017/09/28/world-war-i-when-dissent-became-treason/.

Hochschild, A. (2017b, 28/09/2017). When dissent became treason. *The New York Review of Books, LXIV*, 82–85.

Hogan, L. (1984). *A black national news service: The Associated Negro Press and Claude Barnett, 1919–1945*. Madison, New Jersey: Fairleigh Dickinson Univiversity Press.

Holtzblatt, M., Jermakowicz, E. K., & Epstein, B. J. (2015). Tax heavens: Methods and tactics for corporate profit shifting. *International Tax Journal, 41*, 33.

Hopkins, M. W. (1965). Lenin, Stalin, Khrushchev: Three concepts of the press. *Journalism Quarterly, 42*(4), 523–531.

Horkheimer, M., & Adorno, T. (2001). The culture industry: Enlightenment as mass deception. In M. Durham & D. Kellner (Eds.), *Media and cultural studies: Keyworks* (pp. 71–101). Oxford: Blackwell Publishing.

Horne, G. (2017a). *The rise and fall of the Associated Negro Press*. Champaign, Illinois: University of Illinois Press.

Horne, G. (2017b). *The rise and fall of the Associated Negro Press: Claude Barnett's Pan-African news and the Jim Crow Paradox*. Champaign, Illinois: University of Illinois Press.

Houston, B. (2010). The future of investigative journalism. *Daedalus, 139*(2), 45–56.

Howard, R. (2003). *International media assistance: A review of donor activities and lessons learned*. Oslo: Netherlands Institute of International Relations, Clingendael.

Hudson, M. (2017). Panama papers win the Pulitzer prize. Retrieved from https://www.icij.org/blog/2017/04/panama-papers-wins-pulitzer-prize.

Humphrey, H. (1951). *Memorandum for the president of the United States of America*. Retrieved from Washington, DC.

Huntington, S. P. (1981 [1951]). *The soldier and the state*. Cambridge, Massachusetts: Harvard University Press.

Hurtado, A. (2012). La cultura escrita en sociedades campesinas: la experiencia de Radio Sutatenza en el Suroccidente colombiano. *Boletín Cultural y Bibliográfico, 46*(82), 69–92.

Ichikawa, H. (2018). *Soviet science and engineering in the shadow of the Cold War.* Abingdon, Oxfordshire: Routledge.

IIPJM. (2018). Instituto Internacional de Periodismo José Martí. Retrieved from https://periodismojosemarti.wordpress.com/convocatorias-2/.

Ileason, E. (1953a). *Memorandum to the president of the United States: Dicussion at the 164th meeting of the National Security Council, Thursday, October 1, 1963.* Retrieved from Washington DC.

Ileason, E. (1953b). *Memorandum to the president of the United States: Discussion at the 136th meeting of the National Security Council on Wednesday, March 11, 1953.* Retrieved from Washington DC.

Ileason, E. (1953c). *Memorandum to the president of the United States: Discussion at the 167th meeting of the National Security Council, Thursday, October 22, 1953.* Retrieved from Washington DC.

Ilyenkov, E. V. (2001 [1979]). *Leninist dialectics and the metaphysics of positivism: Reflections on V.I. Lenin's book, materialism and empirio-criticism.* Wappingers Falls, NY: Beekman Publisher.

Immerwahr, D. (2019). *How to hide an empire: A short history of the greater United States.* London: Random House.

Ings, S. (2017). *Stalin and the scientists: A history of triumph and tragedy, 1905–1953.* London: Faber & Faber.

Inikori, J. E. (1989). Slavery and the revolution in cotton textile production in England. *Social Science History, 13*(4), 343–379.

Jackson, P. T. (2009). News as a contested commodity: A clash of capitalist and journalistic imperatives. *Journal of Mass Media Ethics, 24*(2–3), 146–163.

James, C. L. R. (2001 [1938]). *The Black Jacobins: Toussaint L'Ouverture and the San Domingo revolution.* London: Penguin.

Janowitz, M. (1975). Professional models in journalism: The gatekeeper and the advocate. *Journalism Quarterly, 52*(4), 618–626.

Jeffrey, H. P. (1987). Legislative origins of the Fulbright program. *The Annals of the American Academy of Political and Social Science, 491*(1), 36–47.

Jenkins, R. (2001). Mistaking 'governance' for 'politics': Foreign aid, democracy, and the construction of civil society. In K. Sudipta (Ed.), *Civil Society: History and Possibilities* (pp. 250–268). Cambridge: Cambridge University Press.

Jensen, T., & Tyler, I. (2015). 'Benefits broods': The cultural and political crafting of anti-welfare commonsense. *Critical Social Policy, 35*(4), 470–491.

Jones, A., & Waisbord, S. (2010). *International media assistance and aid effectiveness: Conceptual blindspots and institutional incentives.* Paper presented at the APSA 2010 Annual Meeting Paper, Washington, DC.

Josephi, B. U. (2010). *Journalism education in countries with limited media freedom.* Oxford: Peter Lang.

Kale, V. (2015). Sitting down with P. Sainath. Retrieved from https://psainath.org/sitting-down-with-p-sainath/.

Kant, I. (1985 [1783]). *Prolegomena to any future metaphysics*. New York: Liberal Arts Press.

Kaplan, R. L. (2006). The news about new institutionalism: Journalism's ethic of objectivity and its political origins. *Political Communication, 23*(2), 173–185. doi:10.1080/10584600600629737.

Kathryn, M. (2017). We're all in this thing together: Cold war consensus in the exclusive social world of Washington reporters. In B. J. Schulman & J. E. Zelizer (Eds.), *Media nation: The political history of news in modern America* (pp. 63–76). Philadeplphia, Pennsylvania: University of Pennsylvania Press.

Keene, J. (2007). *Fighting for Franco: International volunteers in nationalist Spain during the Spanish Civil War*. New York: Bloomsbury Publishing.

Kenez, P. (1981). *Lenin and the freedom of the press*. Washington, DC: Kennan Institute for Advanced Russian Studies.

Keohane, R. O. (1991). The United States and the postwar order: Empire or hegemony? *Journal of Peace Research, 28*(4), 435–439.

Kerr, D. (2002). Orwell's BBC broadcasts: Colonial discourse and the rhetoric of propaganda. *Textual Practice, 16*(3), 473–490.

Kiesewetter, H. (1998). Regional factors in European desindustrialization from 1955–1995. In C. E. Núñez (Ed.), *De-industrialization in Europe 19th-29th Centuries* (pp. 155–167). Sevilla: Fundación Fomento de la Historia Económica.

Killingray, D. (1986). The maintenance of law and order in British colonial Africa. *African Affairs, 85*(340), 411–437.

Kirkendall, R. S. (1989). *The Harry S. Truman encyclopedia*. Boston: G.K. Hall & Co.

Kitano, N., & Harada, Y. (2016). Estimating China's foreign aid 2001–2013. *Journal of International Development, 28*(7), 1050–1074.

Kitzberger, P., & Pérez, G. J. (2008). *Los pobres en papel. Las narrativas de la pobreza en la prensa latinoamericana*. Buenos Aires: Fundación Konrad Adenauer,.

Klauber, E. (1945). Memorandum from the Acting Director.

Knight, G. (1982). News and ideology. *Canadian Journal of communication, 8*(4), 15–41.

Knock, T. (1992). *To end all wars: Woodrow Wilson and the quest for a new world order*. New York: Oxford University Press.

Koch, T. (1990). *The news as a myth. Fact and context in journalism*. Westport, CT: Greenwood Publishing Group.

Koepnick, L. P. (1999). *Walter Benjamin and the aesthetics of power*. Lincoln, NE: University of Nebraska Press.

Kuhn, T. S. (2012 [1962]). *The structure of scientific revolutions*. Chicago: University of Chicago Press.

Kuitenbrouwer, V. (2016). Radio as a tool of empire. Intercontinental broadcasting from the Netherlands to the Dutch East Indies in the 1920s and 1930s. *Itinerario, 40*(1), 83–103.

Kumar, K. (2006). *Promoting independent media: Strategies for democracy assistance*. Boulder, Colorado: Lynne Rienner Publishers.

LaMay, C. L. (2009). *Exporting press freedom. Economic and editorial dilemmas in international media assistance*. New Brunswick: Transaction Publishers.

Lancaster, C. (2008). *Foreign aid: Diplomacy, development, domestic politics*. Chicago, Illinois: University of Chicago Press.

Latham, M. E. (1998). Ideology, social science, and destiny: Modernization and the Kennedy-Era Alliance for Progress. *Diplomatic History, 22*(2), 199–229.

Latham, M. E. (2000). *Modernization as ideology: American social science and "nation building" in the Kennedy era* (Vol. 4). Chapel Hill: University of North Carolina Press.

Lazaridis, G., & Veikou, M. (2017). The rise of the far right in Greece and opposition to 'othering', hate speech, and crime by civil and civic organizations. *Journal of Civil Society, 13*(1), 1–17.

Le Bon, G. (2010 [1897]). *The crowd: A study of the popular mind*. Fairford, Gloucestershire: Echo Library.

Lee, A. M. (2013). News audiences revisited: Theorizing the link between audience motivations and news consumption. *Journal of Broadcasting & Electronic Media, 57*(3), 300–317.

Leeson, P. T. (2008). Escaping poverty: Foreign aid, private property, and economic development. *Journal of Private Enterprise, 23*(2), 39–64.

Lehman, D. W. (2002). *John Reed and the writing of Revolution*. Athens, Ohio: Ohio University Press.

Lemberg, D. (2019). *Barriers down: How American power and free-flow policies shaped global media*. Columbia University Press.

Lenin, V. (1919). Theses on Bourgeois Democracy and the dictatorship of the proletariat. Retrieved from http://www.workersliberty.org/node/8062.

Lenoe, M. (2004). *Closer to the masses. Stalinist culture, social revolution, and soviet newspapers*. Cambridge, Massachusetts: Harvard University Press.

Lever, R. (2019). Facebook follows Google with funds to support journalism. Retrieved from https://phys.org/news/2019-01-facebook-invest-million-local-journalism.html.

Levine, C. (2017). Mercer family's charitable giving skyrocketed in 2015, new filing shows. The 2016 election cycle brought the Trump-backing billionaires new prominence. Retrieved from https://publicintegrity.org/politics/mercer-familys-charitable-giving-skyrocketed-in-2015-new-filing-shows/.

Liao, J., Cheng, F., Harris, A., & Xu, D. (2018). The new face of China's foreign aid: Where do we go from here? *The Lancet, 392*(10148), 636.

Lilly, E. (1968). The psychological strategy board and its predecessors. Foreign Policy Coordination 1938–1953. In G. Vincitorio (Ed.), *Studies in Modern History*. New York: St. John's University Press.

Lima, H., Hohlfeldt, A., Sousa, J. P., & Barbosa, M. (2014). *History of the press in the Portuguese-Speaking countries*. Lisbon: Media XXI.

Lippmann, W. (1920). *Liberty and the news*. San Diego, California: Harcourt, Brace and Howe.

Lippmann, W. (2010 [1920]). *Liberty and the news*. Mineola, New York: Dover Publications.

Lippmann, W. (2017 [1922]). *Public opinion.* Abingdon, Oxfordshire: Routledge.
Lithgow, M. (2012). Defying the news: New aesthetics of truth in popular culture. *Canadian Journal of communication, 37*(2), 281–302.
Littler, C. R. (1978). Understanding taylorism. *British Journal of Sociology, 29*(2), 185–202.
Locke, J. (2016 [1690]). *Second treatise of government and a letter concerning toleration.* Oxford: Oxford University Press.
Lombardi, J. (2012). Sociedad y Esclavos en Venezuela la Era Republicana: 1821–1854. *Academia Nacional de la Historia (Venezuela). Boletín de la Academia Nacional de la Historia, 95*(380), 103–117.
Lomøy, J. (2011). *Measuring aid: 50 years of DAC statistics 1961–2011.* Retrieved from Paris: https://www.oecd.org/dac/stats/documentupload/MeasuringAid50yearsDACStats.pdf.
Losurdo, D. (2014). *Liberalism: A counter-history.* London: Verso.
Louis, W. R. (1984). *The British Empire in the Middle East, 1945–1951: Arab Nationalism, the United States, and postwar imperialism.* Oxford: Oxford University Press.
Lucas, S. (1999). *Freedom's war: The American crusade against the Soviet Union.* New York: New York University Press.
Lugo, A. (2008). *Fragmented lives, assembled parts: Culture, capitalism, and conquest at the US-Mexico border.* Austin, Texas: University of Texas Press.
Lugo-Ocando, J. (2008). *The media in Latin America.* New York: McGraw-Hill Education.
Lugo-Ocando, J. (2014). *Blaming the victim: How global journalism fails those in poverty.* London: Pluto Press.
Lugo-Ocando, J. (2018). A mouthpiece for truth: Foreign aid for media development and the making of journalism in the Global South. *Brazilian Journalism Research, 14*(2), 412–431.
Lugo-Ocando, J. (2020). The 'changing'face of media discourses on poverty in the age of populism and anti-globalisation: The political appeal of anti-modernity and certainty in Brazil. *International Communication Gazette, 82*(1), 101–116.
Lugo-Ocando, J., Caizalez, A., & Lohmeier, C. (2010). When PSB is delivered by the hand of God: The case of Roman Catholic broadcast networks in Venezuela. *International Journal of Media & Cultural Politics, 6*(2), 149–167.
Lugo-Ocando, J., & Faria Brandão, R. (2016). Stabbing news: Articulating crime statistics in the newsroom. *Journalism Practice, 10*(6), 715–729.
Lugo-Ocando, J., & Nguyen, A. (2017). *Developing news: Global journalism and the coverage of "Third World" development.* Abingdon, Oxfordshire: Taylor & Francis.
Lule, J. (1991). Roots of the space race: Sputnik and the language of US news in 1957. *Journalism Quarterly, 68*(1–2), 76–86.
Luxemburgo, R. (2017 [1922]). *La Revolución Rusa.* Barcelona: Página Indómita.
Ma, V. (2016). Propaganda and censorship: Adapting to the modern age. *Harvard International Review, 37*(2), 46.

MacBride-Commission. (2003 [1980]). *Many voices, one world: Communication and society, today and tomorrow: The MacBride report*. Lanham, Maryland: Unesco/ Rowman & Littlefield Publishers.

Machlup, F. (1962). *The production and distribution of knowledge in the United States*. Princeton, New Jersey: Princeton University Press.

Madrick, J., & Papanikolaou, N. (2010). The stagnation of male wages in the US. *International Review of Applied Economics, 24*(3), 309–318.

Manion, C. (1949). The founding fathers and the natural law: A study of the source of our legal institutions. *American Bar Association Journal, 35*(6), 461–529.

Mann, T. (1952). *Memorandum to Mr. Charles S. Murphy, special counsel to the president, The White House*. Retrieved from Washington DC.

Manning, C., & Malbrough, M. (2012). *The changing dynamics of foreign aid and democracy in Mozambique*. Retrieved from Shibuya, Tokyo. https://www.econstor.eu/handle/10419/81077.

Mano, W. (2008). Africa: Media systems. The international encyclopedia of communication. https://onlinelibrary.wiley.com/doi/abs/10.1002/9781405186407.wbieca033.

Maras, S. (2013). *Objectivity in Journalism*. Wiley.

Marlin, C. L. (1987). Space race propaganda: US coverage of the soviet Sputniks in 1957. *Journalism Quarterly, 64*(2–3), 544–559.

Marques de Melo, J. (2009). Journalistic thinking: Brazil's modern tradition. *Journalism, 10*(1), 9–27.

Martin, R. (1992). Building independent mass media in Africa. *The Journal of Modern African Studies, 30*(2), 331–340.

Martín-Barbero, J., & Rey, G. (1997). El periodismo en Colombia de los oficios y los medios. *Signo y pensamiento, 16*(30), 13–30.

Martinisi, A., & Lugo-Ocando, J. (2015). Overcoming the objectivity of the senses: Enhancing journalism practice through Eastern philosophies. *International Communication Gazette, 77*(5), 439–455.

Martisini, A. and Lugo-Ocando, J. (2020). *Good numbers for bad news statistics, data and the quality of journalism*. London: Anthem Press.

Mattelart, A. (1996). *The invention of communication*. Minneapolis, MN: University of Minnesota Press.

Mattelart, A. (2002). *Geopolítica de la cultura*. Santiago de Chile: Lom Ediciones.

Mattelart, A. (2003). *The information society: An introduction*. London: Sage.

McChesney, R. W. (2010). *Rich media, poor democracy: Communication politics in dubious times*. New York: New Press.

McChesney, R. W. (2002). The US news media and World War III. *Journalism, 3*(1), 14–21.

McCurdy, P. M., & Power, G. (2007). Journalism education as a vehicle for media development in Africa: The AMDI project. *Ecquid Novi, 28*(1–2), 127–147.

McLeod, K. (2002). The politics and history of hip-hop journalism. In S. Jones (Ed.), *Popular music and the press* (pp. 156–170). Philadelphia: Temple University Press.

McManus, J. H. (1992). What kind of commodity is news. *Communication Research, 19*(6), 787–805.

McNair, B. (1998). *The sociology of journalism*. Oxford: Oxford University Press.
McNair, B. (2000). *Journalism and democracy*. Abingdon, Oxfordshire: Routledge.
McNair, B. (2006). *Cultural chaos: Journalism and power in a globalised world*. Abingdon, Oxfordshire: Routledge.
McNair, B. (2018). From control to chaos, and back again: Journalism and the politics of populist authoritarianism. *Journalism Studies, 19*(4), 499–511.
McNally, D. (1989). Locke, levellers and liberty: Property and democracy in the thought of the first whigs. *History of Political Thought, 10*(1), 17–40.
Mehan, J. A. (1981). UNESCO and the US: Action and reaction. *Journal of Communication, 31*(4), 159–163.
Mellado, C., Moreira, S. V., Lagos, C., & Hernández, M. E. (2012). Comparing journalism cultures in Latin America: The case of Chile, Brazil and Mexico. *International Communication Gazette, 74*(1), 60–77.
Mellado, C., & Van Dalen, A. (2017). Changing times, changing journalism: A content analysis of journalistic role performances in a transitional democracy. *The International Journal of Press/Politics, 22*(2), 244–263.
Mellado Ruiz, C. (2010). La influencia de CIESPAL en la formación del periodista latinoamericano. Una revisión crítica. *Estudios sobre el mensaje periodístico, 16*, 307–318.
Merrill, D. (2006). The Truman doctrine: Containing communism and modernity. *Presidential Studies Quarterly, 36*(1), 27–37.
Michalopoulos, S., & Papaioannou, E. (2016). The long-run effects of the scramble for Africa. *American Economic Review, 106*(7), 1802–1848.
Mieczkowski, Y. (2013). *Eisenhower's Sputnik moment: The race for space and world prestige*. Ithaca, New York: Cornell University Press.
Millones, L. (2007). Mesianismo en América Hispana: El Taki Onqoy. *Memoria americana* (15), 7–39.
Mindich, D. (2000). *Just the facts: How "objectivity" came to define American journalism*. New York: New York University Press.
Mindich, D. T. (2000). *Just the facts: How "objectivity" came to define American journalism*. New York: New York University Press.
Moraña, M., Dussel, E. D., & Jáuregui, C. A. (2008). *Coloniality at large: Latin America and the postcolonial debate*. Durham, North Carolina: Duke University Press.
Morris, J. S. (2007). Slanted objectivity? Perceived media bias, cable news exposure, and political attitudes. *Social Science Quarterly, 88*(3), 707–728.
Mott, F. L. (1941). *American journalism: A history of newspapers in the United States through 250 years, 1690–1940*. New York: The Macmillan Company.
Moyo, D. (2009). *Dead aid: Why aid is not working and how there is a better way for Africa*. Basingstoke: Macmillan.
Mrázek, R. (1997). "Let us become radio mechanics": Technology and national identity in late-colonial Netherlands East Indies. *Comparative Studies in Society and History, 39*(1), 3–33.
Muhlmann, G. (2008). *Political history of journalism*. Cambridge: Polity Press.
Mujica, H. (1982). *El Imperio de la Noticia: Algunos Problemas de la Información en El Mundo Contemporáneo*. Caracas: Editorial de la Universidad Central de Venezuela.

Mujica, H. (2006 [1982]). *El imperio de la noticia. Algunos problemas de la información en el mundo contemporáneo.* Caracas: ABN.

Muñoz-Torres, J. R. (2012). Truth and objectivity in journalism: Anatomy of an endless misunderstanding. *Journalism Studies, 13*(4), 566–582.

Murphy, S. M., & Scotton, J. F. (1987). Dependency and journalism education in Africa: Are there alternative models? *African Media Review, 1*(3), 11–35.

Musandu, P. (2018). *Pressing interests: The agenda and influence of a colonial East African newspaper sector.* Montreal: McGill-Queen's University Press.

Mutsvairo, B. (2016). Politics of passion and the pursuit of propaganda in Zimbabwe's state media: A study of the case of The Herald. In B. Mutsvairo (Ed.), *Participatory politics and citizen journalism in a networked Africa: A connected continent* (pp. 157–170). London: Palgrave Macmillan.

Mutsvairo, B., Columbus, S., & Leijendekker, I. (2012). *African citizen journalists' ethics and the emerging networked public sphere.* Paper presented at the 13th International Symposium for Online Journalism 2012, Austin, USA, Austin, TX.

Myers, M. (2014). *Africa's media boom: The role of international aid.* Retrieved from Wasington, DC: https://www.cima.ned.org/resource/africas-media-boom-the-role-of-international-aid/.

Nechyba, T. J. (2000). Mobility, targeting, and private-school vouchers. *American Economic Review, 90*(1), 130–146.

Nerone, J. (2013a). The historical roots of the normative model of journalism. *Journalism, 14*(4), 446–458.

Nerone, J. (2013b). Why journalism history matters to journalism studies. *American Journalism, 30*(1), 15–28.

Nesbitt, F. N. T. (2008). *Universal emancipation: The Haitian revolution and the radical enlightenment.* Charlottesville, Virginia: University of Virginia Press.

Nesbitt, N. (2009). Alter-Rights: Haiti and the singularization of universal human rights. *International Journal of Francophone Studies, 12*(1), 93–108.

Nielsen, K. E. (2001). *Un-American womanhood: Antiradicalism, antifeminism, and the first red scare.* Columbus, Ohio: Ohio State University Press.

Nielsen, R. K. (2015). *Local journalism: The decline of newspapers and the rise of digital media.* London: Bloomsbury Publishing.

Nixon, R. B. (1982). Historia de las Escuelas de Periodismo. *Chasqui: Revista Latinoamericana de Comunicación*(2), 13–19.

Noble, D. (2017). *Forces of production: A social history of industrial automation.* Abingdon, Oxfordshire: Routledge.

Nordenstreng, K. (2011). Free flow doctrine in global media policy. In R. Mansell & M. Raboy (Eds.), *The handbook of global media and communication policy* (pp. 79–94). Hoboken, New Jersey, United States: Wiley-Blackwell.

Nordenstreng, K. (2013). How the new world order and imperialism challenge media studies. *TripleC, 11*(2), 348–358.

North, D. C. (1990). *Institutions, institutional change and economic performance.* Cambridge: Cambridge University Press.

North, D. C. (1991). Institutions. *Journal of Economic Perspectives, 5*(Winter), 97–112.

North, D. C. (1994). Economic performance through time. *The American Economic Review, 84*(3), 359–368.

Nye Jr, J. S. (2008). Public diplomacy and soft power. *The Annals of the American Academy of Political and Social Science, 616*(1), 94–109.

Nye, J. S. (1999). *Understanding international conflicts*. New York: Longman.

OAS. (1948). Charter of organization of American States (A-41). Retrieved from http://www.oas.org/en/sla/dil/inter_american_treaties_A-41_charter_OAS.asp.

Oats, L., & Sadler, P. (2007). The abolition of taxes on knowledge. In *Studies in the history of tax law* (pp. 287–306). Hart Publishing.

Obermayer, B., & Obermaier, F. (2017). *The panama papers*. London: Oneworld Publications.

Ogelsby, J. (1969). Spain's Havana Squadron and the preservation of the balance of power in the Caribbean, 1740–1748. *The Hispanic American Historical Review, 49*(3), 473–488.

Ogundimu, F. F., Oyewo, O. Y., & Adegoke, L. (2007). West African journalism education and the quest for professional standards. *Ecquid Novi, 28*(1–2), 191–197.

Olukotun, A. (2004). *Repressive state and resurgent media under Nigeria's military dictatorship, 1988–98* (Vol. 126). Uppsala: Nordic Africa Institute.

Omu, F. I. (1968). The dilemma of press freedom in colonial Africa: The West African example. *The Journal of African History, 9*(2), 279–298.

Oreskes, N. (2014). Science in the origins of the Cold War. In N. Oreskes & J. Krige (Eds.), *Science and technology in the global Cold War* (pp. 11–30). Cambridge, Massachusetts: MIT Press.

Örnebring, H., & Jönsson, A. M. (2004). Tabloid journalism and the public sphere: A historical perspective on tabloid journalism. *Journalism Studies, 5*(3), 283–295.

Ortega, J. (1993 [1929]). *The revolt of the masses*. New York: W.W. Norton.

Ortega y Gasset, J. (1983 [1930]). *La rebelión de las masas*. Madrid: Orbis.

Osgood, K. A. (2006). *Total Cold War: Eisenhower's secret propaganda battle at home and abroad*. Lawrence, Kansas: University Press of Kansas.

Osiel, M. J. (1986). The professionalization of journalism: Impetus or impediment to a "watchdog" press. *Sociological Inquiry, 56*(2), 163–189.

Osung, M. M. (2018). La radio comunitaria en el entramado mediático del Congo. *Revista de Comunicación de la SEECI*(44), 73–86.

Overholser, G., & Jamieson, K. H. (2005). *The institutions of American democracy: The press*. Oxford: Oxford University Press.

Paine, T. (2004 [1776]). *Common sense*. New York: Broadview Press.

Pakenham, T. (2015 [1990]). *The scramble for Africa*. London: Hachette UK.

Palan, R., Murphy, R., & Chavagneux, C. (2013). *Tax havens: How globalization really works*. Cornell University Press.

Papoutsaki, E. (2007). De-colonising journalism curricula: A research & "development" perspective. *Media Asia, 34*(2), 79–87.

Pappe, I. (2007). *The ethnic cleansing of Palestine*. London: Oneworld Publications.

Parameswaran, R. E. (1997). Colonial interventions and the postcolonial situation in India: The English language, mass media and the articulation of class. *Gazette (Leiden, Netherlands), 59*(1), 21–41.

Park, M.-J., & Curran, J. (2000). *De-Westernizing media studies*. London: Psychology Press.

Parker, J. (2016). *Hearts, minds, voices. US Cold War public diplomacy and the formation of the Third World*. New York: Oxford University Press.

Parry, A. (1967). Soviet aid to Vietnam: The reporter 12 January 1967. *Survival, 9*(3), 76–82.

Parry-Giles, S. J. (1994). The Eisenhower Administration's conceptualization of the USIA: The development of overt and covert propaganda strategies. *Presidential Studies Quarterly, 24*(2), 263–276.

Pasquali, A. (2005). The south and the imbalance in communication. *Global Media and Communication, 1*(3), 289–300.

Paterson, C. (2005). News agency dominance in international news on the internet. In *Converging media, diverging politics: A political economy of news in the United States and Canada*. Lexington: Rowman and Littlefield, 145–164.

Paterson, C. (2011). *The international television news agencies: The world from London*. New York: Peter Lang.

Paterson, C., Gadzekpo, A., & Wasserman, H. (2018). Journalism and foreign aid in Africa. (pp. 1–18): Taylor & Francis.

Paterson, C., & Sreberny, A. (2004). *John Libbey publishing*. New Barnet, Herts: Georgetown University Press.

Pegg, M. (1983). *Broadcasting and society, 1918–1939*. Abingdon, Oxfordshire: Routledge.

Pennycook, G., & Rand, D. G. (2019). Fighting misinformation on social media using crowdsourced judgments of news source quality. *Proceedings of the National Academy of Sciences, 116*(7), 2521–2526.

Peters, C., & Broersma, M. J. (2013). *Rethinking journalism: Trust and participation in a transformed news landscape*. Abingdon, Oxfordshire: Routledge.

Pettegree, A. (2014). *The invention of news. How the world came to know about itself*. New Haven: Yale University Press.

Peycam, P. (2012). *The birth of Vietnamese political journalism*. New York: Columbia University Press.

Picard, R. G. (2008). Shifts in newspaper advertising expenditures and their implications for the future of newspapers. *Journalism Studies, 9*(5), 704–716.

Pickard, V. (2015). The return of the nervous liberals: Market fundamentalism, policy failure, and recurring journalism crises. *The Communication Review, 18*(2), 82–97.

Pickering, S. (2001). Common sense and original deviancy: News discourses and asylum seekers in Australia. *Journal of Refugee Studies, 14*(2), 169–186.

Pineda de Alcázar, M. (2001). Las teorías clásicas de la comunicación: Balance de sus aportes y limitaciones a la luz del siglo XXI. *Opción: revista de Ciencias Humanas y Sociales, 17*(36), 11–29.

Polanyi, K. (2001 [1944]). *The great transformation: The political and economic origin of our time*. Boston: Beacon Press.

Pollard, V. K. (1996). Entering global civil society: Japan's ODA policy-making milieu from June 1992. *Japanese Studies, 16*(2–3), 35–61.

Pollock, E. (2006). *Stalin and the Soviet science wars*. Princeton, New Jersey: Princeton University Press.

Popkin, J. (2010). *You are all free: The Haitian revolution and the abolition of slavery*. Cambridge: Cambridge University Press.

Popkin, J. D. (1990). *Revolutionary news: The press in France, 1789–1799*. Durham, North Carolina: Duke University Press.

Potter, S. (2012). *Broadcasting empire: The BBC and the British world, 1922–1970*. Oxford: Oxford University Press.

Powell, W. W. (2007). The New Institutionalism. Paper. Retrieved from http://web.stanford.edu/group/song/papers/NewInstitutionalism.pdf.

Powers, R. G. (1998). *Not without honor: The history of American anticommunism*. New Haven, Connecticut: Yale University Press.

Pressman, M. (2017). Objectivity and its discontents: The struggle for the soul of American journalism in the 1960s and 1970s. In Bruce J. Schulman & Julian E. Zelizer (Eds.), *Media nation: The political history of news in America* (pp. 96–113). Philadelphia, Pennsylvania: University of Pennsylvania Press.

Price, M. (2002a). *Mapping media assistance*. The Programme in Comparative Media Law & Policy, Centre for Socio-Legal Studies, University of Oxford. Oxford. Retrieved from https://repository.upenn.edu/asc_papers/62/.

Price, M. (2002b). *Media and sovereignty: The global information revolution and its challenge to state power*. Cambridge, Massachusetts: MIT press.

Price, M. (2019). Media development and the market for loyalties. In N. Banequista, S. Abbott, P. Rotham, & W. Mano (Eds.), *International media development. Historical perspectives and news frontiers* (pp. 20–29). Oxford: Peter Lang.

Prieto Castillo, D. (2008). *Radio Nederland Training Center en América Latina: Memoria pedagógica de tres décadas*. San José, Costa Rica: RNTC.

Quinn, B. (2017). UK among six countries to hit 0.7% UN aid spending target. Retrieved from https://www.theguardian.com/global-development/2017/jan/04/uk-among-six-countries-hit-un-aid-spending-target-oecd.

Radosh, R. (2012). A tale of two trials: Soviet propaganda at home and abroad. *World Affairs*, 80–87.

Randall, D. (2000). *The universal journalist*. Pluto Press.

Rao, S., & Lee, S. T. (2005). Globalizing media ethics? An assessment of universal ethics among international political journalists. *Journal of Mass Media Ethics*, 20(2–3), 99–120.

Rapport, M. (2009). *1848: Year of revolution*. Basic Books.

Ratto Ciarlo, J. (1971). *Libertad de prensa en Venezuela: durante la guerra de emancipación hasta la Batalla de Carabobo*. Caracas: Biblioteca de Historia del Ejército.

Ratto Ciarlo, J. (1977). *Historia caraqueña del periodismo venezolano 1808–1830*. Caracas: Cuatricentenario de Caracas.

Read, A. (2008). *The world on fire: 1919 and the battle with Bolshevism*. New York: Random House.

Reed, J. (1919). *Ten days that shook the world*. New York: Boni & Liveright.

Reed, J. (2007 [1919]). *Ten days that shook the world*. London: Penguin Classics.

Reed, J. (2009 [1914]). *Insurgent Mexico; with Pancho Villa in the Mexican revolution*. St Petersburg, Florida: Red and Black Publishers.
Reivich, L. (2007). The fourth face of U.S. imperialism. Retrieved from https://nacla.org/article/fourth-face-us-imperialism.
Requejo-Alemán, J. L., & Lugo-Ocando, J. (2014). Assessing the sustainability of Latin American investigative non-profit journalism. *Journalism Studies, 15*(5), 522–532.
Resis, A. (1977). Lenin on freedom of the press. *The Russian Review, 36*(3), 274–296.
Reynolds Jr, R. D. (1979). The 1906 campaign to sway muckraking periodicals. *Journalism Quarterly, 56*(3), 513–589.
Reynolds, T. (2015). *Economic aspects of the Monroe doctrine during the period 1792–1823.* Paper presented at the Proceedings of the Oklahoma Academy of Science.
Riall, L. (2007). *Garibaldi: Invention of a hero.* New Haven, Connecticut: Yale University Press.
Rich, M. D. (2018). *Truth decay: An initial exploration of the diminishing role of facts and analysis in American public life.* Santa Monica, California: Rand Corporation.
Roach, C. (1990). The movement for a new world information and communication order: A second wave? *Media, Culture & Society, 12*(3), 283–307.
Roach, C. (1997). Cultural imperialism and resistance in media theory and literary theory. *Media, Culture & Society, 19*(1), 47–66.
Rodny-Gumede, Y. (2018). A teaching philosophy of journalism education in the global South: A South African case study. *Journalism, 19*(6), 747–761.
Roeh, I. (1989). Journalism as storytelling, coverage as narrative. *American Behavioral Scientist, 33*(2), 162–168.
Roman, E. (1997). Empire forgotten: The United States's colonization of Puerto Rico. *Villanova Law Review, 42*, 1119.
Romano, A. (1998). Normative theories of development journalism: State versus practitioner perspectives in Indonesia. *Australian Journalism Review, 20*(2), 60–87.
Rosenblum, M. (1977). Reporting from the Third World. *Foreign Affairs, 55*, 815.
Rosenblatt, H. (2018). *The lost history of liberalism: From ancient rome to the twenty-first century.* Princeton, New Jersey: Princeton University Press.
Rosenfeld, S. A. (2011). *Common sense.* Cambridge, Massachusetts: Harvard University Press.
Ross, E. B. (1998). *Matlhus Factor.* London: Zed Books.
Roth, A. (2019). Putin approves law targeting journalists as 'foreign agents'. Retrieved from https://www.theguardian.com/world/2019/dec/03/putin-approves-law-targeting-journalists-foreign-agents.
Roth-Ey, K. (2011). *Moscow prime time: How the Soviet Union built the media empire that lost the cultural Cold War.* Ithaca, New York: Cornell University Press.
Rouner, D., Slater, M. D., & Buddenbaum, J. M. (1999). How perceptions of news bias in news sources relate to beliefs about media bias. *Newspaper Research Journal, 20*(2), 41–51.
Rubio, A. (2017). The beginning of Nueva granada printing, 1738–1782. Letters and typesetters oriented towards printed language. *Lingüística y Literatura*(71), 55–68.

Rueschemeyer, D., Stephens, E. H., & Stephens, J. D. (1992). *Capitalist development and democracy*. Cambridge Polity.

Ruette-Orihuela, K., & Soriano, C. (2016). Remembering the slave rebellion of coro: Historical memory and politics in Venezuela. *Ethnohistory, 63*(2), 327–350.

Ruquoy, P. (2017). Resistance journalism in Haiti: The role of Radio Enriquillo in the coup against Aristide. *Journal of Applied Journalism & Media Studies, 6*(2), 133–139.

Russell, B. (1969 [1920; 1948]). *Teoría y práctica del bolchevismo*. Barcelona: Ariel.

Ryan, M. (2001). Journalistic ethics, objectivity, existential journalism, standpoint epistemology, and public journalism. *Journal of Mass Media Ethics, 16*(1), 3–22.

Ryfe, D. M. (2006). Guest editor's introduction: New institutionalism and the news. *Political Communication, 23*(2), 135–144. doi:10.1080/10584600600728109.

Sadler, P., & Oats, L. (2002). "This great crisis in the republick of letters"-The introduction in 1712 of stamp duties on newspapers and pamphlets. *British Tax Review, 4*, 353–368.

Olmedo, S., & Lugo-Ocando, J. (2018). International cooperation, foreign aid and changes in media agenda: The case of voces. *Journal of Latin American Communication Research, 6*(1–2), 152–169.

Sambrook, R. (2012). *Delivering trust: Impartiality and objectivity in the digital age*.

Samper, A. (1964). *Informe Anual Correspondiente a 1964*. Retrieved from San José, Costa Rica.

Sanborn, C., Portocarrero, F., Coatsworth, J., Aguero, F., & Arrom, S. (2005). *Philanthropy and social change in Latin America*. Cambridge, Massachusetts: Harvard University Press.

Santamaria, S. G. (2018). The sovietization of Cuban journalism. The impact of foreign economy dependency on media structures in a post-soviet era. *Journal of Latin American Communication Research, 6*(1–2), 135–151.

Saunders, F. S. (2000). *Who paid the piper?: The CIA and the cultural Cold War*. London: Granta Books.

Saurin, J. (1996). Globalisation, poverty, and the promises of modernity. *Millennium, 25*(3), 657–680.

Scannell, P. (2005). Public service broadcasting: The history of a concept. In A. Goodwin & G. Whannel (Eds.), *Understanding television* (pp. 20–38). Abingdon, Oxfordshire: Routledge.

Schiffrin, A. (2010). Not really enough: Foreign donors and journalism training in Ghana, Nigeria and Uganda. *Journalism Practice, 4*(3), 405–416.

Schiffrin, A. (2014). *Global muckraking: 100 years of investigative journalism from around the world*. New York: The New Press.

Schiffrin, A. (2017). *Same beds, different dreams? Charitable foundations and newsroom independence in the global south*. Retrieved from Washington, DC: https://www.cima.ned.org/wp-content/uploads/2017/02/CIMA-Media-Philanthropy_Schiffrin.pdf.

Schiller, D. (1981). *Objectivity and the news: The public and the rise of commercial journalism*. Philadelphia, Pennsylvania: University of Pennsylvania Press.

Schiller, H. (1977). *The free flow of information-for whom?* New Jersey, New York: Wiley.

Schiller, H. I. (1975). Génesis of the free flow of information principles: The imposition of communications domination. *Instant Research on Peace and Violence, 5*(2), 75–86.

Schlosser, N. (2015). *Cold war on the airwaves: The radio propaganda war against East Germany.* Champaign, Illinois: University of Illinois Press.

Schramm, W. (1964). *Mass media and national development: The role of information in the developing countries.* Stanford, CA: Stanford University Press.

Schramm, W. (1971). Notes on case studies of instructional media projects. Retrieved from https://eric.ed.gov/?id=ED092145.

Schramm, W., & Atwood, E. (1981). *Circulation of news in the third world: A study of Asia.* Hong Kong: Chinese University Press.

Schudson, M. (1976). *Origins of the ideal of objectivity in the professions: Studies in the history of American journalism and American law, 1830–1940: A thesis* (PhD), Harvard University, Cambridge, Mass.

Schudson, M. (2001). The objectivity norm in American journalism. *Journalism, 2*(2), 149–170.

Schudson, M. (2008). Public spheres, imagined communities, and the underdeveloped historical understanding of journalism. In *Explorations in Communication and History* (pp. 181–189). Abingdon, Oxon: Routledge.

Schudson, M. (2009). Factual knowledge in the age of truthiness. In B. Zelizer (Ed.), *The changing face of journalism. Tablodization, technology and truthiness.* Abingdon, Oxon: Routledge.

Schudson, M., & Tifft, S. (2005). American journalism in historical perspective. In G. Overholser & K. H. Jamieson (Eds.), *Institutions of American democracy: The press* (pp. 17–42). Oxford: Oxford University Press.

Schultze, Q., & Woods, R. (2009). *Understanding evangelical media: The changing face of Christian communication.* Westmont, Illinois: InterVarsity Press.

Scott, M. (2014). *Media and development.* London: Zed Books Ltd.

Scott, M., Bunce, M., & Wright, K. (2017). Donor power and the news: The influence of foundation funding on international public service journalism. *The International Journal of Press/Politics, 22*(2), 163–184.

Scotton, J. F. (1973). The First African Press in East Africa: Protest and nationalism in Uganda in the 1920 s. *The International Journal of African Historical Studies, 6*(2), 211–228.

Seaton, J. (2007). The BBC and metabolising britishness: Critical patriotism. *The Political Quarterly, 78*, 72–85.

Secretary of State, D. f. M., Culture and Sports. (2006). *Broadcasting. An agreement between her majesty's secretary of state for culture, media and sport and the British Broadcasting Corporation.* Retrieved from London: http://www.bbc.co.uk/bbctrust/governance/regulatory_framework/charter_agreement.html.

Segura, M. S. (2018). The influence of international cooperation in Latin American communication field. *Journal of Latin American Communication Research, 6*(1–2), 81–97.

Seldes, G. (1938). *Lords of the press*. New York: Julian Messner.
Sell, W. E. (1957). Doctrine of misappropriation in unfair competition. The Associated Press doctrine after forty years. *Vanderbilt Law Review, 11*, 483.
Serna Rodríguez, A. M. (2014). Prensa y sociedad en las décadas revolucionarias (1910–1940). *Secuencia*(88), 109–149.
Shaxson, N. (2011). *Treasure islands: Tax havens and the men who stole the world*. New York: Random House.
Shoup, L. H., & Minter, W. (2004). *Imperial brain trust: The council on foreign relations and United States foreign policy*. Indiana: iUniverse.
Siebert, F. F. S., & Schramm, W. L. (1956). *Four theories of the press: The authoritarian, libertarian, social responsiblility and soviet communist concepts of what the press should be and do*. University of Illinois Press.
Siegan, B. (2018). *Property rights: From Magna Carta to the fourteenth amendment*. Abingdon, Oxfordshire: Routledge.
Silberstein-Loeb, J. (2014). *The international distribution of news: The Associated Press, Press Association, and Reuters, 1848–1947*. Cambridge: Cambridge University Press.
Simonson, P., Morooka, J., Xiong, B., & Bedsole, N. (2019). The beginnings of mass communication: A transnational history. *Journal of Communication, 69*(5), 518–543.
Sims, N. (2007). *True stories: A century of literary journalism*. Evanston, Illinois: Northwestern University Press.
Singer, J. B. (2007). Contested autonomy: Professional and popular claims on journalistic norms. *Journalism Studies, 8*(1), 79–95.
Singh, K., & Gross, B. (1981). "MacBride": The report and the response. *Journal of Communication, 31*(4), 104–117.
Skjerdal, T. S. (2012). The three alternative journalisms of Africa. *International Communication Gazette, 74*(7), 636–654.
Slater, P., & Connerton, P. (1981). Origin and significance of the Frankfurt School: A Marxist perspective. *Science and Society, 45*(3), 335–336.
Slavtcheva-Petkova, V. (2019). *Global journalism: An introduction*. London: Macmillan International Higher Education.
Smith, A. (1980). *Geopolitics of information: How western culture dominates the world*. London: Faber and Faber.
Smith, H. (1993). Apartheid, sharpeville and 'impartiality': The reporting of South Africa on BBC television 1948–1961. *Historical Journal of Film, Radio and Television, 13*(3), 251–298.
Smith, J. (2006). *Europe and the Americas: State formation, capitalism and civilizations in Atlantic modernity*. Leiden: Brill.
Smith, J. A. (1990). *Printers and press freedom: The ideology of early American journalism*. Oxford: Oxford University Press.
Somerville, P. (1994). Homelessness policy in Britain. *Policy & Politics, 22*(3), 163–178.
Sommerville, C. J. (1996). *The news revolution in England: Cultural dynamics of daily information*. Oxford: Oxford University Press.

Sonne, P., & Fassihi, F. (2012). Tehran's TV channel loses British licens. *The Wall Street Journal*. Retrieved from https://www.wsj.com/articles/SB10001424052970 2046165045771727637811772708.

Sotiron, M. (1997). *From politics to profit: The commercialization of Canadian daily newspapers, 1890–1920*. Montreal: McGill-Queen's Press.

Sparks, C. (2007). *Globalization, development and the mass media*. London: Sage.

Sparrow, B. H. (2006). A research agenda for an institutional media. *Political Communication, 23*(2), 145–157. doi:10.1080/10584600600629695.

Spivak, G. C. (2010 [1988]). Can the subaltern speak? In R. Morris (Ed.), *Can the subaltern speak? Reflections on the history of an idea* (pp. 21–80). New York: Columbia University Press.

Spurr, D. (1993). *The rhetoric of empire: Colonial discourse in journalism, travel writing, and imperial administration*. Durham, North Carolina: Duke University Press.

Starkman, D. (2014). *The watchdog that didn't bark: The financial crisis and the disappearance of investigative journalism*. New York: Columbia University Press.

Startt, J. D. (1991). *Journalists for empire. The imperial debate in the Edwardian Stately Press, 1903–1913*. London: Greenwood Press.

Statler, K. C., & Johns, A. L. (2006). *The Eisenhower administration, the Third World, and the globalization of the Cold War*. Lanham, Maryland: Rowman & Littlefield.

Steel, J. (2013). *Journalism and free speech*. Abingdon: Routledge.

Stengers, I. (2000). *The invention of modern science*. Minneapolis, Minnesota: University of Minnesota Press.

Stevenson, R. L. (1988). *Communication development and the Third World. The global politics of information*. New York: Longman.

Storrs, L. R. (2013). *The second red scare and the unmaking of the new deal left*. Princeton, New Jersey: Princeton University Press.

Straubhaar, J. D. (1989). Television and video in the transition from military to civilian rule in Brazil. *Latin American Research Review, 24*(1), 140–154.

Streckfuss, R. (1990). Objectivity in journalism: A search and a reassessment. *Journalism Quarterly, 67*(4), 973–983.

Subervi-Vélez, F., Rodríguez Cotto, S. and, Lugo-Ocando, J. (2020). *The news media in Puerto Rico: Journalism in colonial settings and in times of crises*. Abingdon, Oxfordshire: Routledge.

Sugden, R. (1986). *The economics of rights, co-operation, and welfare*. Oxford: Blackwell.

Sussman, L. R. (1992). *The culture of freedom: The small world of fulbright scholars*. Lanham, Maryland: Rowman & Littlefield.

Swenson, K. (2018). Rebekah Mercer, the billionaire backer of Bannon and Trump, chooses sides. *Washington Post, January*. Retrieved from https://www.washingtonpost.com/news/morning-mix/wp/2018/01/05/rebekah-mercer-the-billionaire-backer-of-bannon-and-trump-chooses-sides/.

Symons, J. (2014). *The general strike*. Cornwall: House of Stratus.

Syvertsen, T., Mjøs, O. J., Enli, G. S., & Moe, H. (2014). *The media welfare state: Nordic media in the digital era*. Ann Arbor, Michigan: University of Michigan Press.

Takeyh, R. (2000). *The origins of the Eisenhower doctrine: The US, Britain and Nasser's Egypt, 1953–57*. London: Springer.

Tarde, G. (2010 [1895]). *Gabriel Tarde on communication and social influence: Selected papers*. Chicago: University of Chicago Press.

Tarnoff, C. (2005). *Foreign aid: An introductory overview of US programs and policy*. Retrieved from Washington DC: https://apps.dtic.mil/docs/citations/ADA 457380.

Tharoor, S. (2018). *Inglorious empire: What the British did to India*. London: Penguin.

Theoharis, A. G. (1977). *Seeds of repression*. New York: Times Books.

Thussu, D. K. (2005). From MacBride to Murdoch: The marketisation of global communication. *Javnost-The Public, 12*(3), 47–60.

Thussu, D. K. (2006). *Media on the move: Global flow and contra-flow*. Abingdon, Oxfordshire: Routledge.

Tietaah, G. K., Yeboah-Banin, A. A., Akrofi-Quarcoo, S., & Sesenu, F. Y. (2018). Journalism aid: Country of origin and influences on beneficiary perceptions and practices. *African Journalism Studies, 39*(2), 90–103.

Tiffen, R. (1976). A new information order? International agencies and the flow of news. *Southeast Asian Journal of Social Science. Special Issue: "Communication and Social Development in Asia, 4*(2), 65–76.

Tong, J., & Sparks, C. (2009). Investigative journalism in China today. *Journalism Studies, 10*(3), 337–352.

Truman, H. (1951). Letter to the Chairman, Board of Foreign Scholarships, on the Fulbright Program. Retrieved from https://www.trumanlibrary.org/publicpapers/index.php?pid=315.

Truman, H. (1963). *Letter to Honorable Wayne Morse of the United States Senate*. Private Letter. Harry S. Truman Presidential Library & Museum. Independence, MO.

Truman, H. (1964, 06–10–1964). [Letter to William B. Arthur from LOOK Magazine]. Student Research File. Central Intelligence Agency. B File. Box 24.

Tuchman, G. (1972). Objectivity as strategic ritual: An examination of newsmen's notions of objectivity. *American Journal of Sociology, 77*(4), 660–679.

Tully, J. (1982). *A discourse on property: John Locke and his adversaries*. Cambridge: Cambridge University Press.

Tumber, H., & Prentoulis, M. (2005). Journalism and the making of a profession. In H. de Burgh (Ed.), *Making journalists: Diverse models, global issues* (pp. 58–73). Abingdon, Oxfordshire: Routledge.

Uche, L. U. (1991). Ideology, theory and professionalism in the African Mass Media. *African Media Review, 5*(1), 1–16.

UNESCO. (2017). *Model curricula for journalism education*. Retrieved from Paris: https://unesdoc.unesco.org/ark:/48223/pf0000151209.

Uranga, W., & Pasquini, J. M. (1988). *Precisiones sobre la radio.* Buenos Aires: Ediciones Paulinas.

Urribarrí, R. (2011). Redes sociales y medios digitales:¿ alternativa comunicacional en Venezuela? *Comunicación: estudios venezolanos de comunicación*(156), 47–52.

USIA. (1960). *Committee meeting 23 May 1960 (12:45–13:05) international television.* Retrieved from Washington DC.

Varón Gabai, R. (1990). El Taki Onqoy: las raíces andinas de un fenómeno colonial. In L. Millones & S. Castro-Klarén (Eds.), *El Retorno de las huacas: estudios y documentos sobre el Taki Onqoy, siglo XVI* (pp. 331–405). Lima: Ediciones EIP.

Vieira, V. C. C. (2019). From third world theory to belt and road initiative: International aid as a Chinese Foreign Policy tool. *Contexto Internacional, 41*(3), 529–551.

Vokes, R. (2017). *Media and development.* Abingdon, Oxfordshire: Routledge.

Wahutu, J. (2019). Western journalists, learn from your African peers. Retrieved from https://www.niemanlab.org/2019/12/western-journalists-learn-from-your-african-peers/.

Waisbord, S. (2013). *Reinventing professionalism: Journalism and news in global perspective.* Hoboken, New Jersey: John Wiley & Sons.

Waisbord, S. (2019). A sketch of media development. In N. Benequista, S. Abbott, P. Rothman, & W. Mano (Eds.), *International media development. Historical perspectives and new frontiers.* Oxford: Peter Lang Publishing, Inc.

Walker, S. (2018). University founded by George Soros 'forced out' of Hungary. Retrieved from https://www.theguardian.com/world/2018/oct/25/university-founded-by-george-soros-forced-out-of-hungary.

Ward, L. (2010). *John Locke and modern life.* Cambridge: Cambridge University Press.

Ward, S. J. (2015). *The invention of journalism ethics: The path to objectivity and beyond* (Vol. 38). Montreal, Quebec: McGill-Queen's Press-MQUP.

Warner, J., & Iastrebner, M. (2018). What projects are included in the SembraMedia directory? Retrieved from http://www.sembramedia.org/sembramedia-directory/.

Wasserman, H. (2017). *Media, geopolitics and power: A view from the global south.* Champaign, IL: University of Illinois Press.

Weaver, F. (2018). *Latin America in the world economy: Mercantile colonialism to global capitalism.* Abingdon, Oxfordshire: Routledge.

Weilemann, P. (2017). Experiences of a multidimensional think tank: The Konrad-Adenauer-Stiftung. In J. McGann & R. K. Weaver (Eds.), *Think tanks and civil societies. Catalysts for ideas and action* (pp. 169–186). Abingdon, Oxfordshire: Routledge.

Wellington, H. (1978). On freedom of expression. *Yale Law Journal, 88*(6), 1105–1109.

Wesley, C. H. (1917). The struggle for the recognition of Haiti and Liberia as independent republics. *The Journal of Negro History, 2*(4), 369–383.

Whealey, R. H. (2015). *Hitler and Spain: The Nazi role in the Spanish Civil War, 1936–1939.* Lexington, Kentucky, United States: University Press of Kentucky.

White, L. J. (1969). Enclosures and population movements in England, 1700–1830. *Explorations in Economic History, 6*(2), 175–186.

Whitehead, C. (1993). Privatizing housing: An assessment of UK experience. *Housing Policy Debate, 4*(1), 101–139.

Wien, C. (2005). Defining objectivity within journalism. *Nordicom Review, 26*(2), 3–15.

Willse, C. (2010). Neo-liberal biopolitics and the invention of chronic homelessness. *Economy and Society, 39*(2), 155–184.

Wilson, H. S. (2015). *McClure's magazine and the Muckrakers*. Princeton, New Jersey: Princeton University Press.

Winston, B. (2002). *Media, technology and society: A history: From the telegraph to the internet*. Abingdon, Oxfordshire: Routledge.

Wood, E. M. (1991). *The pristine culture of capitalism: A historical essay on old regimes and modern states*. London: Verso.

Woods, J. R. (2003). *Black struggle, red scare: Segregation and anti-communism in the south, 1948--1968*. Baton Rouge, Louisiana: Luisiana State University Press.

Wright, K., Scott, M., & Bunce, M. (2019). Foundation-funded journalism, philanthrocapitalism and tainted donors. *Journalism Studies, 20*(5), 675–695.

Yadav, Y. P. K. (2011). Is social responsibility a sham for media? *Global Media Journal: Indian Edition*. Retrieved from https://studyres.com/doc/22564853/is-social-responsibility-a-sham-for-media%3F-dr.-y

Zelizer, B. (1993). Journalists as interpretive communities. *Critical Studies in Media Communication, 10*(3), 219–237.

Zelizer, B. (2009). Journalists as interpretive communities, revisited. In *The Routledge Companion to News and Journalism* (pp. 225–234). Routledge.

Zelizer, B. (2017). *Resetting journalism in the aftermath of Brexit and Trump*. Paper presented at the Media, Communication and Cultural Studies Association Annual Conference, Leeds, UK.

Index

Afghanistan, 52, 54, 144
Africa, 12, 23, 26, 27, 30, 40, 42, 50, 54–56, 78, 88–89, 93, 95, 97–99, 120, 125, 129, 132, 140, 143, 148, 158, 161, 164, 166
al-Asad, Bashar, 101
Al-Jazeera, 12, 101
Allende, Salvador, 9
Anderson, Benedict, 5, 17
Angola, 8, 52, 79
Argentina, 27, 120
Aristide, Jean-Bertand, 166
Asia, 11–12, 50, 78, 83, 89, 93, 95, 97, 99, 120, 125, 129, 132, 137–38, 140, 143, 145, 148
Asian values, 145
Associated Press, 19, 43, 73
Australia, 2, 130

BBC, 44, 52, 64, 72, 78, 98, 101, 110, 120, 125, 133, 134, 146
Berlin Wall, 8, 12, 115, 122
Bolívar, Simón, 12, 52–56, 91, 137
Bolivia, 162, 165
Bolshevism, 69, 81
Bosnia-Herzegovina, 144
Bozell, Brent, 148
Brazil, 5, 120–21, 165
British Empire, 17, 98
Burleson, Albert S., 59, 71–72, 74

capitalism, 7, 11, 14, 44, 47, 82, 85, 102
Caribbean, 53, 93, 95, 125
Castro, Fidel, 23, 128
Catholic Church, 27, 122, 148, 149
censorship, 72, 74, 146–47, 154, 166
Central America, 144
Central Intelligence Agency (CIA), 11, 82, 83
Centre for International Media Assistance (CIMA), 141–42, 153
Centro Internacional de Estudios Superiores de Comunicación para América Latina (CIESPAL), 50
Chávez, Hugo, 126
Chevening, program, 124, 130
Chile, 6, 9, 11
China, 8, 12, 39, 48, 138, 139, 147
Church, Frank, US Senator (D), 9
CNN, 101
Cold War, 6–8, 11, 13–14, 16, 20, 23, 33, 48, 50–51, 70, 76, 81–84, 86, 88–89, 99, 102, 104, 107, 110–11, 115, 119, 124, 127–28, 130–32, 138, 141, 143–46, 161
Colombia, 65, 129, 168
Columbus, Christopher, 18, 94
communism, 7, 10, 15, 48, 50, 59–60, 62, 72, 76, 81, 86, 88, 110, 112, 114

201

Congo, Democratic Republic of the, 143
contested orchestration, 4
Costa Rica, 125
Council for Mutual Economic Assistance (Comecon), 80
Creole, 165
Cuba, 8, 10, 12, 23, 43, 52, 79–81, 128, 137–39, 144
cybernetics, 114

deontology, 3, 12, 36, 46, 59, 66, 68, 71–72, 81, 90, 102, 113, 125, 160–62, 165, 167
Deutsche Welle, 125
Dominican Republic, 166
Dulles, Allen Welsh, 83

Ecuador, 50
education, journalism, 10, 26, 40–41, 50, 56, 86, 99, 119–33, 140
Egypt, 96
Eisenhower, Dwight D. (Ike), 23, 27, 87–88, 97, 128
El Correo del Orinoco, 55, 99
Enlightenment, 3, 17, 21, 31, 33–35, 37, 39, 42, 44, 49, 64, 68–69, 90, 110–11, 161–62
Ethiopia, 81
Europe, 3–4, 10–12, 29–30, 32–34, 39–40, 43–46, 49–50, 54, 60, 64–66, 71, 75, 78–80, 82–83, 85–86, 89, 91–98, 100, 102–3, 121–22, 125–26, 132, 135, 139–40, 143, 149, 161–64, 166
Evangelical church, 148

Facultad Latinoamericana de Ciencias Sociales (FLACSO), 127
Fourth Estate, 147
France, 43, 50, 54–55
free flow of information, theory, 11, 13, 15, 49, 88–89, 96, 111, 113–15, 167
Fulbright Program, 85–86, 91, 130, 140
Fundación Carolina, 123

Germany, 78, 123, 140–41
Ghana, 26, 115, 134

grammars, journalism, 6, 36, 94, 113, 157, 164–67
Great Depression, 81
Great Transformation, 6, 46
Greece, 45, 82–83
Guatemala, 23, 128

Haiti, 12, 53–56, 91, 116, 137, 165, 166
hegemony, 5, 7, 11, 14, 18, 23, 43–44, 46, 52, 65, 77, 82, 94–96, 102, 112, 133, 139, 164
Humphrey, Hubert H., US Senator (D), 83

ideology, 1, 5, 7–8, 15–16, 18–19, 22, 25, 38, 46, 54, 63, 65, 69, 78, 93–96, 103, 107, 109, 111–14
impartiality, 2, 30, 37, 63–65, 91, 104, 107–8, 110, 113, 115, 117–18, 135, 160–61, 165
India, 23, 26, 39, 51, 53, 65, 97–98, 110, 127, 132, 165
Indonesia, 78, 144–45
information flow, 11, 13, 15, 43, 49, 88–89, 96, 111, 113–15, 147, 167. *See also* free flow of information, theory
information freedom, 167
International Center for Journalists (ICFJ), 123
Iran, 23, 78, 101, 128
Italy, 33, 82–83

Japan, 2–3, 12, 84, 98, 123, 140–41
Johnston, Lyndon B., 128–29

Kant, Immanuel, 51
Kennedy, John F., 27, 128
Kenya, 6, 42
Konrad Adenauer Foundation, 11, 123, 153

Latin America, 11–12, 14, 20, 26, 28, 40, 42, 45, 49–50, 52, 54, 78, 83, 85–86, 88–89, 93, 95, 97, 104–5,

109, 114, 120, 122, 125, 127, 129, 132, 135, 148, 149, 152–54, 166
Lenin, Vladimir Ilyich Ulyanov, 30, 60, 62, 67–69, 74–75, 82
Lippmann, Walter, 22, 34, 44, 63–64, 74–75, 77
Locke, John, 33–34, 48
Luxemburg, Rosa, 66

market of ideas, free, 35, 84, 113–15, 159
Market Society, 2, 6, 18, 20, 38, 46, 48, 82, 95
Marshall Plan, 9
Marx, Marxism, 22, 30, 60, 62, 66, 68–69, 77, 132
McBride Report, 13, 49
McCarthyism, 10, 48, 71, 86
media co-option (also co-opted media), 59, 72, 108, 160
Media Research Center, 148
Mercer, Robert, 148
Mercurio, El, 11
Mexican Revolution, 45, 75
Mexico, 40, 43, 120, 155, 165
Military–Industrial Complex, 81
Moon, Sun Myung, 148
Morocco, 78, 125
Muckrakers, 62, 70–71, 77

Nasser, Gamal Abdel, 96
nation building, 6–7, 27, 33, 43, 57, 59–60, 64, 66, 72, 82, 97, 112, 114, 142–46
new institutionalism (NI), 102
New York Times, 128, 166
Nieman Foundation, 130
Nigeria, 99
non-governmental organisation (NGOs), 8, 11, 13–14, 24, 28, 50, 52, 79–80, 122–26
North Korea, 79, 81, 138, 146
Nuffic, Dutch organisation for internationalisation in education, 130

objectivity, 1, 3, 6, 8, 10, 13, 16, 19, 21–22, 25, 35–37, 45–51, 57, 60, 63–70, 73–78, 81, 86, 89–91, 103–18, 127, 135, 160–62, 165, 167
Office for War Information, 84, 88
Open Society, 11, 101, 123
Operations Coordinating Board (OCB), 87
Organisation for Economic Co-operation and Development (OECD), 2, 141
Organization of American States, 50, 86, 129

Peru, 18, 155
Philippines, 43, 82, 149
Polanyi, Karl, 6, 20, 38, 46, 95
post office, 59–60, 72
Pravda, 69, 81
Prensa Latina, 81
Priestley, Joseph, 51
professional autonomy, 1, 15, 30, 35, 43, 56, 80–81, 112
professional ideology, 1, 8, 63, 109, 160
propaganda, 7, 11, 22, 44, 46, 54, 62, 66, 69, 72, 74–75, 77, 79–82, 84, 86, 88–91, 96–101, 110, 114, 127–28, 131, 145–47, 157, 161
Puerto Rico, 43, 83, 125
Putin, Vladimir, 126

Qatar, 12, 101

Radio Enriquillo, 165–66
Radio France Internationale, 78, 125
Radio Free Europe, 83, 89, 91, 92, 146
Radio Netherlands, 11, 50, 78
Radio Sutatenza, 168
Realpolitik, 145
Red Scare, 10
Reed, John, 45
Reuters, 44, 48, 62, 76, 81, 83, 87
Reuters Institute, 130
Roosevelt, Franklin D., 76
Rostow, Walt Whitman, 15
Russia, 57, 60, 66, 68–69, 71, 74–75, 79, 80, 91, 101, 126, 144, 146–47

Sainath, Palagummi, 165, 167
Schudson, Michael, 2–5, 22, 36, 47, 58, 66, 73, 90, 120
science journalism, 122, 127–29
Serbia, 144
Sierra Leone, 144
socialism, 8, 34, 46, 60, 69, 75, 79, 82, 138
Soros, George, 11, 101, 123, 126, 141
South Africa, 27, 65
Soviet Revolution, 7, 10, 57, 60, 62, 64, 71, 74, 78, 86, 89, 91
Soviet Union, USSR, 6, 8, 10–11, 16, 28, 32, 44, 52, 62, 66, 69–70, 74, 78–79, 81, 87, 89–90, 92, 96, 99, 107, 112–13, 118, 128, 131, 144, 157, 161
Spain, 71, 78, 100, 123, 125, 140
Sputnik, 128
Stalin, Joseph Vissarionovich, 44, 48, 52, 62, 67–69, 79, 81, 96
Stalinism, 44, 67, 69, 79
subaltern voices/class, 6, 23, 160
Sub-Sahara Africa, 50
Syria, 101, 133–34

Tanzania, 42, 97, 99
TASS Russian news agency, 81
Toda Peace Institute, 123
Transnational Journalism History, project, 45
Truman, Harry S., 27, 75, 79, 82–87, 91, 96, 106, 127–29, 135
Turkey, 82, 101

Un-American activities, 34
Unification Church, 148

United Kingdom, Britain, Great Britain, 9, 12, 22, 25, 26–28, 32, 40–41, 55, 58, 63–64, 71, 76, 90, 96, 99, 108, 110–13, 121, 124, 130, 140–41
United Nations Educational, Scientific and Cultural Organisation (UNESCO), 49–50, 89, 96, 111, 114, 127, 132–33
United Press International, 148
United States Information Agency (USIA), 88–89
United States of America, US, 4, 22, 5–11, 15, 22, 25, 27, 31–34, 36, 39, 42–46, 48–52, 55, 58–66, 69–79, 81–92, 95–96, 99, 101, 107–3, 113, 120, 122–24, 126, 128, 130–31, 135, 139–43, 164

Venezuela, 12, 52–55, 65, 91, 126, 129, 137, 152, 165
Vietnam, 8, 10, 39, 79, 82, 95–96, 128–29, 138, 144

Wilson, Woodrow, 10, 59, 72, 112
workers (movements, unions, struggles), 10, 18, 29, 32, 40, 44, 46, 52, 57–58, 62–72, 74–76, 78, 90, 168
Worlds of Journalism Study, 1, 48
World War I, First World War, 19, 59–60, 62, 64, 72, 74–75, 77–78
World War II, 7–9, 11, 26, 31, 33–34, 43, 49, 75, 77–79, 86, 95–96, 98–100, 112–14, 116, 122, 124, 139, 148, 167

Zelizer, Barbie, 5, 27, 163
Zimbabwe, 99

About the Author

Jairo Lugo-Ocando is director of executive and graduate education and professor in residence at Northwestern University in Qatar. He previously served as an associate professor and deputy head at the School of Media and Communication at the University of Leeds and was the head of the MA in Global Journalism at the University of Sheffield both in the United Kingdom. Before entering academe, he served as news editor-in-chief of Venezuela's *Dairio La Verdad* and worked as a journalist and freelance writer for several news organizations in Venezuela, United States, Peru, and Colombia. Lugo-Ocando received his PhD from the University of Sussex, an MA from Lancaster University and a BA in Social Communication and Print Journalism from the Universidad del Zulia in Venezuela.

www.ingramcontent.com/pod-product-compliance
Lightning Source LLC
Chambersburg PA
CBHW050905300426
44111CB00010B/1388